To Emma

Thank you for the constant inspiration!

15.01.2021

The Arab Spring between Transformation and Capture

NEW POLITICS OF AUTONOMY

Series Editors: Saul Newman and Martina Tazzioli

In recent years, we have witnessed an unprecedented emergence of new forms of radical politics—from Tahrir Square, Gezi Park, and the global Occupy movement to Wikileaks and hacktivism. What is striking about such movements is their rejection of leadership structures and the absence of political demands and agendas. Instead, their originality lies in the autonomous forms of political life they engender.

The New Politics of Autonomy book series is an attempt to make sense of this new terrain of anti-political politics and to develop an alternative conceptual and theoretical arsenal for thinking about the politics of autonomy. The series investigates political, economic, and ethical questions raised by this new paradigm of autonomy. It brings together authors and researchers who are engaged, in various ways, with understanding contemporary radical political movements and who approach the theme of autonomy from different perspectives: political theory, philosophy, ethics, literature and art, psychoanalytic theory, political economy, and political history.

Titles in the Series

Spaces of Governmentality: Autonomous Migration and the Arab Uprisings
    Martina Tazzioli

The Composition of Movements to Come: Aesthetics and Cultural Labour after the Avant-Garde
    Stevphen Shukaitis

Foucault and the Making of Subjects
    Edited by Laura Cremonesi, Orazio Irrera, Daniele Lorenzini, and Martina Tazzioli

Italian Critical Thought: Genealogies and Categories
    Edited by Dario Gentili, Elettra Stimilli, and Glenda Garelli

In the Marxian Workshops: Producing Subjects
    Sandro Mezzadra

Anarchisms, Postanarchisms and Ethics
    Benjamin Franks

The Urban Enigma: Time, Autonomy, and Postcolonial Transformations in Latin America
    Simone Vegliò

The Arab Spring between Transformation and Capture: Autonomy, Media, and Mobility in Tunisia
    Oana Pârvan

The Arab Spring between Transformation and Capture

Autonomy, Media, and Mobility in Tunisia

Oana Pârvan

ROWMAN & LITTLEFIELD
Lanham • Boulder • New York • London

Published by Rowman & Littlefield
An imprint of The Rowman & Littlefield Publishing Group, Inc.
4501 Forbes Boulevard, Suite 200, Lanham, Maryland 20706
www.rowman.com

6 Tinworth Street, London, SE11 5AL, United Kingdom

Copyright © 2020 by Oana Pârvan

All rights reserved. No part of this book may be reproduced in any form or by any electronic or mechanical means, including information storage and retrieval systems, without written permission from the publisher, except by a reviewer who may quote passages in a review.

British Library Cataloguing in Publication Information Available

Library of Congress Cataloging-in-Publication Data

Names: Pârvan, Oana, 1985– author.
Title: The Arab Spring between transformation and capture : autonomous media and mobility in Tunisia / Oana Pârvan.
Other titles: New politics of autonomy.
Description: Lanham, Maryland : Rowman & Littlefield Publishing Group, 2020. | Series: New politics of autonomy | Includes bibliographical references and index. | Summary: "This book provides a detailed analysis of the narrative frame of the 'Arab Spring' and unpacks the process of the Tunisian revolution beyond national borders, discussing the importance of migration for different examples of collective action."— Provided by publisher.
Identifiers: LCCN 2020024791 (print) | LCCN 2020024792 (ebook) | ISBN 9781786614766 (cloth) | ISBN 9781786614773 (epub)
Subjects: LCSH: Arab Spring, 2010– | Revolutions—Tunisia—History—21st century. | Mass media—Tunisia—History—21st century. | Tunisia—History—Demonstrations, 2010– | Tunisia—Emigration and immigration—History—21st century.
Classification: LCC DT266.4 .P37 2020 (print) | LCC DT266.4 (ebook) | DDC 961.105/2—dc23
LC record available at https://lccn.loc.gov/2020024791
LC ebook record available at https://lccn.loc.gov/2020024792

Bunicilor mei, cărora le mulțumesc pentru că mă călăuzesc neîncetat

Gheorghe Pârvan (1926–2013)
Maria Pârvan (1928–2017)

Contents

Acknowledgments ix

Preface xi

Introduction 1

1 The "Arab Spring": The Projection of a "Familiar" Revolution 13

2 The Event of Resistance and Its Capture 43

3 A Microhistory of the Tunisian Revolution: The Struggle of the Disenfranchised 69

4 Histories of Dispossession and Contemporary Vanguards 101

5 Mediation of an Event : Circulation of Cultures and Practices of Resistance 145

Conclusion 177

Notes 185

Bibliography 199

Index 217

Acknowledgments

The ideas in this work are the result of a very long series of fortunate encounters and dialogues that I am deeply grateful for.

Before I even started this experience, the support of Franco Berardi "Bifo" was crucial in helping me imagine my research proposal and encouraging me to continue on the academic path. I also thank Federico Montanari for his initial support and Bhaskar Mukhopadhyay for having taken interest in my research proposal.

I have been able to develop this work mainly thanks to the Arts and Humanities Research Council Grant Partnership award. Moreover, thanks to the Erasmus Plus program I have benefited from crucial interactions with scholars and artists at the Orientale University in Naples and the Humboldt University in Berlin. I particularly want to thank the Centre for Postcolonial and Gender Studies in Naples and Doctor Tiziana Terranova for all her stimulating feedback and for giving me the opportunity to be part of a research community of like-minded thinkers and practitioners. I extend my gratitude to the researchers who made Naples my second home: Nina Ferrante, Roberto Terracciano, Olga Solombrino, and Brian D'Aquino.

I am especially grateful to my supervisors, Luciana Parisi and Shela Sheikh, for their illuminating and patient guidance and for teaching me so much more than just how to write my research.

These years have been blessed by the constant support and affection I have received from my colleagues and sisters, Mijke van Drift and Gitanjali Pyndiah. They have meant the world to my emotional and intellectual growth.

I thank my "Tunisian" hosts, Liu' Fornara and Debora Del Pistoia, for their generosity and the stories they've shared.

I am grateful to have come in contact with the films of Ridha Tlili and Walid Fellah, with the art practice of Mohamed Dali Ltaief, and the research and documentaries of Habib Ayeb. Their work has provided the most valuable contribution toward my interaction with the event of the Tunisian revolution.

My special thanks goes to Martina Tazzioli for her friendship and daily discussions. Our debates, her work, and her advice have significantly informed and improved my writing. I also thank Isabel for her affectionate patience and support.

Nici măcar un rând din aceasta lucrare n-aş fi scris fără neîncetata susţinere şi dragoste a părinţilor mei, Ely si Ştefan, care m-au învaţat de când eram mica să pun întrebări şi să nu-mi fie frică de răspunsuri, şi care, cu atata răbdare, mi-au dat putere ori de cate ori—şi n-au fost puţine—m-am simţit descurajată.

Preface

I have been asked many times to justify my research interest in the Tunisian revolution, given that I hold no apparent autobiographical connection to the area. I am Romanian (by birth), Italian (by emigration), a knowledge practitioner in a British institution, and a rather poor Arabic speaker.

Power relations also inform the distribution of expected research interests, since non-Western thinkers in social and human sciences are often expected to become "native informants" of their (supposed) cultures of belonging, whereas researchers coming from the global North are readily encouraged to *explore* foreign "cultures" (especially the ones belonging to the global South) without having to provide extensive justifications or deep autobiographical connections with their areas of interest.

The following are the reasons why I look at these events with a sense of proximity and belonging. First, because I also come from what Antonio Gramsci would have called a "subaltern" nation—namely, post-socialist Romania—where change has often been depicted with skepticism or fascination by the dominant regime of signification, suggesting the exceptionality of political agency.

Like the Tunisians, my life has also been marked by a revolutionary transformation, that of the anti-Communist revolution of 1989. Since I belong to the post-revolutionary generation, I have personally experienced the consequences of one's recent history being shaped by hegemonic narratives, determined by either local or global dominant interests, each with their correspondent discourses. Therefore, I feel a responsibility to reveal and question such narratives when I encounter them.

Second, I believe Tunisia to be one of the symbols and examples of a contemporary political practice many—both in the West and elsewhere—unfortunately choose to ignore or dismiss, even when they hold the best intentions. It is necessary to overthrow the most common Western analytical standpoint and learn from rather than teach or judge the "Arabs" or the "mob," while realizing that their political courage and creativity touches upon the Tunisian Kasbah as well as upon the disenfranchised western suburbs, and that these spaces can become a fertile ground for the politics of the future, only when and if one accepts to engage with them.

Introduction

On December 17, 2010, an event shook the city of Sidi Bouzid in Tunisia instigating a domino effect that would alter the lives of millions of North African citizens. Sidi Bouzid is a city of 400,000 inhabitants in the center of Tunisia. Like many other Tunisian cities, most of its local youth, which make up almost half of the population, are unemployed, and are even more likely to be if they are holding degrees.

Mohamed Bouazizi was a twenty-six-year-old unemployed graduate getting by as a fruit vendor on the streets. When a local policewoman requisitioned Bouazizi's fruit cart and merchandise and met his complaints with a public slap in the face, he decided to express his outrage and desperation in an extreme way. He reached the headquarters of the Sidi Bouzid Governorate, demanding his cart and merchandise back. He then poured gasoline on his body and set himself on fire. He died on January 4, 2011.

However, from that very afternoon, his gesture sparked a long series of protests, which, despite violent repression, evolved into the Tunisian revolution. Against all odds, the Tunisian revolution managed to topple the Western-backed dictatorship of Zine el-Abidine Ben Ali after twenty-three years of undisputed authoritarian rule. At least 338 people lost their lives and 2,147 were injured during a month of generalized mobilization (Mandraud, 2011).

After the Tunisian "spark," other countries of the region were also shaken by expressions of mass dissent. Vast protests occurred in Egypt, Libya, Syria, Yemen, Bahrain, Jordan, and Morocco. Tunisia and Egypt alone managed to put an end to their oppressive regimes with their revolutions. Western observers chose to gather all the mobilizations of 2011 in the North African and Middle Eastern (MENA) region under the umbrella term of "Arab Spring."

The "Arab Spring" is commonly understood as a series of anti-government mass mobilizations, mainly occurring between the end of 2010 and 2012. Because the first instances of protests happened in Tunisia, Egypt, and Libya, alongside Yemen, Bahrain, and Syria, these heterogenous events—each one of them with its specific roots and development—are generalized as "Arab."

However, some thinkers have challenged this feature of Arabness of these uprisings, drawing attention to the African dimension of this period of dissent, which also touched upon Algeria, Burkina Faso, Cameroon, Cotê d'Ivoire (Ivory Coast), Ethiopia, Gabon, Kenya, Mauritania, Morocco, Senegal, South Africa, Sudan, Swaziland, Uganda, Western Sahara, and Zimbabwe (Manji and Ekine, 2012).

The "Arab Spring" and similar contemporaneous movements that arose in different countries (such as the Spanish *Indignados*, the Syntagma Square movement in Greece, the American Occupy Wall Street, and the Turkish Gezi Park movement) were seen as instances of the revitalization of contemporary politics. This is increasingly relevant in an age marked by a post-ideological belief in the "eternal present" of neoliberalism and the "end of history" (Scott, 2014).

Moreover, the "Arab Spring" held an additional point of political relevance since it temporarily interrupted the signification regime imposed after 9/11 devoted to representing "Arab" peoples as "terrorist" threats to the West and incompatible with the Western idea of liberal democracy. On the contrary, what the protesters of the "Arab Spring" pursued (at least according to the Western and regional media discourse) was precisely democracy. Most importantly, "Arab" peoples were able to reach democratic achievements by themselves, with no need for Western interventions (unlike what the "War on Terror" paradigm would suggest).

The literature on the "Arab Spring"[1] is vast. In my view, however, and as I will be arguing, it often fails to account for the political relevance of the event beyond the borders of the MENA region.[2] An important reason why Western knowledge production somehow isolated the Arab Spring politically is connected to the fact that few observers were actually concerned to engage with the Orientalist, Eurocentric construction of the event itself (for this argument, I will mostly draw from the critiques developed by Ahl Al Kahf, 2013; Al-Ali, 2012; El Mahdi, 2011; and Rizk, 2014). Only once the inherent articulations of the Arab Spring narrative are revealed as profoundly reductive and biased distortions is the field open for considering the originality of the political event as such. Precisely because I disagree with a collective representation of the phenomenon and the subtended generalizations implied by the Arab Spring formula—which tend to lump together different events and support the idea of an "Arab" specificity—I will focus mainly on the case of the Tunisian revolution.

By looking at the Tunisian revolution, I hope to shed light on nonhegemonic patterns of reception of and interaction with instances of non-Western resistance (outside and inside the global North). My claim is that a suspension of the hegemonic, stereotypical assumptions around the event makes visible different narrative layers. These layers offer valuable hints regarding contemporary political subjectivity, its strategies, and resistance practices able to challenge global governmentality.

My position of inquiry is embedded into a Western knowledge production institution, but my standpoint is somehow intermediary. What I mean is that there is a borderline between Western and "Arab" thinkers who engage with the Arab Spring topic, no matter the reading each of them chooses to privilege. This epistemic borderline confirms a very strong (and, I argue, problematic) distinction between a Western and a non-Western imaginary of politics. As a consequence, in their analyses, many Western observers tacitly claim a certain distance from the phenomenon (of the "Arab" revolutions), whereas "Arab" observers often claim their proximity to it (whether they're writing from the region or not). As a Western-based knowledge practitioner, I will attempt to write by practicing proximity toward some aspects that make this event distant from my history and political sensibility. I do this mostly because I am convinced that its most innovative features should contaminate the Western political imaginary and help foster future alliances.

The intention of this research is that of revealing and deconstructing the hegemonic narratives that have influenced the shape of knowledge around the "Arab" mobilizations. I have critiqued both the Arab Spring formula as well as the label of "revolution" itself and tried to explore more productive conceptual tools such as "resistance" and political "event."

The "Arab Spring" is an interpretative paradigm born in the North American foreign policy circles, and it carries a fair legacy of Orientalist knowledge on the "Arab" world, especially activated by the War on Terror age of military invasions and Islamophobia. This background facilitates an interpretation of heterogeneous events as an area-specific, unexpected series of popular uprisings for Western-inspired liberal democracy. My argument challenges this approach on several levels. In the first chapter, I will unpack the Orientalist undertones of this kind of generalizing narrative. But beyond that, and focusing on the Tunisian revolution, I will show the specificity of an event of exceptional courage and organization by reflecting on its histories of dispossession and resistance. The Tunisian revolution is my attempt to reveal how an event of resistance can be engaged with respecting its specificity and futurity; how people in Tunisia have unsettled a Western-backed police state by enacting politics from beyond representative bodies such as unions and parties and how those practices have been circulated in Europe.

In this work, I deconstruct the narrative of the Arab Spring and focus only on the Tunisian Dignity revolution. So, I start from a critical reflection in order to design tools of analysis, both theoretical and empirical, able to account for the importance of the Tunisian mobilization for more generalizable reflections on contemporary politics.

As far as the methodology is concerned, I worked on Western literature on the "Arab" revolutions, according to the directions of critique indicated to me by the production of local thinkers, both scholars and journalists, but mostly artists and activists who have provided me with inspirational readings of the events (such as Ahl Al Kahf, 2013; Rizk, 2014; and films of Tlili, 2011, 2013).

Unlike the most common debate regarding the "success" or "failure" of the Arab Spring/Tunisian revolution, the accounts of artists and activists drew attention to the exceptionality and social (as opposed to the political) nature of the phenomenon, which are the aspects I, therefore, chose to focus upon.

Moreover, instead of working with the category of "revolution," and thus supporting its Western genealogy, I turned to philosophical work around the notion of "resistance" by Howard Caygill but also occasionally by Michel Foucault and Gilles Deleuze. I chose these thinkers for many reasons, which will be discussed in each chapter, but most importantly because they have provided valuable examples of how to productively *think* theory *through* different contemporary *events* of resistance. In addition, the theories of the "event" (although apparently incompatible with the articulation of the notion of "resistance"), as discussed by Deleuze and Alain Badiou (in the reading of contemporary researchers such as Simon O'Sullivan, Claudia Aradau, Rodrigo Nunes, and Maurizio Lazzarato), helped me substitute the idea of "revolution" with that of a "network of events of resistance." Unlike the Deleuzian interpretation of the "event," considered as a (nonpolitical) common, infinitesimal variation, or the Badiouan reading of it as an extraordinarily rare and definitive cut, my proposition follows Aradau's definition of the "event of resistance" as a "rupture in the situation from a specific sub-set/category which [. . .] interrupts the power/knowledge relations" (Aradau, 2004: 4). I have thus proceeded by giving an account of this network of events of resistance and by developing diagrams informed by the flows of struggle that have crossed the Tunisian territory and culminated in 2011.

This work mainly relies on three sources of knowledge production: political practice, art practice, and critical theory.

In terms of theories, I take inspiration from critical theorists who have come in contact with social movements such as Foucault, Félix Guattari,

Deleuze, Caygill, Joshua Clover, Tiziana Terranova, Banu Bargu, and Nunes. These thinkers have developed theoretical tools that I find relevant for my inquiry when approaching questions like "What is resistance?" "How can a revolution be narrated?" or "Through which medium do protests spread?"

One of the main difficulties in my research was that of working simultaneously with different orders of (multilingual) knowledge production, from the journalistic to the artistic and theoretical ones, while keeping in mind the intuitions of my brief periods of ethnographic research in Tunisia (in 2013 and 2014). I found that the production of Tunisian artists (whether local or diasporic) provided me with the most valuable indications as to the direction research should take, and I tried to follow these indications in the development of my argument and propositions.

Finally, it's worth addressing why autonomy features in the title of this work. Although there isn't a direct reference to the concept until I discuss the circulation of practices of resistance in chapter 5, autonomy constitutes an important framework. Autonomy (from the Italian *autonomia*) is a political and theoretical heterodox Marxist tradition born around Italy's factories in the '60s and '70s. It is strongly characterized by the interdependence and the constant exchanges between its conceptual innovation and its practices of organization.

Theoretically, autonomy sees the site of production as no longer located in the factory but in society: in Italy, this new, diffused location of production is labeled the "social factory." As a consequence, conflict, too, is relocated within wider society, and the working class is portrayed as the primary agent of revolutionary transformation, to which capital's evolving techniques of accumulation and control are perceived as reactive, thus the notion of autonomy of the working class.

Practice-wise, this tradition indicates a history of politics enacted from a position of "rank and file autonomy," which rejects the mediation of bodies of representation such as unions or parties. This history has inspired the emergence of a line of inquiry called "autonomy of migration" in the '90s when some scholars of migration started looking at mass mobility as a social movement rather than as a mere matter of labor supply and demand.

Within this tradition, it is mainly the work of Dimitri Papadopoulos and Vassilis Tsianos (Papadopoulos and Tsianos, 2007) that supports my theoretical resonance with the autonomy framework, since they discuss how migration can be seen "as one of the biggest laboratories for the subversion of liberal politics" (Idem: 230). This subversion is precisely what I believe the political practices of the disenfranchised Tunisian revolutionaries, then migrants, can be seen as a courageous example of.

CHAPTER OUTLINE

Each of the five chapters will be preceded by an introductory section, which will function both as an abstract and as an opportunity to introduce the argument of the chapter while connecting it to the other chapters. Each of these initial introductions will be titled in accordance with the chapter's focus.

In the first chapter, titled "The 'Arab Spring': The Projection of a 'Familiar' Revolution," I reflect on the impact of the Orientalist paradigm of "Arab Exceptionalism" (Stark, 2011) on narratives such as those of the "Arab Spring" or the "Jasmine revolution." Drawing from the observations of "Arab" thinkers (such as Dakhli, 2013; El Mahdi, 2011; Haddad, Bsheer, and Abu-Rish, 2012; Hibou, 2011; or Rizk, 2014), I claim that these narratives are part of a hegemonic "discursive configuration," which implies many reductive assumptions. I thus argue against the hypothesis of an unexpected and completed revolution, mainly promoted by young, Internet-savvy, nonviolent male citizens, whose struggle is read according to the secular/religious binary as aiming at a Western-like liberal democracy. I chose some examples from the vast literature on the topic in order to point out how ideology and religion can be framed by a non-Western observer (Dabashi, 2012a); how important the spatial takeover becomes as a political strategy of existence (Garelli, Sossi, and Tazzioli, 2013); and how some Leftist theorists (such as Badiou, 2012; Hardt and Negri, 2011, 2012; and Žižek, 2012) often downplayed the political originality of the events in the Middle East, unable to decree the victory of emancipation in countries where armies and religion play such important roles.

Furthermore, in order to resist the Eurocentric representations of instances of non-Western resistance, Foucault's and Guattari's accounts of the Iranian and Brazilian (molecular) revolution suggest the importance of an "anti-strategic" approach: one concerned to be "respectful when a singularity revolts, [and] intransigent when power violates the universal" (Foucault, 1979) when dealing with the people's urgency to rise up. In this sense, when interacting with such events, it becomes crucial to suspend one's expectations and rather embrace the "unconscious that protests" (Guattari and Rolnik, 1986).

In the second chapter, titled "The Event of Resistance and Its Capture," I argue that the notion of "revolution" is not able to account for the specificity of the Tunisian events, nor acknowledge their difference and thus facilitate the futurity of similar practices. Instead, I propose the notion of a "network of events of resistance" based on theories of resistance (Caygill, 2013) and of the event (Badiou, 1988, 2006, 2012; Deleuze, 1992a). Moreover, drawing from Spinozian reflections (read by Nunes, 2013) through Deleuze and Guattari (Deleuze and Guattari, 1980) on knowledge based on recognition as opposed to the one based on the "nomadic thought," my intention is that of building a category that can help me account for the virtual dimension of the event (of the Tunisian revolution) instead of reducing its dimension of the real to the actual one.[3] I, therefore, seek to account for the event's *singularity* in terms of it being a trace of subjectivation (Guattari and Rolnik, 1986), as one holding an experimental originality that is irreducible to Western political categories. My understanding of singularity is drawn from Guattari and Rolnik's work *Molecular Revolution in Brazil* ([1986] 2008). I intend "singularity" as a trace of a process of singularization. I use this term because I want to stress that the singular specificity of this event is not to be framed with the help of Western political categories but rather reflected upon as part of a historical lineage of resistance. Seeing the event in these terms also allows a reflection on what the Tunisian revolution brings as an original contribution to the contemporary struggles from within neoliberalism and police states all over the world.

Comparing the ideas of the event developed by Deleuze and by Badiou, I conclude that features inspired by both philosophers define a notion of event able to embrace the Tunisian revolution. Following the reflections of Nunes (2010) and Aradau (2004), this research identifies some important aspects of the event of resistance. First of all, these types of events require an interruption of the power/knowledge regime. In some cases, the mobilization becomes contagious, and similar protest gestures are emulated making the interruption spread and solidify.[4] These powerful gestures of resistance and interruption are constantly articulated in a myriad of places beyond the square gatherings that usually receive most of the media attention. Finally, a crucial aspect of the events of resistance is the fact that, before they are reabsorbed by the regime of dominant signification, they can lead to important examples of transversality or cross-class alliances, such as I believe the Tunisian revolution was an instance of.

In this sense, the definition of "resistance" is both based on Caygill's philosophy of defiance (2013) and Lazzarato's understanding of it in terms of subjectivation (2014). I argue that resistance has both a reactive and negative nature, and a productive or creative nature, rooted in the dimension of the virtual. Instead of being essentialized, resistance is viewed dynamically (in its ever-changing relationship with its counter-force) and as projecting the possibility of future resistance (Caygill, 2013: 12). Moreover, resistance can be profoundly connective, either unintentionally (when defiance or contestation becomes contagious) or by building intentional political alliances or transversalities.

These gestures of resistance disturb the established order; therefore, they are met with attempts of capture. In the Tunisian case, the protests were first heavily repressed, then acknowledged and/or credited as Facebook-led, and then finally, after the toppling of the president, the revolution was eulogized although its demands remain unheard. These are just some examples of how an event of resistance undergoes capture. In fact, this can occur at a discursive level, where signification is produced in order to actively dominate the field of possibility; for instance, focusing on the protagonism of Western social media rather than on the courage of the impoverished Tunisians challenging a police state (Lazzarato, 2003, 2004). Alternatively, the power apparatus can also intervene by bypassing speech and cognition and by valorizing the flow of affects toward its own agenda. This occurs, for example, in those cases in which accumulated dissent is redirected elsewhere, such as in the case of underprivileged Tunisians who engage in Islamic militancy and end up attacking their even poorer fellow citizens.[5] This way a certain contagion of dissent can also lead to forms of conflict that benefit constituted power, which in this case was not only the Tunisian government but also Islamic militant organizations. I discuss this point precisely because I want to underline some examples in which contagion of dissent carries a transformative and affirmative political validity (these examples will mainly be described in chapters 3 and 5).

In the third chapter, titled "A Microhistory of the Tunisian Revolution: The Struggle of the Disenfranchised," I materialize my diagrammatic transposition of the event. Drawing from Lazzarato's (2014) and O'Sullivan's (2014) understanding of the diagram as a non-discursive intervention, and inspired by the counter-mapping of the Tunisian revolution operated by Glenda Garelli, Federica Sossi, and Martina Tazzioli in *Spaces in Migration* (2013), I develop my own diagrams. Since I understand the revolutionary process as a "network of events of resistance" (which have mainly been pointed out to me by some participants to the revolution), I follow the direction of such events and claim that the Tunisian territory is a true crossroad of flows of struggle, thanks to its position between Europe and the rest of the African continent. In order to fully account for the genealogy and development of the resistance connected to the Tunisian territory, I have extended the time frame to the period 2008–2015.

By employing the works of North African thinkers (such as Dakhli, 2013; Hibou, 2011; and Kilani, 2014), I point to the specificity of the Tunisian setting as one marked by a historically unequal development between the rich coast and capital, and an eternally abandoned western, central, and southern region (that same region the revolution started from), also partially inhabited by the indigenous population of *Imazighen* ("Berbers").[6] It also becomes clear how the majority of the unemployed turn to the informal economy, illegal emigration, and even Islamic militancy in order to achieve dignified living conditions. My microhistory of the event is mostly concerned with the articulations of this great majority of disenfranchised Tunisian citizens (who I first call "underclass," then "mob"). By using diagrams, I draw one possible chronology and geography of the event, following the directions indicated by the single moments of rupture. In other words, I follow the actions of the rioters, of the illegalized migrants, of the refugees and see where they take me, while also reflecting on where they come from and how their practices relate to the past and the future.

I, therefore, hypothesize the existence of four flows of struggle around the Tunisian revolution. The first flow is animated by the Tunisian underclass, mostly young under- or unemployed inhabitants of the poor cities or of the capital's suburbs. They brought about the revolution and reached Tunis from the peripheries of the country, occupying the capital's administrative center, the Kasbah, with their demands for political and social change.

The second flow took shape once the "revolutionaries" had the possibility to cross the border to Europe, thus becoming what Europeans call "undocumented migrants" or *harraga* (literally "those who burn") as they are called by their fellow citizens from the Maghreb. At least 20,000 crossed the Mediterranean, and many have perished in shipwrecks. Those who have reached Europe have propelled a significant and still ongoing wave of migrant struggles.

The third flow is represented by the struggle of the refugees. With the destabilization of the neighboring country of Libya, 200,000 refugees entered the Tunisian territory. Many of them had been hosted by the Tunisians themselves, who nevertheless discriminated against those refugees they identified as "African," mostly citizens holding Sub-Saharan African nationalities. Among the refugees escaping Libya, many crossed the sea, while others chose to stay in Tunisia and fight for their right to asylum and relocation in Europe. They are the protagonists of the flow of struggle of the refugees.

I also consider the flow of Islamic militants, thousands of young disenfranchised Tunisians who have chosen to devote their lives to the Islam-oriented militancy in their country but mostly abroad.

By taking this snapshot of a territory (of which Tunisia is the epicenter) in a particular period (2008–2015), and by reflecting on its flows of struggle, I underline the protagonism of the underclass and of these groups' capacity to challenge both local and global governmentality. My intention is to draw attention to this fundamental yet criminalized political agent, which I initially define as "underclass" or "Lumpenprecariat" (Rizk, 2014). These terms account for the Tunisian social stratification and for the importance of informalization of labor in the context of the revolution. Furthermore, these same categories can be read in relation to the reworked notion of "mob" (as reframed by Aradau and Huysmans, 2009), which precisely refers to the way vulnerabilized groups enact a "rejection of the price of being subject" (Tazzioli, 2016) and consequently expand the notion of the political from a profoundly marginal position.

In the fourth chapter, titled "Histories of Dispossession and Contemporary Vanguards," I start by investigating the absences within the Tunisian revolution. Thanks to the work of the critical geographer Habib Ayeb (2011, 2013), I am able to trace the genealogy of dispossession that has targeted the rural environment, from the colonial settlement until the revolution. In addition to the importance of the rural regions and history, I also acknowledge the "inaudible" presence of Tunisia's indigenous population, the *Imazighen*, in the threads of the revolution.

There seems to be a direct connection between the impoverishment of the countryside and the increasing urban segregation, especially in terms of internal migration toward the northern cities and their suburbs, the *hwem*. The *houma* (plural *hwem*), in fact, appears as the new terrain of identity formation and political organization from below, as characterized in the work of the sociologist Olfa Lamloum (2016). This aspect is particularly important, as the *hwem* are crucial spatial dimensions of the revolution.

Furthermore, in this chapter I engage with the work of the street art collective Ahl Al Kahf,[7] showing how its practice has grown out of the revolutionary event and how it carried the legacy of this opening up of possibilities around and beyond the country.

The protests initiated by Ridha Yahyaoui's suicide in January 2016[8] in Kasserine further demonstrated that the issues raised by the revolution had been disregarded by the government; they also showed that the impoverished Tunisian youth would not entirely be attracted by the Islamic militancy proposal, which had involved many Tunisians after 2013. I address these aspects with the notion of "vanguard," showing the affirmative vocation of many of Tunisia's poorest citizens. Finally, thanks to Bargu's work on the Turkish socialist struggle of the 1990s, I describe the tactics of the struggle of the Tunisians in terms of "necroresistance," reflecting on the ways in which "bare life" can become a political tool for emancipation (Bargu, 2014, 2015).

In the fifth chapter, titled "Mediation of an Event: Circulation of Cultures and Practices of Resistance," I challenge the attitude of technofetishism in relation to the "Arab Spring" and investigate what lies beyond and alongside its social media presence. In doing this, I don't take for granted the role of technology, in general, and of connectivity, in particular. Based on a media studies approach and on the work of Terranova (Terranova, 2004, 2007, 2016), I advance the notion of mediation as a form of creation, organization, and transmission of meaning and affect, able to go against the technologies of containment of dissent, such as representation and modulation of affects. This framework is also intended to account for the way cultures and practices of resistance circulate across borders, such as in the case of the struggle of the porters in Italy in 2013, which employed the language of the Tunisian revolution.

This chapter also addresses the question of the propagation of protests. It hypothesizes that resonance, rather than contagion, is what explains how riots spread across different communities, and that resonance depends on the commonality of the experience of dispossession and state violence (Clover, 2016). A focus on contagion, contamination, or virality as the modality by which protests spread might occlude the political fact that certain risky forms of mobilization are enacted by particular communities. I read this resonance as informed by the commonality of the embodied experience of injustice, declined through space (as an inhabitant of a poor suburban reality), time (as individuals hopelessly waiting for an opportunity to earn money, to work, to travel, etc.), and mobility (as subjects whose movement is constantly contained and criminalized).

Eventually, what I argue is that the Tunisian revolution was born to denounce and fight a form of internal colonialism—of the richer north and coastal areas on the rest of the country—and its expression in terms of state violence, also employed to extract value from the informal survival economy of the country's poorest areas. Moreover, it is crucial to stress that the country's pre-revolutionary economic inequality is strongly tied to neoliberal policies that the Ben Ali regime chose to promote, receiving, in exchange, a positive evaluation from his Western allies, who were in 2011 compelled to reconsider their attitude under the pressure of the popular uprising.

In this sense, my research hopes to indicate some conditions of possibility for politics of emancipation in the post-colonial and post-socialist setting of the contemporary age, marked by the practices of global techno-governance, enforced and justified by the discourses of the War on Terror and austerity. In this situation, instead of depoliticizing and criminalizing the intervention of the "rioter," the "revolutionary," the "unemployed," the "migrant," the "refugee," and the "terrorist," what is necessary is to reflect on the political relevance of these subjectivities, when they are made visible, and on how at least some of them can foster the alliances among political formations in the future.

This work's particular approach—theoretically informed and empirically grounded—can be relevant as an example of framing contemporary phenomena such as revolutions, social movements, mobility, and media.

My interdisciplinary methodology is based on the premise that an event such as the Tunisian revolution carries a significantly creative potential, able to enrich the understanding of contemporary flows of accumulation, global history, and politics from below.

What is generalizable in other areas of study is to allow for an event of progressive politics enacted from below to challenge both media practices and theoretical frameworks and to embrace and develop the conceptual and political fruits of this challenge.

Chapter One

The "Arab Spring"
The Projection of a "Familiar" Revolution

> That's why they put you away, my friend. You were dangerous. You challenged this God of theirs, went in search of this heaven that you had been offered in exchange for your malnutrition, disease, ignorance, and poverty. You wanted to feel this Heaven in your hand, see it with your eyes, not later in the by and by, but right here, right now!
>
> —Sylvia Wynter, *The Hills of Hebron*, 1962

LOOKING *AT* OR INTERACTING *WITH* THE ARAB SPRING?

In the context of the explosive manifestations of dissent that have marked recent history, the representation of the Arab Spring, which occurred in 2011, has a particular significance because it carries a double potentiality. There is the potential of representing it as yet another "revolution of the Other" (Levin [film], 2014) in the struggle for recognition of the same that the West engaged in with the Orientalist readings of these events. Yet, on the other side, the Arab Spring also offers the opportunity of opening up toward an interaction with the Arab collective resistance practices enacted in the Middle East. This type of interaction would require acknowledging that these events' specificity might, in fact, represent a highly productive and inspiring way of opposing contemporary articulations of domination. This could be the first step toward imagining a possible global consciousness (Kaldor, 2003). And "imagination must be nourished" (Boltanski, 1999: 51–54).

This reflection has started from a joined discovery of critical discussions around the politics of representation of the event, such as Rabab El Mahdi's article, "Orientalising the Egyptian Uprising" (2011), alongside the valuable political practice of art collectives, such as Ahl Al Kahf[1] based in Tunisia.

The uprisings in Tunisia and Egypt (which culminated on January 14 and 25, 2011), and the wave of protest that followed in the region, have challenged the analytical categories employed for the understanding of the Middle East. Thinkers across disciplines have underlined, in different ways, the innovative nature of these events, as well as their impact on framing the interaction between the West and the East in the aftermath of the War on Terror.

The main question raised by this chapter regards the patterns of reception of the event by non-Western actors ("Arabs")[2] and led by social categories whose actions are often de-politicized, misread, or ignored, as is the case with the instances of collective action promoted by the urban poor. How can the political relevance of this event be read in the context of global governmentality, going beyond the common interpretative frames originating both from the West and the local post-revolutionary establishment?

My claim is that the Arab Spring paradigm itself constitutes an instance of hegemonic "discursive configuration" that needs to be deconstructed and challenged in all its implicit assumptions. Especially the ones regarding aspects such as the duration, class, and gender composition of the revolution and the way a certain representation of the event is focused on the opposition between religious and secular sensibility.

This chapter represents a first approach to the critique of the narrative of the "Arab Spring." My intention is to underline the performativity of contemporary Orientalizing discursive formations by pointing out some stereotypic features that the 2011 protests in the Middle East have been read through. In this chapter, I also introduce some of the critical reflections (El Mahdi, 2011; Amin, 2012; Rizk, 2014; Garelli et al., 2013; Hanieh, 2013) and practices (of collectives such as Ahl Al Kahf in Tunisia and Mosireen in Egypt and of filmmakers like Ridha Tlili, 2010, 2011, Sami Tlili, 2012, 2013) that have inspired me. Moreover, I discuss the contributions of some Leftist European philosophers in relation to the "Arab Spring" (Žižek, 2012; Badiou, 2012; Hardt and Negri, 2011, 2012). Finally, I seek examples of anti-hegemonic engagements with political moments of rupture in the works of Michel Foucault (on the 1979 Iranian revolution) and of Félix Guattari (on the post-1984 Brazilian "molecular revolution").

Considering the work of Foucault and Guattari on instances of non-Western revolutions—namely, the Iranian and Brazilian "molecular" revolutions—will provide some useful suggestions toward how to approach such intense and still ongoing events with an awareness of the inherent bias of the Western standpoint and an active engagement with the specificity of the mobilizations. Moreover, I will also show how the work of the Martinican psychiatrist and anti-colonial fighter Frantz Fanon has proven a crucial inspiration source for this analysis.

The expected result of this research is a broader understanding of practices of resistance and of their interaction with power and representation, which is not an Arab-specific question but concerns all of us. What is at stake is our status as spectators, (dis)connected (from) to that of the Tunisian revolutionaries, and the transformative potentiality of these events, silenced through a complex mechanism of "otherization" and intermittent visibility.

This sheds light on the contemporary interaction between domination and resistance, on the conditions of possibility of collective struggle, on the global recomposition of the underclass, and on the way in which the "media mask" interacts with all of this.

This initial chapter contains the "seeds" for each of the following chapters. In fact, once I reflect on the discursive formation of the "Arab Spring" in this chapter, I will then suggest possible ways to engage with the event: by reflecting on what philosophical paradigm of the event can account for such moments of interruption of the power/knowledge relations (chapter 2); by building a chrono-geography of the events in accordance with their flows of struggle (chapter 3); by unearthing the practices of minor art and politics connected to the Tunisian revolution (chapter 4); and finally by hypothesizing how cultures and practices of resistance circulate and how propagation of organized dissent can lead to revolutionary transformation (chapter 5).

1.1. ON THE MASK OF THE "ARAB SPRING"

This research will mainly and intentionally focus on the Tunisian uprising that toppled the government of el-Abidine Ben Ali on January 14, 2011. First, however, it is necessary to engage with the development of one term that has and still is influencing our perception of the series of political unrests that have shaken the region of the Middle East starting from December 18, 2010, the date when the Tunisian protests escalated as a reaction to Mohamed Bouazizi's immolation in Sidi Bouzid, a city located in the center of Tunisia. That term is "Arab Spring."

I have chosen to call this term a "discursive configuration" drawing on "discourse" as a "socially produced group of ideas or ways of thinking that can be tracked in individual texts or groups of texts, but that also demand to be located within wider historical and social structures of relations" (Turner, 1996). This discursive configuration is fed by particular hegemonic assumptions, and it produces a set of narratives able to self-replicate and automatically reproduces hegemonic meaning configurations when confronted with moments of rupture and discontinuity. This is the way in which the dominant signification regime operates the re-incorporation of moments of disruption. This is also why the stereotypical features of the media discourse around the Arab revolutions have been referred to in terms of "domination narrative" (Rizk, 2014).

In my case study, the Tunisian revolution, the discursive configuration is articulated on two levels. At a global level, the event is re-signified thanks to the Arab Spring narrative, while at the local level, the Tunisian authorities focus on a broad institutionalization of the "14th of January" revolution by emphasizing its completion. Moreover, there are (at least) three moments to be identified in both the global and the local discursive configuration regarding Tunisia: the pre-revolutionary moment, the revolutionary climax, and the post-revolutionary moment. Before 2011, the West would consider Tunisia its partner (both commercial and political), while the government would promote the myth of the Tunisian "economic miracle" (Hibou, 2011: 9). During the revolution, the West saluted the Arab Spring, while the Tunisian governments celebrated the glorious achievements of the "14th of January" revolution. In the aftermath of the revolution, the West went back to its concerns about "terrorist" threats (after the electoral victory of the Islamists of Ennahda on October 23, 2011) and "illegal" migration, while the Tunisian authorities were also considering the revolution completed and preferred to shift the attention toward the fight against terrorism.

Throughout this research, I will develop a thorough critique of the term "revolution." First, I will point out the stereotypes inherent in the paradigm of the Arab Spring (in this chapter), and later (in chapter 2) I will move away from the revolution framework in order to privilege the analytical lens of the "network of events of resistance," which I consider more useful to account for the micro-levels of resistance that the 2011 revolution was a result of. I will acknowledge the importance of these moments of rupture by employing reflections derived from post-structuralist theories of the event.

However, this research does not intend to label conceptions of revolution as being always Orientalist, neither am I suggesting that theories of the event can be the solution to Orientalist narratives on Tunisia. In this sense, the critique of the term and the framework of "revolution"—as it will be developed in this and the following chapters—uniquely regard the way this term has been weaponized to their own interests by states and dominant groups (which the revolution was a challenge to). My critique does not regard the way the term "revolution" may be employed by all social groups or political actors. In fact, I will often use the term in the text as and when it is employed by the protagonists of the Tunisian revolution.

In the following section, more focus will be granted to the Arab Spring as a discursive configuration and its stereotypical assumptions. What is immediately liable for critique is that the media has homogenized a series of extremely different political events under the generic umbrella term of Arab Spring. If one were to give a unitary definition to such heterogeneous events, one should at least differentiate between so-called successful revolutions (Tunisia, Egypt), revolutions transformed into civil wars (Libya, Syria), and all the other attempted revolutions forgotten by Western and Arab media (Yemen, Bahrain, Jordan, Morocco) (Valeriani, 2012).

At the same time, the political stakes of the protests are caught in between the conflicting gestures of naming and self-naming. On the one side, the events are formatted and evaluated by external actors, such as some Western observers with their own agenda; on the other side, the active participants in the protests choose to name the events they've contributed to in their own different ways, as discussed later.

The political implications of the "Arab Spring" term become even clearer once the genealogy of its coinage is explicit. The self-declared inventor of the term is Marc Lynch, a Middle East scholar writing for the American journal *Foreign Policy* on January 6, 2011, in an article titled "Obama's 'Arab Spring'?" The term alludes to different Western historical transformations (especially the European 1848 "Spring of the Peoples" and the anti-Soviet 1968 "Prague Spring"). As a consequence, the term has been recognized to be intentionally carrying liberal meanings as "part of a US strategy of controlling (the movement's) aims and goals" and labeling the events in North Africa as uprisings inspired by an America-style liberal democracy (Massad, 2012 in Haddad et al., 2012).

But more significantly, the Arab Spring contains a stereotypically Western understanding of the Arab dimension—one particularly proliferated against the backdrop of the War on Terror—and distinguished by the projection of the so-called Arab Exceptionalism, as dubbed by Samuel Huntington. This frame is intended to convey the generic Arab/Islamic world's resistance to representative democracy (Stark, 2011) as well as its inclination toward authoritarianism and inter-religious conflictuality.

Furthermore, it has to be noted that the exceptionalism animated by anti-"Arab"/Islam racism is a paradigm that has been initially promoted by the United States in the geopolitical setting of the "oil crisis" of the 1970s under the form of neo-Orientalism (Said, 1997; Terranova, 2007). From an Arab perspective, a common word game shows the impact of the geopolitical rise of the fossil fuel on the long lineage of Arab resistance. In fact, it is commonly accepted that "from 1973 onwards, the oil manna (*al fawra*) has taken the place of revolution (*al thawra*)" (Amin, 2012: 151). Recently, the neo-Orientalism paradigm of the 1970s has been "updated" through the lens of post-9/11 Islamophobia.

As El Mahdi notices, in the immediate aftermath of 2011, the "Arab Awakening" substituted the "Arab Exceptionalism" narrative, while subtending the total political "sleepiness" or absence of democracy of the countries included in the Arab Spring scheme (El Mahdi, 2011). In this way, the "Arab Awakening" perspective overlooked a broad tradition of anti-colonial struggles, pan-Arab awareness, and political theory and practice, many of which had historically challenged the West's striving of domination in the area. In this sense, more than being aligned with the Western values of liberalism, the Tunisian uprising revealed the possibility of evading the classical and liberal framing of revolutions because it pierced through "that neoliberal present as time stalled, without hope for emancipatory futures" with "far-reaching effects on how we think about the nature of political action and justice" (Scott, 2014).

Furthermore, it is important to stress how the series of protests in Tunisia and Egypt, at least starting from 2007, have all been articulated in opposition to "neoliberalism as a state-led project" (Hanieh, 2013) or to the "state-led monopoly capitalism" (Amin, 2012). Most precisely, these protests had repeatedly been a response to a certain model of redistribution focused around a massive operation of polarization: immiseration, on the one side, and accumulation, on the other side, both of which fostered by Western-compliant autocratic systems (Hanieh, 2013).

This being said, the Tunisian upheavals can be called "revolution" insofar as it's the direct participants who have chosen to call it so, and bearing in mind the Arabic term's genealogy. In this sense, "revolution" becomes a viable term to name these events only as long as this "terminology (is) chosen by active agents themselves to name their own actions rather than seeking to categorize a political process through the use of standard terminology" (El Houri, 2016).

However, I suggest a definition yet to come since, as Anthony Alessandrini explains, "Revolutions change things, and among the things that they change, or should change, are the categories through which we view such changes. New subjectivities and new singularities demand new frameworks, both of understanding and of solidarity" (Alessandrini, 2014).

Who names the events and *what names are employed* become crucial in order to understand the power relations around the Tunisian revolution. In this sense, beyond the Arab Spring umbrella term, there are specific names that have been connected to the Tunisian revolution and have also been broadly critiqued by the Tunisians. Each and every one of them contains one specific assumption, which will be deconstructed in the following section.

The "Jasmine revolution," for example, stresses the nonviolent aspect of the upheaval, but, more significantly, it forecloses the protagonism of the internal areas of the country by using the symbol of a flower only growing in the richest neighborhood of the Tunis, Sidi Bousaid. As a counterpart of the jasmine, and in order to restore the importance of the internal and Western rebellions, some have suggested names such as the *Hindi* revolution, referring to the flower of the cactus growing in the desert internal areas (Dakhli, 2013); the Fig revolution (Tlili [film], 2011); or the alfa grass revolution (Ayeb, 2011).

Moreover, the much-celebrated revolution of the "14th of January," the date when the president Ben Ali left the country, has been critiqued for its imposition of an end to the mobilization. It was ironically called the "revolution under 5 minutes" (Tlili, 2011) as opposed to what activists perceive as a "revolutionary becoming" (Ahl Al Kahf, 2013) and what more commonly Tunisians refer to as the *processus* when referring to the ongoing "transition" process toward "democracy."[3]

Most Tunisians would employ the Arabic term to indicate their revolution as *al-thawra*, which holds a different historical lineage when compared to the Western "revolution" and its historical examples. In fact, the Latin term carries an inherent Orientalist gaze when applied to non-Western settings insofar as it implicitly sets Western historical precedents as the norm. In this same way, as Angela Giordani points out, the Arabic term *al-thawra* is irreducibly tied to the anti-colonialist and anti-imperialist struggles in the "Arab" world but is also intended as a concrete instance of rebellion that functions as a means to reach the more transcendent *inquilab*, translatable as "institutional change,"[4] "necessary to bring about the Arab nation's rebirth, or *ba'th*."

> So, while the popular anti-imperialist uprising of *thawra* was the expression of the *umma*'s (Islamic community) will-to-power, *inquilab* was what would give the *umma* its historical form as a "modern national entity" capable of re-entering the trajectory of self-realization and awakening (*nahda*) from which it had been supposedly deflected by Ottoman, imperialist and Zionist domination. (Giordani, 2013: 7)

From the generic Arabic term of *al-thawra*, largely employed in the postcolonial period for its reference to victorious struggles against different forms of domination, I'll return to the Arab Spring discursive configuration and explore the set of stereotypical assumptions it carries.

It is imperative to closely identify the latencies of this totalizing Arab Spring framework, taking inspiration from the way Tunisians and Egyptians have articulated resistance to the narrative. Dismissing these stereotypes for Tunisia is the first step toward dismissing them for all the other countries.

One of the first scholars to have exposed the "revolution grand-narrative" linked to the Arab Spring is El Mahdi, who clearly pointed at a biased interpretation by both the international media but also by "academics, politicians, and the local elite" engaged in "orientalizing the Egyptian Uprising,"

> constructed as a youth, non-violent revolution in which social media (especially Facebook and Twitter) are champions. The underlying message here is that these "middle-class" educated youth (read: modern) are not "terrorists," they hold the same values as "us" (the democratic West), and finally use the same tools (Facebook and Twitter) that "we" invented and use in our daily lives. They are just like "us" and hence they deserve celebration. (El Mahdi, 2011)

Although El Mahdi's analysis concerns the Egyptian case, it is very relevant in the process of deconstructing the Arab Spring in general and can be applied to the Tunisian case in particular. In this sense, thinkers like Magid Shihade have pointed out how the understanding of the Arab Spring had been permeated by Orientalism, Eurocentrism, and the Western conception of "modernity" (Shihade and Shihade, 2012).

The critique constituted by expressions such as "Orientalising the Egyptian uprising" (El Mahdi, 2011) or the "domination narrative" (Rizk, 2014) is important because it challenges some of the aspects of the event for the way in which they have been framed by the Arab Spring discursive configuration.

The first most pervasive and complex aspect of this discursive configuration is the temporality of the event in terms of how both its emergence and its duration are understood. According to the Arab Spring reading—and bearing in mind its more "successful" examples, namely, Tunisia and Egypt—the revolutions are implicitly considered as an unexpected and completed (either achieved or "failed") outburst of democratic practices.

Privileging the sudden rebellion against the dictator facilitates at least two important erasures. The first is the pre-2011 lineage of struggle, with its social demands, which goes beyond the mere goal of toppling the "dictator." The second is the complicity of the West with its former ally, depicted globally as the only one accountable for the social inequality, which led to the revolution.

On the contrary, unlike what is being implied by the Arab exceptionalism paradigm, Tunisia has an extensive tradition of political dissent, social movements, and struggles in the period of Ben Ali's government, which were faced with a pervasive repressive state apparatus (as illustrated by Garelli et al., 2013; Massarelli, 2012; Hibou, 2011; Ben Mhenni, 2011; Dakhli, 2013; Beinin and Vairel, 2013). Some of the more recent examples are the collective protests organized by the main trade union (UGTT), by the League of Human Rights, by the union of the unemployed graduates (UDC), and by the Yizzi Fok blogger network in 2007. Furthermore, the most significant pre-revolutionary mobilization is the one in 2008 in Gafsa (Del Pistoia and Duchemin in *Osservatorio Iraq*, 2016: 19). In fact, "while they seemed a 'surprise' for numerous observers, the demonstrations of December 2010 and January 2011 *echoed* other strong and contentious social movements, notably the revolts in the Gafsa mining basin in 2008" (Dakhli, 2013, my emphasis).

In an attempt to resist the reduction of the revolution's temporal horizon, many Tunisian participants have challenged the "failure" narrative promoted by both liberal and radical Western observers (Francois and Sadik, 2013), which is mostly based on the victory of Islam-inspired parties such as Ennahda in Tunisia and the Muslim Brotherhood in Egypt. This is because depicting the Tunisian revolution as "failed" implies a limit asserted by external observers, autonomously deciding on the beginning and the end of the revolutionary process. As Walid El Houri points out in this critique of the failed revolution paradigm, "The idea of speaking about failure or success of an ongoing event, ends that event, it establishes a point of conclusion, a perceived suture" (El Houri, 2016).

I'm not arguing here for a notion of "permanent revolution," but I am rather referring to the fact that Tunisians perceive themselves as part of an ongoing transformative process despite the awareness of many post-revolutionary difficulties and setbacks.

Leyla Dakhli is very eloquent in describing this collective perception: "While protests were continuously undertaken in the country, a form of disappointment and discouragement manifested. The feeling of a betrayed revolution now visibly coexists with the understanding that the revolutionary process is still ongoing" (Dakhli, 2013).

Like in the case of the Arab exceptionalism paradigm, which influenced the Western perception of Tunisia before, during, and after the 2011 revolution, the focus on gender has also been modulated in different ways.[5] As far as the revolution is concerned, the gender composition of the protestors has been either overlooked or saluted as rare, privileging the focus on the young male participants and their masculine-centered agency. Confirming the Orientalist view of the subjection of Arab women, initial media accounts ignored the women's participation in the revolution or celebrated the gestures of individual women as exceptional, unexpected acts of courage (Al-Ali, 2012).[6] On the contrary,

> for decades [women] had been active members in trade unions, political opposition parties and more informal networks and organizations that were all instrumental in the recent political developments. Women have been very much

involved in the virtual communities of bloggers and Facebook users. And during the height of the actual protests to oust Ben Ali and Mubarak, women of all generations and social classes were on the streets in large numbers. (Al-Ali, 2012: 27)

In this regard, my case study and further investigation will not specifically focus on examples of protagonism of women and girls in the political arena in Tunisia. I am aware that I will be privileging the collective actions centered around young, poor urban men, engaged in extreme forms of protest and mobility, in their journeys from the countryside to the city, toward Europe and toward the Islamic militancy fronts in the East. Nevertheless, there are multiple forms of collective action, mainly led and enacted by girls and women across different social classes, that would deserve further attention but that this work will not focus upon.[7]

This brings me to what might be the most delicate aspect of the Tunisian (and Egyptian) uprising—namely, the class belonging of the people involved in the protests and the consequent nature of their demands. As El Mahdi has pointed out, most of the Arab Spring narrative has concentrated on generic "youth" being the promoters of the uprisings and "middle-class young people" becoming its representatives, both in traditional media outlets and in social media.

> In this construct, the media and academic analysts lump together the contradictory and often conflictual interests of "yuppies" (young, urban, professionals of (Western) connections and backgrounds) with those of the unemployed, who live under the poverty line in rural areas and slum-areas. Under this banner of "youth" and "yuppies," upper-middle-class young people are portrayed as the quintessential representative of this uprising. (El Mahdi, 2011)

In this regard, one of the members of Mosireen Egyptian video collective, Philip Rizk, has published a thorough rejection of the "representative" role assigned to the middle-class young people during the Egyptian revolution, depicted as mediators of what the liberal West wanted to perceive as a friendly, "familiar revolution," according to a narrative he called "domination narrative" (Rizk, 2014). "We became the translators of a collective uprising we were far from representative of. [. . .] This process drowned out the voices of the majority. No matter how hard we tried to argue otherwise, we fit the part—middle class, internet-savvy, youth, and thus revolutionary" (Ibidem).

This class aspect is directly linked to the violence with which these uprisings have managed to oust their dictators since the "middle class, internet-savvy" youth is not expected to employ violence as a contestation tool. The

Arab Spring's stereotypical peculiarity—similar to that of the "Jasmine revolution" narrative—lies in its alleged peaceful methods, mostly provided by the access to new media, especially social media, able to sustain the spreading of news and the organizing of gatherings. This is also the reason for the emergence of definitions such as "Facebook revolution," "Twitter revolution," or, more generally, "Revolution 2.0" (Ghonim, 2012). The violence and the accentuated focus on social media are closely connected and cannot be separated. Social media is also often employed as an explanation to the implicit Orientalist question, "How did the 'Arabs' succeed to topple their dictators?" and is thematized as a magic tool of social change. On the contrary, as the series of precedent struggles in both Tunisia and Egypt prove, violence has, unfortunately, always been present. If we avoid considering struggles themselves as a reaction to structural violence—either direct or indirect, in terms of social exclusion or state violence—we definitely cannot ignore the violent response of the state, in both cases, without which the "martyrs" of the revolution wouldn't have existed. During the Tunisian revolutionary climax alone, 338 people were killed and 2,147 were injured (Mandraud, 2011). This is to dismiss the possibility of a nonviolent revolution, alluded to by the classic "Tahrir Square" gathering frame. As Rizk and El Mahdi suggest, the underclass's struggle is far from the bucolic "Facebook revolution":

> *Did you hear the voices of the underclass?* Did you see the family members of the martyrs clad in black mourning in their homes? Did you see images of unnamed civilians gunned down by snipers on the roofs of the police stations? Did you see police officers opening prison doors in order to undermine this revolutionary moment and wreak havoc on nearby communities? Did you see protesters storming police stations on January 28th, seeking vengeance for years of unaccounted-for torture, violence, and psychological domination? Did you see the Molotov cocktails prepared by women and lowered from their balconies to avenge the maiming of their sons and neighbours? *This is not non-violent.* Only the fixation through the lens of a camera on Tahrir Square in daylight could appease you with that impression. (Rizk, 2014, my emphasis)

As Rizk points out, violence has been highly present in the protests. In fact, following the trail of violence offers a significant view over the way the protests unfolded, as it links the violence of the authoritarian state and its massive police apparatus to the resilience and determination of the protesters, which employed a vast range of means to resist and keep challenging the power of their governments.

In fact, a form of violence that hasn't been considered enough, with a deep political charge, concerns different degrees of self-harm. It was an action of this type, enacted by Mohamed Bouazizi in Sidi Bouzid, that sparked the

Tunisian revolution itself. Unfortunately, extreme cases of self-harm continued occurring both in Tunisia and in the territories crossed by the Tunisian migrants after the revolution.

Therefore, it can be concluded that the nonviolent image of the uprisings is ignoring or misreading crucial and dramatic features of the upheavals. First of all, that of a large employment of lethal violence on behalf of the government; then that of the unarmed active defense on behalf of the protesters, alongside their practices of self-harm and suicidal violence.

As for the usage of social media before the toppling down of the dictators, in both Egypt and Tunisia the Internet was placed under severe censorship, which is why both countries saw the involvement in the protests of groups defending formerly persecuted bloggers. Furthermore, before 2010, corporate Western companies fully supported the authoritarian limitation of freedom of expression, like when Vodafone switched off the cell phone service at the request of the Egyptian regime (Mejias, 2012).

In this sense, the access of some of the protesters to the Internet was undoubtedly useful for both spreading the news and organizing gatherings but worked only once the governments no longer enforced the censorship.

My point is that "it takes more than a social media platform to organize and sustain a grassroots protest movement" (Ibidem). Furthermore, the most common optimistic approach toward the democratizing impact of the use of social media, which some call "liberation technology," "does not seem very interested in questioning the roles and structures of the institutions that own and control social media networks" (Ibidem). Moreover, social media was mostly accessible to the middle-class, urban, Internet-savvy youth, which is, as explained before, an important participant, yet a minority in the composition of the revolutionary body.

When considering another fundamental aspect, that of religion, it must be pointed out that the Egyptian and Tunisian revolutions have been initially regarded with suspicion and then glorified for their total lack of religious claims.[8] How can the religious belief of the protesters be accounted for without stigmatizing or romanticizing it? In the Western gaze, secularism is the only path to be taken toward "democracy," although the West has largely ignored the Tunisian radical Left, for instance, that has constantly advocated for the importance of secularism. Moreover, former rulers of the country, like Habib Bourguiba and Ben Ali, had politically weaponized secularism as an exemplary move toward Western-style modernization and as a strategy to neutralize political opposition connected to political Islam right after independence.[9] In opposition to secularism, the West appears to fear fundamentalism and theocracy as the only possible alternatives to "democracy." Muslim countries are often represented as affected by intra-religious or sectarian conflicts, like the Shia-Sunni conflict currently enflaming Syria. In this way, sectarianism and the violence connected to it are "naturalized" and associated with a religious community already extensively represented as "pre-modern" and oppressive when compared to the West, even more so after 2001.[10] Despite the post-revolutionary conflicts, the uprisings have been an occasion of broad collaboration, enacted especially during the protest gatherings and the occupations, not only among secular and believers but also between different groups of Muslims, as Hamid Dabashi explains:

> The challenges posed by these revolutions to divisions within Islam and among Muslims—racial (Arabs, Turks, Iranians, etc.), ethnic (Kurds, Baluchs, etc.) or sectarian (Sunni and Shi'a in particular)—has at once agitated and (*ipso facto*) discredited them. These revolutions are collective acts of overcoming. They are crafting new identities, forging new solidarities, both within and without the "Islam and the West binary"—overcoming once and for all the thick (material and moral) colonial divide. (Dabashi, 2012a: 10)

Finally, as far as the political demands are concerned, the nature of the demands advanced by the underclass was a radically social one focused on employment, equal territorial development, and fighting corruption and police brutality, as exemplified by the most popular slogan: "Bread, freedom, dignity!" However, the Arab Spring narrative prefers privileging the generic struggle against the national dictatorship previously sustained by the Western countries, represented not only as violently repressive but most of all corrupt and unable to manage the country's economy adequately. Rizk hypothesizes the reason of such a narrative deviation in the sense that

> these discourses silenced the structural dimensions of injustice and concealed the role of neo-liberal policies promoted by the likes of the International Monetary Fund, the European Union and the United States of America in deepening the stratification between poor and rich. They made you forget that it is out of these structures of injustice that the desire for social justice is born in the first place. (Rizk, 2014)

What will emerge from the discussion of these assumptions is that the Tunisian revolution was the result of a broad alliance across the society, led by the country's disenfranchised categories.

Many Western readings, with their focus on religion-based conflict as well as the state's "official story," which glorifies the fall of the dictator, therefore neutralize important political aspects of the mobilization and eventually silence the ongoing social conflict. As a consequence, the protagonism of the underclass and the radicality of their demands, centered on redistribution of wealth and end of state violence, which challenge both the local power and their foreign supporters, are being overlooked.

It is possible, at this point, to reflect on the discursive configuration of the Arab Spring as a mask, following Peter Weibel's reflections. The point he makes is that

> while researching on the relationship between media and revolution, one must not interrogate the subject, but the object; not who speaks, but what is being shown and hidden. Because power reveals itself in what cannot be seen—in the media-as-a-mask—even if we're not talking about a mask "beyond" which something is really hiding. (Weibel, 1990, my translation)

Like any *medium*, the narrative of a revolution, or of a series of revolutions such as the "Arab Spring," can be seen as a mask containing numerous intentionally silenced aspects. The functionality of this media representation is that of taking possession of the depicted event while capturing and neutralizing its subversive potentialities. The Arab Spring discursive configuration thus forged is difficult to overturn from its initial functionality. Its internal mechanics must be made visible in order to expose its aims of domination. In other words, and as I will be further discussing in the next chapter, the representation of the event, in the case of narratives such as the Arab Spring, holds a particular type of performativity, which finds itself often in conflict with the aims of the people who animated the revolutionary event.

These narratives are disempowering in at least two directions: toward the collective that has revolted and toward the spectators who must make an effort to recognize and relate to the instance of resistance while being distracted by either the dismissal of it as a "failure" or by its simplifying glorification. How can one start to frame these events, and what would a more sensitive approach imply? More precisely, beyond the generalizing aims of the Arab Spring narrative, how could one engage with the event of the Tunisian revolution without attempting to appropriate or weaponize it? Can an account of the Tunisian revolution, since the Arab Spring is but a deceiving umbrella term, foster and respect the resistance of its protagonists rather than attempt to contain its potential? In the following section, I will provide a rough, and unavoidably incomplete, mapping of some of the different approaches scholars have so far adopted in looking at the events, while focusing on two significant examples.[11]

1.2. READING THE "ARAB SPRING"

The readings of the events connecting the "Arab" uprisings have been numerous and diversified. It has to be noted that ever since the protests in Tunisia overcame the threshold of global visibility—with the massive demonstrations and riots following Mohamed Bouazizi's self-immolation act on December 17, 2010—the majority of the Western media has employed few innovative categories or narrative frames, in the sense that many readings provide stereotypical interpretations drawing mostly on foreign policy expertise. Some unitary readings of the Arab Spring follow particular editorial lines depending on the publication the author collaborates with, such as *Reuters* (Noueihed and Warren, 2012), *BBC* (Gerges, 2014), *The Financial Times*, and *The Economist* (Osman, 2013).

A common feature of many of the interpretations of the events is the focus on the aspect of discontinuity. Regardless of the observer's political stance, the "Arab" uprisings are generally considered the end and/or the beginning of some temporal, political, and social unit, a clear border in contemporary history.

The second most frequent focus of the "Arab" uprisings literature is on the communicational aspect, celebrating the democratizing role of Western social media, especially Facebook and Twitter (Castells, 2012; Mason, 2012), but also the importance of blogging and online "citizen journalism" opposing the state censorship and contributing to the advent of what most indicate as the "new Arab public sphere" (Lynch, 2012). Some authors have concentrated on gathering and systematizing testimonies coming from one specific or more of the countries affected by the uprisings (Al-Zubaidi and Cassel, 2013), interested in "giving voice" to local accounts and subjective recollections from different angles, such as the migration experience (Garelli et al., 2013) or the activist practices (Massarelli, 2012).

An important phylum of literature is constituted by the interpretations of the so-called Leftist theorists (Žižek, 2012; Badiou, 2012; Hardt and Negri, 2011, 2012), which I illustrate later in this section. Alongside these orientations, numerous scholars have engaged in shedding light on particular aspects of the uprisings from different perspectives. They have reflected on the construction of obedience in the pre-revolutionary period (Hibou, 2011); on how authoritarianism in the Middle East was a functional actor in the economic domination on behalf of the West (Hanieh, 2013); on how protesting bodies interacted with the performativity of space (Butler, 2011; Weizman, 2014); or on how these uprisings were a promise to overcome "the West and the rest" paradigm (Dabashi, 2012a). These heterogeneous approaches are useful in enriching the interdisciplinary mosaic of concepts and analyses needed for a better interaction with such recent and still unfolding events.

Eventually, a new orientation of literature emerged from thinkers critically questioning the dominant narrative of the Arab Spring, some of whom I have already quoted,[12] who come from an anti-Orientalist theoretical ground (cf. Haddad et al., 2012) or from independent political and artistic collectives such as Mosireen in Egypt and Ahl Al Kahf in Tunisia, whose works I will be engaging with in chapter 4. I will be thoroughly exploring only some of these works to show the extensive framework of alternative reflections and practices concerning the Tunisian revolutionary process.

One of the earliest analyses of the Arab uprisings belongs to the Iranian comparative literature scholar Dabashi's provocatively titled *The Arab Spring: The End of Postcolonialism* (2012a). Dabashi greets the advent of a "renewed liberation geography" inaugurated by the Arab uprisings. While opening up the possibility of building a new public space, based on the ongoing engagement of grassroots voluntary associations such as trade unions, women's associations, and students' groups, he refers to the "end of postcolonialism." What he means is that "the revolutions are simultaneously a rejection not just of the colonial oppression they have inherited but, *a fortiori*, of the postcolonial ideologies that had presented and exhausted themselves as its antithesis in Islamist, nationalist or socialist narratives" (Dabashi, 2012a: 9–10).

With their practices, the revolutionaries have thus emptied the binary West-East, while removing the West's representative authority connected to the traditional Orientalist ways of perceiving the East as a region in need of Western support and examples in order to "progress." Dabashi indicates this with a literary metaphor as a collective open-ended novel instead of an epos where the narrative development is monopolized by one character.

While Dabashi's account is undoubtedly very useful and detailed, considering his scholarship regarding social movements—and especially because of his sensitive understanding of the religious collaborative aspect of the uprisings—the dismissal of what he historically refers to in terms of "postcolonial ideologies" (namely, "Islamist, nationalist or socialist narratives") indicates a possibly too abrupt rupture with historical political traditions. In fact, he operates a clear cut with what he sees as the anti-colonial ideologies of the past—namely, nationalism, socialism, and Islamism—while privileging the protagonism of a highly collaborative civil society based on voluntary organizations. Although most of the participants in the protests, at least in Tunisia, belonged to an apolitical category—united by a shared experience of severe poverty and existential precariousness rather than by previous forms of organization—ideologies shouldn't go ignored. Leftist tradition strategies have informed the pre-revolutionary labor struggles in both Tunisia and Egypt (notably the Mahalla strike in Egypt and the Gafsa Intifada in Tunisia, both in 2008[13]), while political Islam has flourished electorally after the fall of Ben Ali and Mubarak (Merone, 2013a, 2013b, 2015a). Despite the previous regimes' commitment to depoliticizing their peoples (Amin, 2012) and the harsh repression of ideological claims during their rule, ideologies, whether connected to a religious or to a working-class sensibility, should not be imagined as interrupted but rather as developed.

An original approach from a European perspective comes from *Spaces in Migration: Postcards of a Revolution* (Garelli et al., 2013). This research explores the relationship between the experience of the Tunisian revolutionaries (many of whom were inhabitants of the poorer areas of the country) and their subsequent migration across the Mediterranean toward Europe. The authors depict the revolution as taking place in the reconfiguration enacted by the bodies permeated by the desire to take space back and mark it with the full presence of their existence.[14] Occupying the privatized spaces dominated by Ben Ali's dictatorship, such as Avenue Habib Bourguiba and the governmental square of the Kasbah, and challenging the European anti-migration policies, put in place in order to immobilize and erase the existence of those same bodies, run on parallel lines. Tunisia and Europe share the counter-revolutionary drives symbolized by the urge to impose "silence and imperceptibility," challenged by the "guerilla" of presence and insistence of the revolutionaries/migrants. The authors (Glenda Garelli, Federica Sossi, and Martina Tazzioli) insist that "this is also a revolution: this turning of space into one's own within a regime of invisibility, employing strategies of existence and insistence in order to locate *a political presence in the folds of silence and imperceptibility*" (Garelli et al., 2013: 4, my emphasis).

While reflecting on the different "regimes of visibility" that harness the existence of revolutionaries, both as protesters and as illegal migrants, *Spaces in Migration* considers the interaction between these disruptive experiences and the dominant regime of speech and visibility, commonly concentrated on the "politics of testimony" as the privileged method of engaging with the Other, either the "Arab" protester or the illegal migrant. Within this collection of essays, Sossi's critique of this approach, inspired by Jean-François Lyotard's notion of *différend* (Lyotard, 1989: 13), seems to resonate with Gayatri Spivak's notorious question, "Can the Subaltern Speak?" (Spivak, 1988). In stepping away from speaking *for*, the gesture of speaking *with* is also charged with many challenges, as I have also tried to problematize in the preface (Alcoff, 1991). Sossi warns us that

> we run the risk of not deeply interrogating ourselves on the absence of speech and of visibility from the part of those who let themselves be spoken about and be seen, that is those we bear witness for. Why don't they speak? Or why do they speak without being heard? Why are they in part invisible even when devising their strategies for insisting in space? Trying not to bear witness but to

be "together" alongside them, means letting the *différend* be itself, not thinking that it could be resolved, neither through testimony nor otherwise. (Garelli et al., 2013: 162–63)

Many accounts of the Tunisian revolution (and even more so those regarding the Arab Spring) could easily be critiqued for their intentions to "solve the *différend*," as Sossi explains. In other words, these accounts are being critiqued for forcing the application of Western categories on the political imaginary and practices of non-Western citizens, with no intention of addressing the inherent bias of the Western standpoint.[15] Moreover, rather than reflecting on the specificity and innovative nature of such mobilizations, most analysts chose to depurate them of any radical political content—be it religious or socialist—while reducing them to an anti-dictatorship social media revolution. While this is generally the orientation of the supporters of the liberal reading of the events, based on the Western interests in the region, radical observers also operate a sort of "dissolution of the *différend*" when they use or dismiss the upheavals according to their theoretical expectations. All the ones I will give an overview of paradoxically suggest a sense of distrust in approaching a revolutionary practice perceived as dangerously close to religious sensibility, somehow declining something like a Leftist "Arab Exceptionalism."[16]

The Arab uprisings have aroused great interest and enthusiasm on behalf of many radical theorists who have viewed the events as announcing a significant wave of political revitalization. I have chosen to work on the Leftist readings of the Arab Spring because of the expectation that these particular theorists could provide useful elements regarding the political potential of the event.[17] However, as I illustrate, even these more politically receptive observers are influenced by the mainstream narrative, which they rarely question, and by the distrust toward the Islamic world. Therefore, they often project Western standards on the events rather than embracing their political singularity.

Alain Badiou and Slavoj Žižek, for instance, have attempted a unitary interpretation of different phenomena in the Arab and Western world, thus connecting the Arab uprisings to the anti-austerity movements in Europe and the United States as well as the riots inflaming Paris and London's suburbs, while Antonio Negri and Michael Hardt have opted to explore the new politics of organization of the Arab protesters, later extended in their book *Declaration*, which also analyzed the Occupy movement (Hardt and Negri, 2012).

What all these authors have in common is a strong concentration on the rupture caused by the revolutionary event, sometimes perceived with euphoria—as the opening of a new revolutionary era—other times with nostalgia, since it is perceived as not possessing the necessary project or awareness able to enact the expected transformation. In this sense, radical thinkers often interact with and interpret the mainstream media image of the Arab Spring and its different situations of rebellion without addressing the inherent bias of the construction of the event as such.

In his *The Year of Dreaming Dangerously* (2012), Žižek makes a clear distinction between Tunisia and Egypt on the one hand, and Libya and Syria on the other hand, in terms of a radical emancipatory struggle, definitely present in the first cases but shadowed by civil war and foreign military interventions in the second cases. The political trajectory of the Arab uprising is depicted as a merely liberal one, like in the case of anti-Communist East European revolutions of 1989: "The official circles and most of the Western media celebrate them as being essentially the same as 'pro-democracy' revolutions in Eastern Europe: a desire for Western liberal revolutions in Eastern Europe: a *desire for Western liberal democracy*, a desire to become like the West" (Idem: 74, my emphasis).

The author has an overall distrustful vision of the events, eventually decreeing the Egyptian summer of 2011 to "be remembered as the end of the revolution," since Islamists and the army have gained the power and suppressed the emancipatory potential unchained by the January uprisings. On the other hand, the philosopher advocates for the future uprising of the poor who, he claims, have been "largely absent in the Spring uprisings, which were dominated, initially at least, by educated middle-class youth" (Idem: 75).

As opposed to Žižek, Badiou identifies a strong ideal, almost transcendent, dimension to the uprisings and the riots punctuating the contemporary age in relation to their possibility of bringing about "the Rebirth." The rebirth is understood as the "emergence of a capacity, at once destructive and creative, whose aim is to make a genuine exit from the established order, of History" (Badiou, 2012: 15), while also fostering the rebirth of the "Idea," intended as "the idea of Communism" (Idem: 6). The transformation, the rebirth, is driven by the riots, seen by the author as true "guardians of the history of emancipation," in the three forms of their potential development: the immediate, the latent, and the historical riot. The latter is possibly followed by the revolution, which should possess within itself the resources for an immediate seizure of power (Idem: 32).[18] When compared to the 1848 "revolution" in Europe, the "Arab riots" are seen as not producing a new state and society situation but rather as the beginning of a new historical sequence (Idem: 47–48). The validity of the mobilization lies in the fact that it reawakens history. "When History reawakens, it is the reawakening that matters. This is valid by itself. As for the results, we shall see" (Idem: 99). The transformative "event" (as will be further discussed in the next chapter) marked by the riots and uprisings is seen in terms of the eruption of the "inexistent": the underclass, the exploited, the repressed.

Badiou's systematization of the functioning of the political event contains relevant intuitions, mostly for its focus on the riots, as opposed to the dominant narratives, which consider riots a mere nonpolitical expression of self-destructive violence. Nevertheless, this would also be Badiou's critique of the first form of riot, the "immediate" one. Although Badiou's reflection is very relevant in looking at the articulation of the political event, a possible limit could be the criteria for the "Reawakening of History." Although this moment of reawakening is described only in abstract terms—through its intensification, contraction, localization, organization system, and political Truth—it holds a rigid predetermined form, which might overlook innovative examples of contemporary forms of resistance. On the other hand, the centrality of the abstract and solemn notion of Idea, still linked to the Communist system of beliefs, seems to be far removed from the ideological pragmatism of young revolutionaries in both Tunisia and Egypt. Rather than remaining faithful to the Communist Idea, both groups have, in fact, shown to be more focused on the search of the appropriate theoretical tools to deal with the contingencies of the struggle for radical social justice, against internally and externally driven conservative setbacks. As Rizk observes in an interview, with some skepticism toward the application of Communism-inspired Ideas in Egypt, "In order to break any logic of reform, of reformulation of the old, we don't need a socialist vision, we don't need a Marxist vision, we need to undo the old and see where this will take us" (Harb, 2013).

Furthermore, in their article in *The Guardian* titled "Arabs Are Democracy's New Pioneers" (Hardt and Negri, 2011), Hardt and Negri broadly apply their theorizations of "multitude" and "the common" as reading tools of the uprisings. According to the authors, one of the most interesting aspects of the protests is their leaderless organizational structure since "the multitude is able to organize itself without centre." As a consequence, the broad usage of new media is viewed as the symptom, rather than the cause, of this center-less organization since "these are the modes of expression of an intelligent population capable of using the instruments at hand to organize autonomously." As opposed to Žižek's "desire to become like the West," which he uses to label the Arab uprisings, Negri and Hardt see the Arab multitude going in a more radical direction: "The insurrections of the Arab youth are certainly not aimed at a traditional liberal constitution that merely guarantees the division of powers and a regular electoral dynamic, but rather at a form of democracy adequate to the new forms of expression and needs of the multitude" (Hardt and Negri, 2011).

Dictated by the youth's "general sense of frustrated productive and expressive capacities," the constitutional answer to these needs should enable the creation of a "common plan to manage natural resources and social production," since this would be a way to challenge neoliberal capitalism. Nevertheless, the authors point out the fact that the Arab world has significant obstacles to overcome before fulfilling the multitude's aspirations since "the Islamic rule is completely inadequate to meet these needs." They thus identify the Muslim belief as a limit to the full expression of the revolution's potential. Although the thinkers' definition of "Islamic rule" isn't clear, their concerns echo those of the liberal dismissals of the "Islamic Winter," oversimplifying the relationship between religion and state, still highly debated and negotiated after the uprisings in both Egypt and Tunisia.[19] Moreover, Hardt and Negri chose to concentrate particularly on freedom of speech and the access to social production. These are undoubtedly part of the causes of the protests, but certainly not sufficiently impellent to determine a highly risky mobilization across the Tunisian and Egyptian society against fierce police states, in comparison to the pressure of unemployment, poverty, and state abuse. In fact, the focus on social media and freedom of speech, also central in the Arab Spring narrative, sheds light only on the priorities of a minority of the participants of the revolution, not to say that it silences the demands for radical social justice, in terms of redistribution of wealth and labor as well as an end to state violence.

In conclusion, I believe that the work of scholars who have been reflecting on the economic dynamics of the MENA area for years holds some of the most useful readings of the 2010–2011 events. In this sense, Adam Hanieh's work from 2013, *Lineages of Revolt*, contains some truly valuable suggestions, sustained by years of critical research in the area.

What emerges very clearly from this work is that the protests framed under the Arab Spring label are far more than just rebellions against authoritarian governments aiming at Western-type democracy. In fact, Hanieh argues, the 2011 revolutions are fundamentally the sign of an increasing opposition against the neoliberal project—promoted by the West and its interest groups—and its autocratic supporters. In this sense, the region is a particular example of how neoliberalism and authoritarianism can collaborate, which is what happened at least from the late 1970s, in the interest of national and global capital, therefore "ensuring the ongoing subordination of the region's political economy to the forms of accumulation in the core capitalist states of the world markets" (Hanieh, 2013: 46).

The uprising led by the urban poor of the central Tunisian cities—placed under a constant and increasing forceful dispossession process by their state—resonates with the wider picture illustrated by Hanieh: "Immiseration and accumulation are forcefully connected—neoliberalism has effectively acted to redistribute wealth from the region's poor to the wealthiest layers of society by subsuming every aspect of social life under the logic of capital" (Idem: 73).

In this sense, the Tunisian revolution emerges as a fundamental gesture of contestation of the neoliberal project and of the alliance between global and local capital whose functioning is dependent on the police state and which the protests managed to expose the fragility of.

1.3. HOW TO RESIST REPRESENTATION: FRENCH THEORY AND THE NON-WESTERN REVOLUTIONS

Eventually, what all the accounts of the Arab uprisings confront the observer with is the question of representation and its inherent power relations. In a broader context of reflection against the dominative agency of representation, French thinkers of critical theory provide useful insights regarding potential lines of flight in terms of both thinking and acting against representation, intended here as the Arab Spring discursive formation. In this section, I reflect on the way Gilles Deleuze and Guattari discuss the alternative to a knowledge practice based on representation in their 1972 work *The Anti-Oedipus*. Furthermore, I will draw from two examples of engagement with non-Western revolutions that are relevant for this research: Foucault's work on the 1979 Iranian revolution (Foucault, 1979) and Guattari's practices around the Brazilian "molecular revolution" (Guattari and Rolnik, [1986] 2008).

In the third chapter titled "Savages, Barbarians, Civilized Men" of Deleuze and Guattari's *Anti-Oedipus*, the authors reflect on the different mechanisms of signification and the resulting orders of representation set to capture flows of desire. The French philosophers suggest avoiding the imperative of the unitary narrative, marked by a transcendent totalizing agent, and tolerating contradictions and fragmentary accounts. Moreover, they encourage focusing on the "continuum" of flows that is the plane of contingency, while considering the disobedient signifieds that maintain their nature only provisionally, before they get integrated into the main narrative or "axiomatic." These are, hence, the hypothetical features of alternative narrative configurations able to question the hegemonic narrative: not unitary, nor totalizing, focused on the fluidity of contingency, disobedient and provisional. And these are the accounts and readings of the Tunisian revolution this research is interested in as opposed to the monolithic and paralyzing Arab Spring or the state narratives around it.

Two scholars in particular provide relevant practical precedents in making sense of examples of rebellion set in non-Western environments. Both of them have analyzed specific cases of political events in their researches, succeeding in sensitively framing transformation processes while they were still unfolding.

The first is Foucault, and I will be looking at his 1979 journalistic work framing the Iranian revolution. He was commenting on the event as part of a new concept of bringing intellectuals and journalists together in detailed investigations on the ground according to a program of "reporting ideas" with the philosopher acting as "moderator of power" and philosophy "on the side of counter-power" (Foucault, 2007: 374). "On condition that philosophy stops thinking of itself as prophecy, pedagogy, or legislation, and that it gives itself the task of analysing, elucidating, making visible, and thereby intensifying the struggles that take place around power, the strategies of adversaries within relations of power, the tactics employed, and the sources of resistance" (Foucault, 2001: 537).

The harsh Leftist critique to his opening up to the Iranian "political spirituality" (Foucault, 2001: 708) forced him in the late 1970s to take a very radical stance regarding his understanding of what uprisings were about, of their relationship to religion and spirituality, with his electrifying final response article "Useless to Revolt?" published in *Le Monde* on May 11, 1979. His approach in this article and in his reflection connected to the 1979 events provides an example of how one can engage with the unfolding resistance of somebody else, thereby respecting the other's specificity and approaching it in ways that preserve the event's futurity rather than containing the events narratively with tropes of failure, as has been done in the case of the "Arab Spring."

Foucault is talking about how history is challenged by resistance, by the irreducible urgency of subjectivities to interrupt the chain of oppression, even at the cost of their own sacrifice, regardless of their number, and about how they expose the fragility of power:

> The impulse by which a single individual, a group, a minority, or an entire people says, "I will no longer obey," and throws the risk of their life in the face of an authority they consider unjust seems to me to be something *irreducible*. Because no authority is capable of making it utterly impossible. (Foucault, 1979, my emphasis)

To the Leftist thinkers—some of whom still maintain their skepticism today, such as Badiou, Negri, and partially Žižek—who consider the religious nature of the uprising not dignified of being recognized for its emancipatory potential, Foucault answers with respect toward the Iranian people, and his words seem to sadly resonate even today when the Arab world is still caged by the Arab exceptionalism stereotype:

I am not in agreement with anyone who would say, "It is useless for you to revolt; it is always going to be the same thing." *One does not dictate to those who risk their lives facing a power.* Is one right to revolt, or not? Let us leave the question open. People do revolt; that is a fact. And that is how subjectivity (not that of great men, but that of anyone) is brought into history, breathing life into it. (Foucault, 1979, my emphasis)

To this regard, Foucault sums up the principles of what he calls "theoretical morality" in approaching the uprisings. As opposed to the calculations of strategists, he chooses to be "antistrategic: to be *respectful when a singularity revolts, intransigent when power violates the universal*" (Ibidem, my emphasis). Most surprisingly, in his unedited manuscripts of "The Birth of Biopolitics," Foucault establishes a close relationship between resistance and governmentality as the interplay that generates the political, since "politics is no more and no less than that which is born with resistance to governmentality, the first uprising, the first confrontation" (Senellart in Foucault, 2007: 390).

The passage to Guattari and to his exploration of the *Molecular Revolution in Brazil* (Guattari and Rolnik, [1986] 2008) is necessary because, in the heterogeneous material collected in this book, Guattari deals broadly with the question of productive resistance, referring to plenty of historical examples and contemporary situations. This approach, based on forms of political organization unfolding in Brazil after the end of the military dictatorship in 1984, provides a valuable practice-based and open-ended method of engaging with events set beyond the horizon of Eurocentric expectations and precedents. Most importantly, this method helps engage with events that challenge the cultural and economic domination of Eurocentric interests.

The book, originally published in Portuguese (translated in English in 2008) with the title *Cartographies of Desire*, documents Guattari's travel across Brazil in 1984, after the end of the military dictatorship, when Luiz Inácio Lula's Workers' Party was part of the radical debates enflaming the country. In this work, revolution is intended as an unpredictable *"repetition that changes something, a repetition that brings about the irreversible"* (Guattari and Rolnik, 2008: 258–59, my emphasis). Guattari focuses on the "molecular" aspects, which indicate a deep transformation of the relationships on three distinct levels: infrapersonal—at work, in dreaming; personal—in terms of self-domination; and interpersonal—in the invention of new forms of sociability in domestic, romantic, and professional life (Idem: 62–63).[20] The transformation occurs through processes of singularization opposing the production of subjectivities driven by Integrated World Capitalism. Resistance, as will be discussed in the second chapter, is seen in its productive nature, as "invention" of autonomy (Idem: 16). It captures the elements of the situation, it constructs its own types of practical and theoretical references, without remaining dependent in relation to the global power [. . .]. Once groups acquire this freedom to live their processes, they acquire an ability to read their own situation and what is taking place around them. It is this ability that will give them at least some possibility of creation and make it possible to preserve this very important character of autonomy. (Idem: 62)

Surprisingly, in this work Guattari also comments on the 1979 Iranian revolution, underlining the subversive potentiality of religion and of the Muslim Arab world in general:

The appearance of a series of religious phenomena unites a whole nation against the oppressor. People went to their death in their thousands because there was an explosion because there was a *subjective revolution*. It all became institutionalized under Khomeini, and even so it hasn't ended. The whole Muslim Arab world rejects capitalist subjectivity. (Idem: 76, my emphasis)

Guattari's reflection contains a double empowering lesson. On the one hand, it intensifies the "unconscious that protests" because it recognizes desire struggling in places like Brazil, Poland, Italy, and even Iran in the 1980s; on the other hand, it also leaves total freedom to productive resistance, investigating it without attempting to dominate it, rather leaving it open-ended with the exhortation to build it, rather than project it.

Following the work of Foucault in Iran, with his focus on respecting the uprising subjectivity no matter their religion, and that of Guattari in Brazil, with his focus on the molecular dimension of a social revolution, the claim of this research is that the Tunisian revolution must not be framed according to Western political categories and expectations but rather embraced for its singular articulation that cannot be reduced to Western standards. In this sense, its representation in mainstream narratives can be opposed by reflecting on the stratification of layers of visibility and invisibility. In this way, the intention is that of constructing a new level of meaning of this event's singularity, based not only on the "unconscious that protests" but also on a process of re-signification of its hegemonic representation.

Before proceeding to the discussion of the notion of event of resistance in the next chapter, and since I have already made clear how Guattari and Foucault's approach have inspired my research, it is worth mentioning again that Fanon has also been a constant reference point throughout this study. His humanist view has allowed me to imagine future political formations beyond Eurocentric horizons, which is one of the main lessons of the Tunisian revolution. I will list just some of the main reasons why the Fanonian theory and practice has largely supported my approach toward the event of the Tunisian revolution. First of all, Fanon has shown the importance of a situated knowledge production, unfolding from the "zero point of our orientation" (Hudis, 2015: 4). In Peter Hudis's words, he stressed the fact that "we can only know the world—and change it—from the vantage point of our situated experience. But the fact that I am the zero point of my orientation does not mean I cannot reach out to, and know, others" (Ibidem). This focus on the "situated knowledge production" is crucial to the specific methodology I have developed in this work, as I illustrate at the end of this section.

Thanks to the Fanonian inspiration, the relationship between a post-'89 migrant as myself and a revolution shaking the "Arab" world became more apparent. In fact, I lived the encounter with the Tunisian revolution as an instance of intra-subaltern recognition, since both the Tunisian protesters and I are, to different degrees, fabricated as post-colonial subjects (Popovici, 2014; Tichindeleanu, 2010; Tlostanova, 2017). Furthermore, Fanon's humanist project of "decolonization as the creation of new men" (Fanon, [1961] 2004: 2) was animated by many years spent on the barricades of the Algerian anticolonial struggle.

Moreover, in addition to Fanon's privileged connection with Tunisia, where he continued his political activity after being exiled from Algeria, his biography traces an impressive geography of colonial pasts and resistance from the Caribbean to France, North Africa, and Sub-Saharan Africa. In this sense, it can be argued that Fanon's work is an attempt to make the African continent, whole again. "After carrying Algeria to the four corners of Africa, move up with all Africa toward African Algeria, toward the North, toward Algiers, the continental city. What I should like: great lines, great navigation channels through the desert. Subdue the desert, deny it, assemble Africa, create the continent" (Fanon, 1967: 180–81 in Hudis, 2015: 109).

In this sense, the challenge of the African-Arab divide, as well as Fanon's critical reflections on the dangers of neocolonialism and of the national bourgeoisie in the post-independence period (Fanon, 1961), have all been vital suggestions in order to engage with the Tunisian event.

As I mentioned before, the specific methodology that I adopted in this research is one significantly informed by my situated experience. In the following paragraphs, I will briefly outline how this experience has influenced the development of this work: both content-wise and methodologically.

Prior to the beginning of my doctoral research in 2013, I was living and working in Bologna, Italy. Located in the center-north of the country, Bologna was an important passage point for a lot of Tunisians who had emigrated after the revolution. Between 2011 and 2013, this is how I first came in contact with people who had been impacted by the revolution. At the time, I was involved in an activist network for housing rights for squatters and completing an internship at the city's minors' penitentiary. In both environments, Tunisian citizens were over-represented. For example, in Rome, it was the Tunisians organizing large-scale housing squats alongside the Italian networks. Moreover, after 2010 there were more informal workers on the Italian streets coming from Tunisia. At the time, the majority of the young men hosted by the penitentiary were Tunisians.

During those same years, I remember carrying a banner during an antieviction march with the main chant of the Tunisian revolution, written in Arabic by the fellow marchers from Arabic-speaking countries: "Bread, freedom, dignity!"

In 2013, I attended the World Social Forum in Tunis and was telling two young men that there were many of their fellow Tunisians in Italy. They answered that all those "people were not Tunisians, that they came from the South."

I listed all these experiences and encounters to show where my main research questions derived from and why I was unsatisfied with the way this event was represented in mainstream media and foreign policy scholarship. In this sense, the sources that I started from were a lot of observations, personal interactions, and informal discussions, all of which can be categorized as ethnographic material alongside the later discovered art practice of Ahl Al Kahf and critical theory.

My research questions emerged directly from the event, mediated by my experience of it: the three years of encounters with Tunisians in Italy (between 2010 and 2013) and my two trips to Tunis (in 2013 and 2014). Every chapter addresses one of the questions, weaving together relevant theoretical approaches, ethnographic intuitions, and, occasionally, media analyses (mainly focused on street art). My main initial questions regarded how the event could be interacted with in a non-Orientalist manner and who were the categories that led the revolution.

In order to address these questions, I proceed unpacking different aspects in each chapter, as follows.

In the first chapter, I have exposed the construction of the "Arab Spring" paradigm drawing from critical theory (following a critique of ideology approach), as well as from political economy and migration studies.

In the second chapter, I will leave aside the framework of "revolution" in order to focus on the micro-level of movements and ruptures that led to the revolution. Drawing from political theory, I will reflect on the notions of resistance and event, while employing affect theory to show how moments of resistance can be captured.

The third chapter will be my concrete proposal for how to interact with the event in a non-Orientalist manner; namely, by preserving its specificity and futurity. The alternative chrono-geography of the event will be based on local historiographic accounts, diagrammatic and counter-mapping practices, and critical security studies. This last field of analysis will provide the redefinition of the term "mob" (Aradau and Huysmans, 2009), which will help further develop the reflection on the subject of the Tunisian revolution.

In the fourth chapter, I will identify this subject as the urban and suburban impoverished population or through the triad figure of the rioter/undocumented migrant/"terrorist." Sociological and critical geography works will provide useful elements to define the genealogy of this category. Furthermore, a close media analysis of the production of the Ahl Al Kahf collective (between 2010 and 2013) will add crucial elements to understanding the Tunisian political and social context.

Finally, in the fifth chapter I will address the idea of propagation and communication of dissent, drawing from media theory in order to reflect on the media that operate alongside the much-praised social media.

From the beginning, this research was an attempt to think *through* a specific event, to develop event-driven theory. Here's why the practice of Guattari, Foucault, and Fanon were so valuable. In this sense, the biggest challenge was to bridge the gap between theory and event. This gap was at once historical (some of the political theory I used was developed in the 1970s, for example) and geographical. Would it be relevant to apply theories developed elsewhere (in France, UK, US) to a context like post-colonial Tunisia?

One of the main intentions of this work is to dismantle the assumption of exceptionalism of the "Arab" world, conceived by some as separate and in opposition to the Western-like democratic paradigm. Rather than supporting the idea of exceptionalism, in chapters 3 and 4 I will account for Tunisia's specificity through the particular paths and genealogy of the groups that led the revolution. I am, in fact, interested to show how the so-called West and East are similar (in terms of dispossession and mobilizations of the impoverished) and interdependent (economically) rather than separable and different. This I will also try to achieve by discussing the relevance and applicability of each concept—be it "revolution," "event," "resistance," or "underclass"—to the contemporary Tunisian context.

CONCLUSION

This research reflects on the political relevance of the Tunisian revolution and suggests critical patterns of reception by drawing the attention to the event's specificity. The aim is that of looking at the event while preserving its difference and futurity, therefore revealing its political singularity.[21] In order to do so, many of the Western readings of it, such as the Arab Spring or the term of "revolution," have been suspended in order to reflect on their implicit instrumentality. In this sense, I have theorized the existence of a complex "discursive configuration"—articulated in both the global and local narratives of the event—engaged in reintegrating this moment of intense discontinuity in the regime of dominant signification by representing it as an either "achieved" or "failed" liberal revolution. Unfortunately, even the most radical observers from the West have adopted interpretative positions informed by the mainstream narrative around the events, in some cases perpetuating the Arab exceptionalism paradigm, by depicting Islam as a limit to emancipation and privileging the participation of the middle class. This is why I chose to draw attention to the multiple layers of visibility of the event, which have mostly overshadowed the crucial struggles of the urban poor while preferring to focus on the middle-class intellectuals and artists sharing a common and comforting political language with the West. As a result, it appears fundamental *where* one looks when speaking of the Tunisian revolution, what instances of struggle are included under this label. Spectators (like me, maybe you), therefore, are all but passive witnesses of the events and possess, instead, a highly performative role in defining the practices of resistance one can be inspired by and a supporter of. In this sense, the words of Foucault ("be respectful when a singularity revolts") and Guattari ("the whole Muslim Arab world rejects capitalist subjectivity"), although dated, resonate as powerful intensifiers of the radical potential of the Tunisian revolution.

Is there any philosophical reflection able to account for this moment of discontinuity overcoming all the limits of the representation (of the Arab Spring or the "revolution") that have been so far critiqued? What categories can help account for the impact of this uprising in the global world if we are to reject the Arab Spring narrative?

In the next chapter, I will discuss theories of the event and go deeper into the analysis of what a rupture—which can eventually develop into a "revolution"—is made of, as an event of resistance, and how power attempts to capture it. Alongside the critique of the narrative aspects of the mainstream reading of the events developed so far, the next chapter will reflect on the abstract level of the interplay between resistance and power in order to provide useful categories to approach the Tunisian revolution from a different perspective, able to expose its overshadowed features and political relevance.

Chapter Two

The Event of Resistance and Its Capture

> What is important for philosophy, for politics, ultimately for every human, is what Bataille called experience. Namely, something that isn't the affirmation of the subject within the foundational continuity of the subject's project, but is rather in this rupture and in the risk through which the subject accepts its own transmutation, transformation, abolition, in its relation with things, with the others, with truth, with death, etc. That's the experience. It's risking to no longer be oneself.
>
> —Michel Foucault, interviewed by *Le Nouvel Observateur*, 1979

THINKING *THROUGH* THE EVENT

In the previous chapter, this research outlined the reductive features surrounding the Arab Spring discourse, significantly connected to the "Arab exceptionalism" paradigm. As an alternative, the focus was placed on thinkers such as Michel Foucault and Félix Guattari, who have provided examples of accounts of non-Western revolutions—specifically the Iranian and Brazilian ones—able to respect their irreducible nature and avoid framing them with Western-specific political categories. In fact, the mobilizations connected to the so-called Arab Spring and my case study—the Tunisian revolution—have often been read through Western lenses, both in terms of political standards and expectations. This approach has caused a reduction of the event's potentiality, since it wasn't able to account for the novelty of it, neither for the way Western actors could interact with it as supporters.

In this sense, my interest lies in developing a set of operative tools through which to analyze the event, and the responses to it, with the clear aim of preserving its irreducible specificity, which I will refer to as "singularity."[1]

For this purpose, I will discuss philosophical paradigms able to relate to instances of rupture such as the Tunisian revolution. The first gesture in this direction will be to shift from the notion of revolution (and from its traditional historical references) toward concepts of "event" and "resistance," which I find more versatile, less objectifying, and more likely to embrace the virtual dimension of the struggles that I am interested to engage with. Working on theories of the event developed by Gilles Deleuze and Alain Badiou, I will discuss the limits of their views in terms of "proliferation politics" (Deleuze) vs. "rarefied politics" (Badiou) (as thematized in Nunes, 2010, 2013) and attempt to read them in a "productive differential" manner (Thoburn, 2003). I will put forward the concept of "event of resistance" as an operative tool, intended as a "rupture of the situation from the subset which makes a universalizable claim and enacts generic equality" (Aradau and Huysmans, 2009). Furthermore, I will define "resistance" taking Howard Caygill's work on defiance as a starting point (Caygill, 2013) to indicate its dynamic rather than essentializable nature, but also its orientation toward the future. This reflection on the interruption represented by the event of resistance will then be put in relation with different features (that I draw from scholars who engage with the Deleuzian thought) such as the event read in terms of contagion of "affective charges" (Nunes, 2014); the event as holding the mode of the problematic, "raising questions that are an invitation to invent new answers" (Lazzarato, 2004); and the event intended in terms of breaking utilitarism and habit while facilitating enabling affects (O'Sullivan, 2008, 2014). Finally, I will address instances of capture of the event, not only at a discursive level but also at an affective level, in those cases in which accumulated or intensified affects (such as dissent) are speculated upon. In this chapter, I will frame these examples in terms of "nano-modulation" of affects (Parisi and Goodman, 2005).

Throughout this chapter and the next one, I will attempt to craft a knowledge practice starting from the Tunisian revolution as an "exemplary terrain" (Scott, 2014). I will look at it in terms of "event" and "resistance," while exploring its flows and drawing a diagrammatic understanding of them based on the counter-mapping practices I will discuss in section 3.2. The intention is also that of respecting the futurity of the resistance and the alliances connected to the event, rather than submitting it to a flattening success/failure frame.

This is why I have chosen to contest the category of "revolution" and its inherent Western origin since it appears as if solely employing this term, without critically reflecting on it, determines a dismissal in looking at contemporary non-Western revolutions, which are simply "never good enough." What would be an alternative category that could be employed in order to account for the Tunisian revolution's singularity? Is it possible to emancipate the event from an epistemic approach based on its constant comparison to Western standards?

My hypothesis is that the Tunisian revolution can be viewed as a network of events of resistance since this approach allows us to pay attention to an underground micro-level of the mass movement while suspending a knowledge practice based on recognizing and replicating Western categories or historical precedents.

As follows, the notion of resistance will be further defined thanks to the work of Caygill while looking at the political dimension of the event and combining the reflections of Badiou and the Deleuze-Guattari couple.

Eventually, the question of capture of resistance will be raised and discussed with a deeper understanding than the mere critique to mainstream representation instances such as the Arab Spring. In fact, in this first approach to the research question "What is resistance?" I will be claiming that resistance is articulated as a bug or a germ. Thus, its potential contagion is hindered in an immunitary way[2] by the apparatus of capture, intended as the dominant power system, with both discursive and non-discursive modalities.[3]

This chapter's theorization of the "event of resistance" will provide the operative tool for my engagement with the Tunisian revolution in terms of flows of struggle in chapter 3. Furthermore, the understanding of resistance as contagion will be problematized and integrated with a reflection on the centrality of resonance in chapter 5.

2.1. FROM REVOLUTION TO THE EVENT OF RESISTANCE

The act of naming the Tunisian revolution goes beyond the mere representation or articulation of hegemonic discourse as this inquiry has shown so far.[4] The goal of this chapter is that of taking the reflection on the Tunisian events beyond the paradigm of "revolution" and seeing what productive insights this gesture can provide. This term will not only be considered here in its classical meaning, that of an irruptive popular overthrow of a ruling establishment; what will mostly be under scrutiny is the way its employment can reduce the specificity of the events. In this sense, I will be proposing an alternative framing of the mobilization.

When applied to the Tunisian events, the term "revolution" presents numerous limitations, mostly because of the way it is employed in hegemonic narratives, both by the Tunisian state and by the Western states. It is often overlooked that the historical references of the term in the "Arab" world are mostly inspired by instances of anticolonial struggle, as Angela Giordani shows in her discussion of the Arabic term *al-thawra*, illustrated in the previous chapter (Giordani, 2013).[5]

My intention is to take a step backward from the main revolutionary achievement, the toppling of Ben Ali on January 14, 2011, toward the preliminary episodes and other connected moments that have built up the historical event in the first place, starting with the massive struggles in the mining basin of Gafsa (Gobe, 2010), and paying attention to events unfolding from 2008 up to 2016, in this way shedding light on a few aspects of the Tunisian *processus*.

In this sense, my claim is that it would be more productive to frame the Tunisian mobilization not as a "revolution" but as a constellation or *network of events of resistance*,[6] as preliminary instances of systemic rupture of the Tunisian *status quo*, which have progressively accumulated and spread throughout the territory. This approach allows restoring a decentralized image of the revolution, shifting the attention from the hyper-mediated gatherings of the capital to examples of conflict at the periphery of the country. Claudia Aradau has reflected on this notion of the "event of resistance" and has defined it, drawing from Badiou's work, as "a rupture in the situation from the specific sub-set/category which makes a universalizable claim and enacts generic equality" (Aradau, 2004: 10). Moreover, Aradau draws from Jacques Rancière to describe the political nature and lifespan of the event of resistance, as an occurring, which "interrupts the power/knowledge relations and becomes a non-event (non political) when it is incorporated into the existing relations of power/knowledge" (Aradau, 2004: 4).

"Resistance" as such is not supposed to make a declared political claim. Nor must it contain a recognizable consistency in terms of discursive organization—a clear "message"—linked to an articulated, alternative political project. On the contrary, the latter are features expected to characterize what is classically labeled as "revolution." For these reasons, the term "resistance" is more versatile and is capable of accounting for, while not being reductive of, a wider spectrum of practices (not all of which are emancipatory, of course).

In this sense, as further developed, resistance is animated by a "desire of justice" and an "extreme courage," while articulating both a gesture of reaction against oppression alongside the creative construction of an alternative to the *status quo*, possibly preserving the agents' capacity of future resistance (Caygill, 2013: 12).

While imagining, as this research tries to do, a framework that can create convergences between the Western and non-Western events of resistance, what must be overcome is the tendency, mostly of many Western observers, to enact recognition-based knowledge practices when approaching non-Western phenomena. In my case study, the recognition approach (drawing from Baruch Spinoza in Deleuze and Guattari, 1980; Nunes, 2013, 2014) is performed through a Eurocentric reading of the Tunisian revolution on which different actors project Western-specific political categories such as "democracy," "development," "liberal freedoms" and historical precedents such as the French revolution, the French May '68, or the fall of the Berlin Wall. In this way, they reduce or totally ignore the specificity of the Tunisian context of struggle, marked by a post-independence, authoritarian, and Western-backed political elite.

I draw this critique of a certain understanding of non-Western revolutions from Spinoza's reflection on the different kinds of knowledge (illustrated in Nunes, 2010) and on the way this same idea has been developed in Deleuze and Guattari's *A Thousand Plateaus* (1980). In Nunes's words, Spinoza theorizes the existence of two senses of "thought": one centered on "recognition, identity and representation," which "reduces the real to the actual, separating the latter from the virtual conditions that make it differ from itself *in time*" (Nunes, 2010: 14, original emphasis). On the contrary, "nomadic thought" "sees in the actual object the singular expression of problematic, inconsistent virtual conditions" (Nunes, 2010: 14). The first approach is concerned with "extracting constants," while the second simply "engages in a continuous variation of variables" (Deleuze and Guattari, 1980: 433). In addition, adopting the mainstream position of the Western observer also implies a certain distance or disinvolvement from the object of recognition. In this case, those who reduce the Tunisian revolution to imitations of Western mobilizations, whether in terms of expectations or historical precedents, distance themselves from the event turned object, implicitly suggesting that they aren't part of it, despite the operativity of their readings of the event itself, which become part of its modalities of circulation. Drawing from Brian Massumi's reflection on the experience of eventfulness, it can be said that the recognition-based knowledge approaches the experience of struggle "as if [it] were somehow outside it, looking in, like disembodied subjects handling an object" (Massumi, 2002: 219 in Nunes, 2013: 15).

So, what could be a different epistemic approach toward events such as the Tunisian revolution? One that would avoid enacting a Eurocentric, objectifying reading of it? My claim is that the understanding of the event must be interactive and must seek to respect the event's *singularity* in order to acknowledge its exemplarity for how it invokes the futurity of political alliances between flows of resistance across the West-East colonial divide.

In this work, "singularity" refers to a series of phenomena. First of all, it is the trace of the singularization (drawing from Guattari), intended as subjectivation, thus actualization of the virtual through examples of political resistance. Moreover, when I invoke the singularity of the Tunisian revolution, what I mean is that the event—in its capacity of creative disruption of the *status quo*—holds a charge of originality and experimental practices that are irreducible to the Western political paradigms. Therefore, a consequent adjustment of the analysis categories is necessary in order to give an account of and approximate the specificity of the events, especially from a Western standpoint.

In this sense, a more receptive disposition toward the surrounding events might be desirable since, as Maurizio Lazzarato recalls, "those who hold answers prepared in advance [. . .], miss the event" (Lazzarato, 2003).[7] The research will, thus, attempt to develop its operative tools toward accounting for contemporary historical events, such as the Tunisian revolution, and their singularity, by providing the necessary reflections able to answer to the different questions. In fact, in this and in the following chapters, I will weave together philosophical readings, empirical work, and aesthetic analyses in order to reflect on the features of the event of resistance. Moreover, in this chapter, I will also initiate a reflection on how practices of resistance are met by the apparatuses of power, especially by drawing on examples of hegemonic representation and modulation of affects.

In this sense, I have chosen to consider different theories of the event as a starting point for developing an adequate analytical tool able to account for the singularity of the Tunisian revolution. I am interested in the significance of the concept of event in terms of rupture and discontinuity, and I want to link it to the political domain and the emergence of a particular political subjectivity in the broad context of the Tunisian revolution.[8]

The idea of the event in the critical field of philosophy has been central to many reflections from antiquity such as the Stoics up until the contemporary age in the work of thinkers such as Jacques Derrida. However, this discussion will only engage with two specific articulations of this philosophical-political conception of the event—namely, the ones developed in the work of Badiou and that of the Deleuze-Guattari couple.

Deleuze holds no interest in concepts such as "political subjectivity," unlike Badiou. However, all three thinkers share a significant political involvement, mostly marked by their different degrees of participation to the French May '68 (as discussed in Deleuze and Guattari's double biography: Dosse, 2011). This means that they have long reflected (and conflicted) in philosophical terms on instances of collective action and their significance, which is what my research is also attempting to do.

Moreover, Badiou, Deleuze, and Guattari's combined reflection provides useful tools for framing non-Western events of resistance. In the following discussion, I will comment on the theories of event developed by them in different works, supported by the interpretation of three contemporary thinkers who have also been interested, from different angles, in the idea of resistance: Simon O'Sullivan, Aradau, and Rodrigo Nunes.

It can be said that Badiou and Deleuze are the opposite extreme terms of a scale "measuring" the "occurrability" of an event—intended, in this case, as the political event. For Deleuze, an event is common and indicates an infinitesimal structural variation, while Badiou describes it as an extraordinary and rare occurring, which determines a definitive cut. As Alexander Galloway and David Berry explain, it's the "cells dividing [...] versus the storming of the Winter Palace" (Berry and Galloway, 2015: 10). Where on this scale can the Tunisian revolution be positioned? My claim is that neither of the two approaches is fully viable in reading the event's singularity, but a combination of the two, seen in terms of a "productive differential" (Thoburn, 2003: 41), appears to provide the necessary analysis tools, especially thanks to the contemporary theorists reworking them. As a consequence, my methodological approach in order to account for the event will be a mosaic of the Badiouan and Deleuzian/Guattarian intervention.

Deleuze begins reflecting on the event in his early works, inspired by the Stoics' inquiry, such as *Difference and Repetition* (1968) and *The Logic of Sense* (1969); he continues to address the question of discontinuity in other terms in his work with Guattari in *The Anti-Oedipus* (1972) and *A Thousand Plateaus* (1980), finally returning to the term later on in *The Fold: Leibniz and the Baroque* (1988). Eventually, in his later essays (collected in Deleuze, 1995, and Deleuze, 2001), Deleuze applies the philosophy of the event to social circumstances. In "What Is an Event?" (1988), the French thinker imagines the event's discontinuity in a Parmenidean "perpetual flux, with bits and pieces constantly entering and exiting" (Deleuze, 1992a). The event is the differential and infinitesimal result of the interaction between "chaos" and a "screen": "chaos would be the sum of all possibles, that is, all individual essences insofar as each tends to existence on its own account; but the screen only allows compossibles—and only the best combination of compossibles—to be sifted through" (Deleuze, 1992a). The most important feature of the Deleuzian event is that it is conceived as a reciprocal determination (O'Sullivan, 2014) between the actual and the virtual. Therefore, "the actual acts upon the virtual, forcing continuous (virtual) multiplicities to differentiate into new individuals and new relationships among them" (Nunes, 2010: 12).

By applying the category of the Deleuzian event to the Tunisian revolution, there is no danger—unlike with the Badiouan event—of legitimizing triumphalist or dismissive readings of the revolution. Both Deleuze and Guattari are concerned with accounting for an event's virtual dimension. Commenting on May '68, they see the event as "irreducible to social determinism, to causal series [. . .] in disconnection (*décrochage*) or rupture with causalities: [. . .] a bifurcation, a deviation from the laws, an unstable state that opens a new field of possible" (Deleuze and Guattari, 1984: 215 cit. in Nunes, 2010: 13, original emphasis).

By exercising this type of gaze upon an event, be it May '68 or the Tunisian revolution, they don't reduce the real to the actual but see the virtual in the actual (Nunes, 2010: 13). This approach enriches a knowledge practice aimed at revealing the singularity of an event, in the sense that it possesses an increased receptivity toward its irreducible difference in terms of its virtual dimension. Relating to an event in terms of actual-virtual reciprocal determination allows a broader applicability than Badiou's idea of the relationship between the Subject and the Truth or the Idea, as I will discuss later in this section. Also, the Deleuzian event is able to account for the contagious nature of instances of defiance (which will be thematized later through Nunes's reflection), which is an important dimension of the network of resistance events I have indicated as the Tunisian revolution.

The limits of Deleuze's approach regard its applicability in the political field. Since it intentionally lacks categories such as "political subjectivity," the reflection of Deleuze and Guattari—and of the later Deleuze—draws the image of an event that is "too natural," which "does not subjectivize [. . .] prescribe, claim or resist anything," only as an "ephemeral interruption of the situation" (Aradau, 2004: 9), unable to build up some sort of political consistency, in terms of the event's continuity and further efficiency in challenging the *status quo*.

On the contrary, Badiou possesses a very specific understanding of the political event and its resulting subjectivity. Badiou's thought on the event has been central to many of his works, such as *Being and Event* (1988), *Logics of Worlds* (2006), plenty of interventions (Badiou, 1992, 1998a, 1998b, 2001, 2003), and, of more relevance to this research, *The Rebirth of History* (2012), which specifically deals with the "riots and uprisings" of 2011 that I've already briefly outlined in the previous chapter. For Badiou, the event is seen as the vehicle of Truth, working toward inclusion so that "some elements that are presented but not represented in it (such as undocumented migrants) count as counted as one" (Nunes, 2010: 8). In Badiou's terms, the event is a gateway to a transcendent dimension animated by the Idea of Communism (Badiou, 2012: 6) and the pure truth of universal undifferentiated belonging (Nunes, 2010: 7). The event operates a temporary interruption of economy and the state, allowing the unbinding that the state itself is there to prevent, since the state is "founded not on the social bond that it would express but on the unbinding, which it forbids" (Badiou, 1988: 126 cit. in Nunes, 2010: 6). The unbinding moment that corresponds to the disruption, therefore, transforms itself in a claim for inclusion, as was pointed out before, an inclusion of the "presented but not represented," or—as addressed in 2012—of the "inexistent." In fact, in his 2012 reflection *The Rebirth of History*, Badiou sees the event as the eruption of the "inexistent in the field of intensive existence" as opposed to the sheer extensive being, and the "restitution of the inexistent possible," where the "inexistent" refers to the "underclass, the exploited, the repressed" (Badiou, 2012: 92). This is possible when certain conditions are fulfilled such as intensification ("the creation of an intense time" lived with 24/7 involvement by occupiers or protesters), contraction (around a multifaceted, active, thinking minority), and localization (identifying a site of unity and presence). The event also needs an organization system (as a way of preserving its authority), a Subject (generally a political organization, as a constant guardianship of an exception and mediating "between the world and the changing world"), and a political truth (the political product of the event, which preserves its intensification, contraction, and localization as a real presentation of the generic power of the multiple) (Badiou, 2012: 81–92). The whole idea of "Rebirth," referred to in the title of the text, points to the capacity to exit the established order of History, propelled by "the idea of Communism, revisited and nourished by what the spirited diversity of these riots, however fragile, teaches us" (Badiou, 2012: 6).

In the following discussion, I will address some limitations to the Badiouan conception of the event, mostly based on how it is described in *The Rebirth of History*, and I will try to identify useful integrations to the theorist's thought, able to further define what notion of the event of resistance could be more suitable to analyze the Tunisian revolution.

First, the understanding of what precedes the event, as being "presented but not represented" or even "inexistent," which is the term that Badiou chooses to employ when referring to "the underclass, the exploited, the repressed," seems to legitimize the narrative of the unexpected, sudden revolution. According to this reading, the event is not only unexpected but comes out of the void, setting a relationship with the Truth and inaugurating the "*restitution* of the inexistent." The image of the void preceding the event seems to be reductive of the complex series of acts of resistance and affective flows, which make an event such as the Tunisian revolution possible in the first place. In fact, looking at the breaking point while ignoring its historical roots easily cancels many of its features and facilitates hegemonic interpretations since they do not have to take into account the specificity of the preliminary steps toward the event they're looking at. But in Aradau's reading (of the more recent articles of Badiou, 1992, 1998a, 1998b, 2001, 2003), the notion of "void" and "inexistent" acquires a protagonist role in bringing about change and transformation. The relationship between void and plenitude is interpreted in terms of dominated versus dominating categories. To be more precise, in Badiou's examples, the proletariat functions as the void of the capitalist system (Badiou, 2002: 73). Therefore, negative entities such as the "void" or "inexistent" actually hold the power over the creation of possibilities "like a point of exile where it is possible that something, finally, might happen" (Badiou, 2000: 85), driven by "an element of the situation that manifests itself in the event as the anomaly that challenges the inegalitarian logic the situation is based upon" (Aradau, 2004: 11). This reading makes it clear that the "inexistent" is never absent, but always virtually present, so in this way it preserves the lineage of resistance struggles that the Tunisian revolution is the result of.

Second, Badiou has a somewhat rigid understanding of the organization of the consistency of the event, expected to build on intensification, contraction, and localization while putting forward an organization system, a political Subject, and a political Truth. This frame generates unavoidable dismissals of any "event" not able to engage with these standards. As opposed to what appears as a rigid description, Aradau highlights a broader definition of the event as an irruption of the political, described by Badiou in his later works. He defines it as "something that in the categories, slogans, the statements it puts forward is less the demand of a social group or community to be integrated into the existing order than something, which touches upon the *transformation* of that order as a whole" (Badiou, 2001: 101, my emphasis).

This definition is more likely to be applicable to instances of contemporary struggle. Moreover, in terms of the political organization of mass movements, Nunes provides an original understanding of the 2011 protests, which he sees as examples of "networked politics," following "the same form as the dominant models of economic and social production" (Nunes, 2013: 8). These instances are, therefore, based on "distributed leadership" and are activated by a "germ of action," which "spreads to nodes, and hubs that respond to it and amplify their reach," making "large-scale effects such as the Arab Spring, 15M and Occupy—mass movements without mass organization"—possible (Nunes, 2013: 17).

In addition, Nunes critiques Badiou's understanding of the political for its extraordinary rarity, "which stems, precisely from the rarity of subjective breaks encapsulated in an 'event'" (Nunes, 2013: 11). Comparing the Badiouan event with Deleuze's idea of it, Nunes interprets the debate in terms of rarefied politics (Badiou) versus proliferation politics (Deleuze). What Nunes sustains is that an impasse is determined between the two thinkers in the way they depict the status of the event. For Badiou, the event holds an exceptional status, raising the question "What are the conditions of an event for almost nothing to be an event?" On the contrary, Deleuze (and Guattari) privilege the event as being common, so Nunes imagines Deleuze and Guattari asking, "What are the conditions of an event if everything is to be an event?" (Nunes, 2010: 6, 22). While the rarefied politics paradigm limits the political to very rare cases, the proliferation one presents the difficulty of fully distinguishing "substantial structural change." "If politics is everywhere—if change is everywhere—how much change is enough? How can substantial structural change be woven out of the potential for infinitesimal structural variation, and what are even the terms by which we can determine 'substantial'?" (Nunes, 2010: 18).

In this regard, Nunes provides two fundamental hints as to the best way to approach instances of struggle beyond the rarefied politics/proliferation politics impasse. First, what he suggests is to decentralize the focus on resistance from "the most advanced sector of the class" to "the myriad of places [in which] resistance manifests itself in (local responses, counter fire, active and sometimes preventive defensive measures)," reflecting on the way practices of resistance aim to create "transversal connections between these discontinuous active points, from a country to another and inside the same country so as to make the 'revolutionary process' into a polycentric, but wide-scale, systemic challenge" (Nunes, 2013: 12 drawing from Foucault; Deleuze, 2001).

Second, unlike Badiou's idea of the event as a definitive cut, Nunes argues that "movements of resistance do not constitute a system in exterior competition with capital, but are internal to it, and are not simply trying to adapt, but to change the system that is their environment" (Nunes, 2013: 8).

In his theorization of the event, based on the 2011 mass movements, when the virtual emerges in the actual world through practices of resistance, it becomes communicable (although not necessarily according to discursive patterns).[9] That is to say that events communicate also according to non-discursive codes based on the geography of virtuals, on how different distant communities challenge the impossible conditions of existence. Their circulation doesn't only involve intentionality on behalf of the direct participants to the event.[10] This is why, when looking at the 2011 global protest waves, Nunes underlines the importance of the event in its dimension as a traveling, virtual vehicle of "affective charges" (which can obviously also carry deadly lines of flight) as:

> A process of contagion whereby a sensible change, first actualized in a relatively small number of bodies, words, actions (for example, the occupiers at

Gezi Park in Istanbul), becomes, by virtue of those actualizations, communicable to ever larger numbers of people who come across it either by direct contact in the physical layer (people, places) or mediated contact through other layers (corporate media, social media). In this case, what spreads and replicates is at once information—words, images, narratives, actions, etc.—and the *affective charges* that travel with it. (Nunes, 2014: 21–22)

In this sense, the political event's main mode is that of the "problematic" because it expresses both the intolerable and the new possibilities of a certain age. The event doesn't represent "the solution to a problem, but rather the opening up of possibilities that raise questions and are an invitation to invent new answers" (Lazzarato, 2004: 6). As such, it houses a double "creation, individuation or becoming":

The creation of a possibility and its effectuation, the latter of which clashes against the dominant values. And that is where the conflict arises. [. . .]
These new possibilities, once they are created, they are real, but they don't exist beyond the signs, the languages and the gestures that express them. They need to be realised or effectuated in apparatuses, in institutions, in material concatenations. To effectuate or to realise means to develop that which the possible implies. (Lazzarato, 2004: 6, 9, my translation)

To briefly recapitulate, against the recognition-based approach of the category of "revolution," the "event of resistance" allows a broader applicability and a more sensitive proximity to the singularity of a mass movement. The event of resistance enacts a dynamic practice of defiant rejection that is both reactive, affirmative—as further discussed in the following section—and reflexive of its own futurity. The event can be viewed as an instance of active discontinuity, not as a definitive cut or as an infinitesimal variation; and it bears lines of continuity with moments of resistance from the past and the future. In fact, I find it productive to overlap models that focus on how the event is a complete rupture with models that are centered around the complexity and connectedness of the micro unities (intended in terms of events of resistance) that constitute what emerges as a global event of revolutionary change.

Therefore, its virtual dimension is crucial, it manifests itself in a myriad of occasions (and locations) beyond the "most advanced sectors of the class" (Nunes, 2013: 12), which have to be interconnected in order to amplify their impact. It bears a form of organization that mirrors that of the dominant models of economic and social production, which the "networked politics" is an example of. The aim of the event of resistance is that of radically transforming its environment rather than positioning itself outside it. Furthermore, the process of contagion alongside the transversal political alliances that it generates is a way of making sense of contemporary constellations of events of resistance (such as the ones I describe around the phenomenon of the Tunisian revolution).

Finally, Lazzarato's work—mainly inspired by the Seattle anti-globalization movement[11]—adds important features to the notion of event. First of all, as stated above, he argues that the event's mode is that of the problematic, engaged in pointing at questions rather than providing answers. Second, he sees the event as a double becoming, made of a moment of invention, in which possibles are created, and of a moment of repetition, in which those same possibles are implemented within the social field through instances of repetition, effectuation, and propagation. Lazzarato's scholarship on the representation of the political event is a valuable contribution to the debate around theories of the event; first, because he reflects on how media interacts with contemporary political mobilizations, and second, because he complexifies his approach by working on practices that aren't monopolized by the discursive and its processes of signification. In the next section, I will draw from these ideas and questions with the intention to define resistance in relation to the event that is my case study.

2.2. WHAT IS RESISTANCE?

As mentioned above, Caygill provides a significant understanding of the concept of "resistance"[12] in his work *On Resistance: A Philosophy of Defiance* (2013). I choose this theorization of resistance particularly because Caygill relates his reflection to many and different historical events, and this approach, as well as his conclusions, engage productively with my case study. Caygill not only draws from different intellectual traditions (from Immanuel Kant to Foucault), but he also attempts to develop the philosophical implications of examples of historical resistance, which the Tunisian revolution can be assimilated to. In his view, "resistance is motivated above all by a desire for justice, its acts are performed by subjectivities possessed of extreme courage and fortitude and its practice guided by prudence, all three contributing to the deliberate preservation and enhancement of the capacity to resist" (Caygill, 2013: 12).

Caygill's understanding of resistance has some significantly original features. First, it is never considered as a pure moment but rather in a dynamic manner as a "reciprocal play of resistances that form clusters of resistance and counter-resistance" (Caygill, 2013: 5). Second, resistance has an inherent necessity to "preserve and enhance the capacity to resist" (Caygill, 2013: 4). Third, resistance possesses two temporal and intentional dimensions. One regards a reactive response to instances of domination in the present (what Friedrich Nietzsche critiques as *ressentiment* and Caygill thematized as "sacrifice" when dealing with the Paris Commune); the other one regards an orientation toward the (ideal) future social organization. The latter constitutes a constructive, affirmative resistance, engaged in "creating a new democratic world beyond resisting the old," by enacting what Caygill calls an "expansive political form," a notion which he draws from Karl Marx's *Addresses* on the Paris Commune (Caygill, 2013: 38).

In this sense, resistance is a line of flight; an unexpected occurring that transcends the actual world, while at the same time questioning it. It expresses an inherent drive toward transformation. This dimension of resistance is always informed by the virtual, all that which exists and all that is yearned for. Most importantly, this line of escape is determined by an actualized world that operates with oppressive modalities. It is as a response to a form of oppression that "something happens—a molecular event, a point of indeterminacy—that knocks us off course and on to another vector, producing a mutant line of desire" (O'Sullivan, 2008: 96). That which oppresses the virtual capacities of a specific category fuels this desire of escape. As such, "concrete political agents and objects break free from existing modes of political representation by creating a prefigurative alternative composition within and alongside older ones" (Deleuze and Guattari, 1987: 177, 142 cit. in Nail, 2013). When escaping oppression, resistance thus can be thought to be drawing lines of flight within the same system it questions (as explained previously drawing from Nunes, 2013: 9), while determining a line of contact with some of its virtual parallels, as those "affective-events and moments of non-sense that connect us with the virtual, with 'our' outside" (O'Sullivan, 2008: 98). So far, I'm employing the work of Caygill and Nunes in order to account for two important aspects; namely, for the functioning of practices of the political that operate beyond paradigms of representation (such as the party or the trade union) and for the ways in which resistance can lead to the production of the new, as a way to acknowledge the creative nature of resistance.

In his later work, in dealing with capitalism and the production of subjectivity, Lazzarato gives us useful insights regarding dynamics that can easily be connected to this aspect of resistance. Lazzarato's starting point is Guattari's reflection on the Integrated World Capitalism and Foucault's notion of "subjectivation" and "care of the self," by means of which he deviates the debate around politics away from the focus on language, the subject, and economic production. In this sense, just like capitalism, the practices involving resistances to it or, more precisely, production of subjectivity opposed to the capitalist regime referred to as "subjectivation" or "subjective mutation" are explained as "an existential affirmation and apprehension of the self, the others, and the world." "It is on the basis of this non-discursive, existential, and affective crystallization that new languages, new discourses, new knowledge, and a new politics can proliferate" (Lazzarato, 2014: 16). Instead of dismissing "strikes, riots, revolts" as examples of immature political mobilization, Lazzarato points to them as indispensable "moments of rupture with and suspension of chronological time, of the neutralization of subjections and dominant significations." These events, he claims, don't determine the emergence of "immaculate, virginal subjectivities" (Lazzarato, 2014: 19) but rather of *focal points* of proto-subjectivation and proto-enunciation, later to be made consistent by political "experimentation, research, and intervention aimed first of all at the production of subjectivity rather than (only) at the economic, the social, the linguistic" (Lazzarato, 2014: 219). Inspired by Mikhail Bakhtin, Lazzarato ties resistance to the act of enunciation, intended as the "power of self-positioning, self-production, and a capacity to secrete one's own referent" (Lazzarato, 2014: 18). Political enunciation implies "taking risks, posing a challenge," being "capable of governing (oneself) and of governing others within a situation of conflict" (Lazzarato, 2014: 230–31), and it is made possible by "points of nonsense" (Lazzarato, 2014: 223). Resistance is thus untied from language or cognition and regarded as an act of "self-positioning, of affirmation, showing itself in a gesture of refusal without speech" (Lazzarato, 2014: 176), thus preceding both thought and speech. In dealing with resistance as an act, while drawing a parallel with the act in schizoanalysis, Lazzarato points to a fundamental feature of it as being *causa sui* and *non ex nihilo*. In other words, the act is not deterministic, but depends on a sort of contingent accumulation of conditions of possibility and can only take shape thanks to an active creative intervention. As Lazzarato explains, citing Guattari:

> In schizoanalysis, there is no determinism because the act occurs only when there is a *surplus of possibilities* when there is a "possibility of playing a completely new tune when there are relative fields of potential creativity established." Potentialities and possibles that must be created. (Guattari, 1985 cit. in Lazzarato, 2014: 216, my emphasis)

Following this line of thought, Lazzarato rehabilitates revolt—symbolized by moments of discontinuity, or resistance, such as riots and strikes—as the "emergence of focal points of subjectivation" and "the sign of the capacity to interrupt, suspend the dominant significations" (Lazzarato, 2014: 186). In this sense, a revolution is framed by the Italian philosopher as an "assemblage of discursive and non-discursive elements which function and circulate in a diagrammatic register" (Lazzarato, 2014: 267). For Lazzarato, diagrams are a different functioning system opposed to the representational one. They are "a separated category (of images) whose functions are operational, rather than representational." In this sense, "diagrammatic signs, *by acting in place of things themselves*, produce machinic rather than significant redundancy" (Lazzarato, 2014: 86–87, my emphasis). This concept of the diagram, alongside a series of events of resistance, will be the starting point of the reconfiguration of the Tunisian revolution in the next chapter. This diagrammatic approach will allow me to engage with the event without projecting a predetermined narrative structure. Rather, I will draw from the stories of struggles that I have come in contact with in Tunisia and attempt to give a snapshot of how I believe different groups relate to the territory as an epicenter or crossroad of flows of resistance.

Lazzarato's reflection frees resistance and even revolution from the burden of complying with precise standards of political expectations. In this respect, there is a curious resemblance between his definitions of "revolution" (Lazzarato, 2014: 20) and that of "desire" (Lazzarato, 2014: 255–56). Both terms are articulated around the "impossibility [they] make real" (Lazzarato, 2014: 20). In this way, when "following the rupture of previous equilibriums, relations appear that had otherwise been impossible" (Lazzarato, 2014: 255–56).[13] The "impossible" mentioned by Lazzarato[14] is precisely related to that virtual dimension that the transformative aspect of resistance is informed by. Resistance first interrupts the common functioning of the relations of domination to then open up previously unimaginable possibles.[15]

The second aspect of the event of resistance is connected to its productive nature. In the process of opposing an oppressive drive, something new is created, whether it's a secret resistance practice helping the oppressed to bear the violence they're subjected to or an alternative social organization experimenting with alternative social roles.

This productive building is not related to any transcendent dimension; rather, it remains immanent, in the sense that it is articulated as "a recombination of the already existing elements in and for the world (a new dice throw as Deleuze might say)" or a repetition with a difference (O'Sullivan, 2008: 91). This moment follows that of the rupture of the chronological time and of the dominant signification and determines specific effects such as the suspension of habits and of the common utilitarian interest, substituted by new refrains and habits (Idem: 96). In this new context, particular encounters foster the development of enabling affects—joy as opposed to paralysis—and the unfolding of a different existential speed (Idem: 95).

Yet a simple interruption of habit or the acceleration of the tendencies of power is not sufficient to draw an emancipatory line. The new is produced through cohesiveness and consistency (O'Sullivan, 2008: 97), and it affects first of all the relationship with the self, followed by the relationship with the others and the world. As Lazzarato explains, self-affection, which implies altering one's capacities to affect and be affected, is one of the main effects of political enunciation. By definition, strikes, struggles, revolts, and riots—as well as the more recent "occupy" practices—operate in the space left vacant by the dominant modalities of organization; thus they imply a reorganization of those same relations in a non-predetermined, experimental way.

Eventually, the space of construction can become the operative space of liberation in that it implements splinters of the virtual through active practices of emancipation, whether we're talking about the best strategy to counter the governmental militias (as has happened in Tunis with the organization of neighborhood self-defense groups) or the way feminist activists have developed a debate with conservative religious Tunisian citizens while sharing time and building sociality during the occupation of the governmental square of the Kasbah in Tunis (Massarelli, 2012: 62).

The last aspect of the event of resistance concerns its connective dimension. Events of resistance can operate connections either in nonintentional modalities, as contagion, or with intentional modalities, as transversal alliances with other groups enacting resistance. Both contagion and transversal alliances are crucial for the achievement of a mass movement.[16] In the case of contagion, the spread of the "affective charges" can occur regardless of the intention of who is directly involved in practicing specific resistance practices. On the contrary, resistance *qua* transversal alliances is intentional and sometimes the result of the recombination of matter and of the new encounters determined by the moment of rupture.

Resistance enhances its consistency and agency against oppression when lines of connection between different practices of resistance are drawn. This happens on both what could be called a vertical level, where a dialogue is established with events of resistance beyond one's contemporary time, as well as on a horizontal level, where connections are established between resistances cohabiting the same historical period. These alliances can occur either between categories that struggle and categories of support, such as the Tunisian disenfranchised supported by the more guaranteed workers such as lawyers or teachers, or between equally struggling categories such as the unemployed from Tunisia and Egypt, for instance.

In fact, in Deleuze and Guattari's vision, an active line of flight is characterized by "the *creation of transversal relations* that can mobilize the social body to an ever-greater extent" (Nunes, 2010: 15, my emphasis), thus fostering processes of singularization. In these instances, "groups acquire the ability to read their own situation and what is taking place around them," and develop the "ability that will give them at least some possibility of creation and make it possible to preserve this very important character of autonomy" (Guattari and Rolnik, 2008: 62).

Given this relationship between the connective dimension of transversality, the conjunction of flows, and the process of singularization leading to some form of autonomy, it is worth relating this to Massumi's description of autonomy as being defined by "[ones's] connectedness, the way [one] is connected and how intensely, rather than [. . .] the ability to separate off and decide by [one] self" (Massumi and Zournazi, 2009).

To summarize, the event of resistance holds at least three fundamental aspects that have been so far discussed. First, resistance is a rupture or a glitch, a break in a dominant regime that itself holds the possibility of something new, the germ of a different world (Guattari, 1996: 189–99 cit. in O'Sullivan, 2008: 96).[17] Second, resistance as rupture has its roots in the realm of the virtual and makes the impossible become real, bringing about a suspension of the dominant signification machine. It implements new forms of life, which question habits and the utilitarian logic, and which occasionally also leave more space for the pursuit of enabling affects, such as joy, and for the alteration of the speed of everyday life. Third, resistance has the potential to produce alliances with other instances of resistance, which increase its force through transversality and connectedness. In the next section, I will focus on the different ways the potential of resistance is challenged by apparatuses of power, at both the discursive and non-discursive level.

2.3. APPARATUSES OF CAPTURE

The following section will be concerned with the way power articulates the resistance that has been so far described. One of the claims of this research is that the capture of resistance is operated through both discursive and non-discursive modalities, or signifying and asignifying modalities, to follow Lazzarato's terms. In this sense, the power systems that are challenged by moments of rupture such as a revolution generate representations alongside instances of affect modulation, as tools of countering the disorder determined by resistance. In Tunisia, this has been visible, for example, with the state promoting a eulogized narrative of the revolution (at a discursive level), and in the phenomenon of the Islamic militancy, for what pertains to the way accumulation of affects—in this case dissent—can lead to "deadly lines of flight" (as discussed in chapter 4).

Drawing on Deleuze and Guattari's reflection, both Lazzarato and Nunes share a specific orientation regarding the modality of organization of resistance and emancipation politics. Although their approaches are different, they seem to agree with the claim (inaugurated by *The Anti-Oedipus* in its understanding of capitalism and schizophrenia) that resistance to systems of power can only take on the same modality of power itself (Nunes, 2013: 9). It is as if power and the resistance to it would mirror each other except for their divergent goals: one aims at appropriation, the other at the emancipatory transformation. This explains Lazzarato's focus on asignifying semiotics, which he considers a privileged modality employed by power in shaping the production of subjectivity, but also the preliminary ground of resistance formation. Furthermore, this also explains Nunes's interest in the organizational model of the networked politics animating the mass movements of 2011 (Nunes, 2014).

This aspect has been pointed out to prepare the presentation of what appear to be two important approaches of capture of resistance; namely, representation and modulation. Representation is crucial for the Arab Spring and specifically for the Tunisian revolution. These events have been largely covered and thematized by corporate and state media and have catalyzed the production of images and narrative, which have largely influenced the perception of politics in 2011 and afterwards. In this research, representation is analyzed critically as a strategy of capture intended to neutralize the radical demands of the Tunisian revolutionaries by normalizing and transforming them through the mainstream narrative scrutinized in the previous chapter.

Representation is a partially useful starting point to reflect on the media dimension of the event of resistance and the way it is circulated thanks to discourse, narratives, and images. In his 2003 article "Struggle, Event, Media," Lazzarato deconstructs the idea of representation of the event as an expressive double of it. Instead, he points out that the event "doesn't exist outside that which is supposed to express it": the chants, the images taken by cameras, the newspapers, the net, the phones, which allow it to circulate like a viral contagion across the planet. "Images, signs and statements are thus possibilities, possible worlds, which affect souls (brains) and must be realized in bodies" (Lazzarato, 2003: 7). That is also why the Arab Spring discursive formation works as a device that limits the domain of the possible in relation to this event.

This claim is important in the case of the Tunisian revolution for at least two reasons. First, because it indicates that mainstream narratives do not *refer* to an event's genuine "content" but rather that they *interact with* the event of resistance as such. Second, it is important because acknowledging the operativity and interest of representation reveals how alternative, critical accounts of the event are resisting possible attempts of capture and neutralization. The way the responses to mainstream representation can be articulated will be exemplified in chapter 3, with the development of a different framing of the event, and in chapter 4, with the description of the artistic production around the Tunisian revolution. Whether Lazzarato is dealing with the representation of struggles or the advertisement event, he contests the traditional claim according to which representation expresses content. With its prompts (language, signs, and images), he depicts representation as able to affect and stimulate thought and action, rather than just presenting content (or a signified, as it would be called in Structuralist terms).

In *Signs and Machines*, eleven years after the article discussed above, Lazzarato once again analyzes the dynamics of the signification politics around resistance, developing deeper insights into the functioning of representation. The latter is seen as part of an encoding modality based on semiology of signification (Lazzarato, 2014: 67), concerned with establishing a bi-univocal relationship between the sign and its referent. The process of producing signification is inseparable from the act of taking power since it deliberately operates a selection and imposes a referential regime, which, by virtue of "neutralizing all polyvocality and multidimensionality of expression" (Lazzarato, 2014: 73), prevents "becomings, heterogeneous processes of subjectivation" and "imposes 'exclusive disjunctions' (you are man, you are woman)," recognizing only the identities defined by these significations (Lazzarato, 2014: 78). Thanks to this encoding activity, "meaning becomes 'automatic'" (Lazzarato, 2014: 73).[18]

In the case of the communication industry, this production of signification is achieved thanks to a specific operation of isolation. When "normalizing" an event, the "media's first concern is to isolate the person speaking from the connections that make up his collective assemblage," eventually forcing the isolated spokesperson to "express himself according to the media's codes, temporalities, and syntactical and lexical constraints" (Lazzarato, 2014: 167). An example of this is the way media have identified middle-class technology-savvy youth as representatives of the Tunisian and Egyptian revolutions, despite them being a minority of the revolutionaries, chosen only for the familiarity of their pro-democracy language. What is left out, in this case, is the entire collective intersection of flows that might have fostered a specific event of resistance. Thus, the event gets trivialized in the sense that no space for difference and becoming is ever allowed, while identities and discourses appear as the constant repetition of predictable patterns. In this sense, *"the two forms of representation in the system of signs and political institutions go hand in hand and any kind of political break with them demands that both one and the other are overcome"* (Lazzarato, 2014: 202–3, my emphasis).

Along this line of thought, if resistance is to be regarded as an instance of contagion, or a germ or glitch—as I suggested above—the representation could be regarded as an immunitary type of response from the power apparatus. One by virtue of which the opening up of possibles articulated by the event of resistance and its rupture is possibly stitched back in its original form; obviously, it isn't possible to perfectly reverse the process started by the event. By normalizing the event's singularity, both in terms of novelty as well as in terms of its radical demands, the germ of resistance is isolated and its movement across collective assemblages is restricted through reductive readings, which can include criminalization or the total suppression of the event as news.

I am aware that pointing to the coexistence of resistance and contagion is paradoxical since contagion operates like a two-way system or flow and as such can both affect and be affected by power. However, drawing from the Tunisian revolution, and the further and still ongoing ramifications of the event, I have concluded so far that one of the functioning modalities of resistance is contagion, which allows the spreading of dissent under shared conditions of oppression. In this sense, the rupture of the event of resistance, which I want to associate with instances of emancipatory defiance, circulates thanks to its "affective charges," rather than thanks to mass organization, as Nunes explains (Nunes, 2014).

In fact, while the representation strategy basically deals with a discursive articulation of the event of resistance, modulation regards the dimension of affects, thus bypassing the discursive and cognition, with the same aim of limiting the impact of defiance.[19] This plane is by no means separated from the one of the discursive, signifying intervention. Yet it holds the potential of determining more profound and unexpected effects. Massumi defines affect in his introduction to *A Thousand Plateaus* as "an ability to affect and be affected," "a prepersonal intensity corresponding to a passage from one experiential state of the body to another and implying an augmentation or diminution in that body's capacity to act" (Massumi, 1987: xv). "Affect" refers to the set of virtuals, which emotions and identities are a reduction of. It is marked by a continuous movement and articulated around two poles represented by the coefficient of vital energy it is able to propel: whether positively (joy) or negatively (paralysis). Because it is a "pre-personal category, installed before the circumscription of identities" (Lazzarato, 2014: 99), affect is also a cognition-free zone and as such it is not centered on language. Since it is neither linguistic nor cognitive, it spreads according to a mimetic communication pattern. Its functioning is based on the fact that "conceiving a thing like ourselves to be affected with any emotion" triggers the actual experience of a similar emotion (Lazzarato, 2014: 98–99). In other words, affect spreads through contagion, rather than cognition.

As I will point out in chapter 5 (in the section "Processuality and Topologies" [5.2.2]), issues of resistance and revolution bring forward questions around how transformation unfolds at a micro in relation to the macro level in the punctual and in the general. So far this relation between the micro and the macro has been addressed showing the difference between the network of events of resistance and the event perceived more globally (the Tunisian revolution). It is with the passage from the micro to the macro level that resistance arguably acquires an increased representational character in the sense of a more consolidated discursive identity alongside the composition of forms of political representation. Yet, as Lazzarato observes, this fundamental process in absence of which nobody would speak about a "revolution," namely, "the passage from the micro to the macro, from the local to the global must not be done through abstraction, universalization or totalization, but rather through the capacity to keep together and progressively assemble networks and patchworks" (Lazzarato, 2004: 137).

As Nunes points out, the circulation of the event (in its emancipatory declination) is contagious. The constituted powers counter the spreading of emancipation through a narrative type of capture or by unleashing opposite affective charges, such as the fear around the "threat of terrorism," for example. Both resistance politics and dominant governance articulate their intervention on two levels: the discursive and the affective, thus mobilizing both cognition and contagion for their goals. As pointed out by Edward Said in his *Covering Islam* (1997), by the mid-1970s Orientalism developed into neo-Orientalism, influenced by new techniques of power such as public relations, advertising, communication management, and infotainment. The articulation between the West and the East thus moved to a new ground of information warfare where hegemony stopped operating at a logico-discursive level in order to influence knowledge and started employing the modulation of affects in order to consolidate empirical facts. Rather than building a narration and appealing to the cognitive ability of the public, truths were now based on "something that is taken for and functions as an empirical fact." This is what Massumi calls the "affective fact," which grants an extralogical empirical credibility to the affective impact, and consolidates that same credibility through repetition "mainly by repeating the charge, rather than revealing the proof" since "repetition of a warning, (or of a charge) or even its name, can be enough to effect the passage to empirical fact" (Massumi, 2005 cit. in Terranova, 2007).

This is how the valorization of intensified affect occurs, not by simply imposing it but rather by speculating on its very flow. In Massumi's words on the relationship between capitalism and affect: "Capitalism starts intensifying or diversifying affect, but only in order to extract surplus value. It hijacks affect in order to intensify profit potential. It literally valorises affect" (Massumi and Zournazi, 2009). In this way, the pre-individual subjectivity is also put to work, or more precisely speculated upon, by exploiting its "affects, rhythms, movements, durations, intensities, and asignifying semiotics" (Lazzarato, 2014: 99).

The next step in the modulation of affects is that of altering a specific affective temporal dimension by determining its infinite self-replication and creating the scene of a legitimated intervention of the apparatus of capture by producing conflict. In dealing with the post-9/11 age of terrorist threat, Massumi calls this type of set of practices "preemption." With this term, he refers to "when the futurity of unspecified threat is affectively held in the present in a perpetual state of potential emergence[y]" (Massumi, 2007: 23). I believe preemption is crucial when dealing with the way political action connected to the "Arab" world has been presented in the West, against the backdrop of the Islam/anti-Western terrorism nexus. In fact, the Arab Spring has been praised for its nonreligious claims and dismissed once Islam-connected parties, like Ennahda in Tunisia and the Muslim Brotherhood in Egypt, had been democratically elected.

While preemption builds the ground for the intervention of the power apparatus, building up a legitimation based on the "affective fact" and its hammering repetition, there is yet another behavior that the power apparatus can foster in its activity of capture of the flows of desire, which propel the germ of resistance. To illustrate this reaction beyond the boundaries of the immunitary response, what is needed is a dive into the science of nanotechnologies, which points to a different understanding of the viral dynamics. While this is another level of discussion, it suggests how contagion of affects can become productive for the apparatus of capture. I am here referring to examples such as the Islamic State organization, which harvests and builds accumulation on the dissent of the disenfranchised youth throughout the West and the "Arab" world.

In this sense, nanotechnology has been reflecting on alternative interactions with viral agents in which their existence and communication is no longer hindered for immunitary reasons. On the contrary, this type of nanomodulation "will stimulate microbes to communicate and will no longer prevent such propagation but anticipate the emergence of such patterns in the first place, [it] would *use the bugs' own communication language to sabotage their organization*" (Parisi and Goodman, 2005: 6, my emphasis).

In this case, the apparatus no longer attempts an immunitary isolation of the germ but rather stimulates its development to promote its own negentropic agenda. The parallelism that I have in mind here is when dissent is not repressed or neutralized through narratives of an "achieved revolution," but rather intensified and extracted value from in an attempt to appropriate the potential of such phenomena of collective dissent. These are the terms in which in chapter 4 (section 4.3) I will be reading the way Islamic militancy developed in Tunisia after 2013. This type of modulation is not to be intended as a determination of the germ's activity but rather as a predisposition of the conditions of possibility for it to develop in a certain direction (which will never be fully predictable anyway).

The biological approach and the concepts of *preemption* and *modulation*, as well as *nano-modulation*, provided a constructive way to make sense of how certain resistance movements—such as the ones surrounding the Tunisian revolution involving both the unemployed, the migrants, as well as the refugees, which will be discussed later—develop contagious dissent by transforming possibly emancipatory drives in what Deleuze and Guattari would call "deadly, self-poisoning lines of flight," such as "terrorism." This way of reasoning is also informed by the observation of the Spanish philosopher Santiago Alba Rico, who pointed out that "the post-revolutionary Jihadism cannot be defined as a radicalization of Islam, but on the contrary, as an Islamisation of radicality" (Alba Rico, 2015). This line of thought will be further developed in chapter 3 (in the section "The Flow of Islamic Militants").

For the sake of clarity, this research is not interested in contributing to the debate around Islamist armed struggle as a form of fascism. Rather, the interest is that of trying to address the transformation of the explosive emancipatory flow, triggered by the accumulation of dissent, into an almost fully captured and profitable violence flow.

CONCLUSION

In this chapter, the intention was to construct an analytical tool able to account for the singularity of the Tunisian revolution, which—as other instances of non-Western revolutions—has been normalized and reduced by an attempt to assimilate it to Western political and historical references.

What does the hypothesis of the Tunisian revolution as a *network of events of resistance* make visible as opposed to its hegemonic reading? First of all, this approach indicates that resistance cannot be essentialized but must be regarded in the dynamic interplay of resistance and counter-resistance that characterizes it, alongside its contagious dimension. Moreover, resistance is articulated as a gesture of negation and interruption of oppression but also holds an affirmative, productive dimension, which is oriented toward the future and brings about experimental reorganizations of the actual, while embracing the virtual that unlocks the potential of the actual.

By analyzing the event of resistance through Badiou and Deleuze's thought, what becomes clear is the paradox of connecting a dialectic/opposition-based idea—Caygill's resistance, Badiou's event—with the Deleuzian event, marked by a total absence of the idea of interruption/discontinuity as opposition. Drawing from the Tunisian case study, my understanding of the micro and macro unfolding of resistance toward what ends up being a revolutionary transformation is the following: The process starts from any one instant of unmanageability that propagates through a network and makes possible a progressive accumulation of practices of interruption until the mutations generated can no longer be reabsorbed by the governing machine and end up shifting the very modality of the functioning of that same system. My claim is that event and resistance can be considered together, as an instance of local and active discontinuity, which is able to amplify its impact, possibly reaching revolutionary possibilities, if it operates a connection with similar instances. I will refer to this aspect partially in chapter 3 (in the section on "The Flow of the Underclass") and in chapter 5, showing how the revolution was a result of a coalization between the riots of the unemployed and protests promoted by the unionized laborers.

As such, the event of resistance is decentralized, contagious, and operates within its systemic environment rather than outside it. The highly contagious potential of resistance explains both how it manages to develop mass movements without mass organization and also the way power responds to it. The attempts of capture are thus framed as immunitary strategies of limiting the contagion, through a combination of discursive and non-discursive methods involving representation and modulation of affects that both help to "normalize" that type of dissent, which has unchained resistance throughout the "Arab" world in 2011.

The concepts I've discussed so far—the event of resistance, the different features of resistance, and the reflection on how affect can be hegemonically valorized through modulation—are the starting point of one alternative manner of interacting with the event of the Tunisian revolution.

After this theoretical approach, the next chapter will be concerned with the practical way of framing the Tunisian revolution as a network of events of resistance. When and where are these instances to be located? What consistency can the event acquire if one is supposed to follow a different logic from the representational one?

Chapter Three

A Microhistory of the Tunisian Revolution

The Struggle of the Disenfranchised

If you light our fire
Our revolution
will be like the wings
of a butterfly.

—Poem read in Ridha Tlili's *Revolution under 5 Minutes*, 2011

We made the democratic revolution [. . .] we are here to help you do the same.

—Collective of Tunisians from Lampedusa in Paris, 2011

ONE POSSIBLE RECOMPOSITION OF THE EVENT?

In the previous chapter, I challenged and expanded some conceptions of "resistance" and "event," building the hypothesis that framing the Tunisian mass mobilization of 2011 as a network of events rather than a "revolution" would help account for the micro-levels of its political specificities, which the mainstream narratives have foreclosed. In this sense, this chapter is intended to empirically explore the consequences of this shift in framing the events by attempting a diagrammatic reading, intended as a "short-circuit of the discursive" (O'Sullivan, 2014: 9), a visual illustration of the ongoing flows of rebellious practices. The intention is that of revealing and preserving the futurity of the event's resistance as opposed to declaring it exhausted. In this way, the "network of events of resistance" will be imagined in terms of flows, drawing lines of struggle across the Mediterranean territory (between 2008 and 2015).

This chapter is the most historiographically dense one as it attempts to engage with the Tunisian revolution applying the previously developed notion of "event of resistance." This is my suggestion of a way to listen to the event and draw attention to some of its roots, consequent articulations, and contingent intersections. In order to avoid applying Eurocentric standards and projections, I will seek this event's specificity and show how the Tunisians' cry for "Bread, freedom, dignity!" in 2011 was caused by the uneven regional development of the "two Tunisias," exacerbated by the government's neoliberal policies and its aggressive policing apparatus. By adopting an approach inspired by "counter-mapping" intended as a "challenge to hegemonic visibility, in the attempt to post a counter-visibility" (Garelli et al., 2013: 168), I will suggest a diagrammatic engagement with the event based on a series of events of resistance that I will reorganize visually in four different flows of struggle. Bearing in mind to account for the processual temporality (and spatiality) traced by these events, I will recompose one possible chrono-geography of the event, which stretches from 2008 to 2015 and from Paris to Syria. According to these diagrams, the Tunisian territory will appear as a crossroad of flows of struggle for four categories, which can occasionally overlap. The Tunisian underclass—the under- and unemployed population of urban and suburban communities—represents the first category. The second category is the one of the Tunisian illegalized migrants toward Europe, called *harraga* (literally "those who burn," referred to the burning of their IDs or their lives in the process of crossing the Mediterranean Sea). The third category focuses on the struggle of the refugees fleeing from Libya after the break of the civil war. Finally, I will look into the diagram drawn by some of the significant actions of the Tunisian Islamic militants after 2011.

Since I am interested in what kind of political subjectivity is to be connected to this event, I will underline the importance of the triad figure of the Tunisian "rioter/illegal migrant/militant," relating it to a reworked notion of "mob," centered around the way mobility practices of stigmatized groups (such as illegalized migrants) allow "excluded social groups to enter the political process and accede to equality" (Aradau and Huysmans, 2009: 592).

This experiment aims at contributing methodologically toward the constitution of different patterns of reception of and interaction with instances of resistance enacted by subjectivities who are often misrecognized in terms of their political validity, whether because of their distance from the Western standpoint (*qua* "Arabs") or because of their class identity (*qua* "mob"). This is why I have so far framed the events as an example of the "revolution[1] of the Other," in order to draw attention to the other-ization processes inherent to the Arab Spring paradigm.

In this sense, the Tunisian context must be considered for its irreducible historical characteristics, mostly with regards to the categories that have been the protagonists of the revolution such as the unemployed. Moreover, reading the revolution in terms of flows will reveal that Tunisia is, in fact, a *crossroad* of struggles, many of which have been directly triggered by the fall of the Tunisian president or by other events connected to the Arab Spring. I have thus decided to expand the gaze to all these struggles and follow the unfolding of some of them.

As opposed to the common focus on the Internet-savvy youth (which I've critiqued in chapter 1, section 1.1), this work claims that the Tunisian revolution was propelled by the underclass, which in this chapter will be provisionally redefined as the "mob," drawing from Claudia Aradau and Jef Huysmans's reflection.[2] The "mob" will refer to the group that defies both local and global instances of governance with its resistance practices. Hopefully, this approach to the events will help reveal the recent political sensibility born out of the poor internal areas of the country. I am also interested to reflect on how the "mob" confronted local colonialism and neoliberalism, both in their national declination as well as in their global articulation, in terms of anti-immigration policies, for example.

With its focus on mobility practices, this chapter will be the starting point for the future reflection on the political relevance of the "vanguard" in chapter 4.

3.1. THE SPECIFICITY OF THE TUNISIAN REVOLUTION: BETWEEN BREAD RIOTS AND BREAD RACE

In order to better comprehend the nature of the Tunisian *al-thawra* ("revolution" in Arabic), what is needed is a brief focus on the country's specificity, which will reveal some of the historical mechanisms that have led to the mass mobilization and the fall of Ben Ali's regime.

First of all, it is relevant to point out that Ben Ali's government promoted the idea of the Tunisian "economic miracle." As Beatrice Hibou clarifies, the economic system mainly based on the textile industry and tourism had been "running out of steam since the end of the 90s" (Hibou, 2011: xxi). Therefore, the rhetoric of the miracle "was the result of the spin put on economic data [and] it comprised a fundamental mechanism of the exercise of domination, especially since it depicted in no way the reality of millions of Tunisian citizens" (Hibou, 2011: xxi). This fiction was all the more oppressive since it foreclosed the alarming increase in unemployment throughout the internal and western areas of the country, which made access to the labor market literally impossible for a growing number of Tunisian young citizens. The revolts up to January 14 and "the first and the second occupation of the Kasbah resoundingly showed [. . .] that the representation of Tunisia as a modern, Western country constructed around its capital and its big cities, was for a long time, disconnected from the rest of the country" (Garelli et al., 2013: 13).

The main specificity of the Tunisian territory is its inherent development disparity between the north and coastal area (the so-called Tunisian Sahel region)—where the richest cities are located: Tunis, Sfax, Sousse, and Gabès—and the internal and western areas (where the main rebel cities are located such as Sidi Bouzid, Gafsa, Kasserine), alongside the southern cities (like Ben Guerdane) at the border with Libya. Most of these areas also hold a particularly arid and increasingly desertlike climate, making everyday life even more challenging. This unequal development has marked Tunisia ever since its independence as a nation in 1956, and is arguably, as discussed in chapter 4, a colonial trend.

The poorer areas outside the Sahel region, such as Gafsa (in the center-west of the country)—engaged in the exploitation of phosphate in the last hundred years—have been traditionally rebellious. Gafsa exploded during the 2008 riots and strikes against the nepotistic hiring process in the mines, but it is also famous for having been heavily repressed by Bourguiba during the 1984 bread riots and, further back in time, in 1952 by the French colonizers. "In the collective memory of the inhabitants of the Gafsa oasis," these instances of resistance "convey [. . .] their exclusion from power after having massively taken part to the national liberation as well as the fact of not being masters of their own destiny" (Kilani, 2014: 200, my translation).

In addition, the internal poor areas—where the revolution started—are also populated by citizens of Imazighen (also known as "Berber"[3]) origins, a nomadic indigenous people who inhabited the region before the conquest of the Arabs. The Imazighen have animated some of the most important resistance movements, such as the anticolonial struggle and victory against the French colonizers, partially led by the Amazigh fighter Lazhar Chraiti (Tlili [film], 2013).

Maybe the best data to express this regional gap are currently the ones regarding unemployment and poverty, although the previous regime has been systematically altering them. The richest regions also hold the added value industries of tourism and textile production and make up most of the jobs of the country. On the other hand, the west mainly deals with agriculture, which—given the harsh climate—pushes many inhabitants to migrate toward the richer cities (Missaoui and Khalfaoui, 2011: 136). In fact, the urban population of Tunis and the main cities is constantly growing due to internal migration.

In 2008, for example, "everyone knew that the region of Sidi Bouzid [in central Tunisia] had 10 and a half times more poor people than Monastir (on the coast): 1.2% against 12.8%" (Idem: 41). Among the unemployed, the young graduates, politically organized in the Unemployed Graduates Union since 2007, are a major category. Statistically, unemployed and poor people mainly live in the west of the country. In terms of data, the unemployment in the west for young people is almost three times higher than on the coast. For instance, in 2009, 60 percent were looking for a job in Kasserine (in the center-west) as opposed to 20 percent in Nabeul (part of Grand Tunis). Data from 2005 show that poverty as well is unequally distributed, with 12.5 percent in the center-west and 5.5 percent in the south-west as opposed to a national average of 3.8 percent (Idem: 135).

Yet data hardly or only partially capture the sense of desperation and urgency that the Tunisian events were triggered by. However, data give some hints as to the degree of poverty and frustration felt by the majority of the unemployed youth of the western regions. And this somehow contributes to explaining why and with what expectations that same group defied Ben Ali's rule and took its demands to the capital in the course of the march that took hundreds of Tunisians from the south of the country to Tunis. Moreover, the uneven development provides some hints regarding the gap between the two components of the Tunisian revolution: the fight against dictatorship opposed to the fight for bread and dignity, united in the revolution's most popular slogan: "Bread, freedom, dignity!" After January 2011, this "divided society" paradigm was transposed in the debate around the so-called political vs. social character of the revolution. Therefore, a distinction was perceived between the demands of Sidi Bouzid's inhabitants—survival, work—who had inaugurated the protest, and the demands of the revolutionaries from Tunis, which were centered on freedom (Garelli et al., 2013: 33).

However, this picture wouldn't be complete if we didn't look into the pragmatic resources and solutions that the population had developed to counter this endemic poverty. The most important ones are the networks of the informal economy, migration, and, lately, the involvement in the Islamic social movement and occasionally militancy, mostly abroad.

There is a very eloquent expression that indicates the centrality of informal economy for the survival tactics before 2011: the *course à ikhobza*, which is a colloquial expression in the Tunisian dialect translatable as "the bread race" (Meddeb, 2011). It refers to all the practices the young unemployed had to enact in order to provide for their livelihood, "faced with an authoritarian, clientelist, corrupt power," which they downplayed "using creativity and inventiveness" (Garelli et al., 2013: 10).

There is always an important connection between the practices of the "bread race" and the unrests, which have announced and brought about the revolution. In fact, the three preliminary episodes most often cited as "preparing" the revolution—the uprisings in Gafsa (January–June 2008), Ben Guerdane (August 2010), and Sidi Bouzid (December 2010)—were all triggered by the state closing those margins of maneuverability necessary for the "bread race." In Gafsa in 2008, for example, people had been deceived into applying for jobs eventually granted to the establishment's clients; in Ben Guerdane in 2010, the border with Libya, vital for the small local smugglers, was closed; while in Sidi Bouzid, a policewoman dispossessed an illegal street vendor. "Bread" thus becomes the vital and incontestable "red line" of the Tunisian underclass, the symbol of their own survival and expression of

> their desire to satisfy their vital needs just like other sectors of the population. Bread is the pre-eminent example of normality that must be accessible to all, or which should legitimately be so. And this is especially true since official speeches for over a decade had been constantly vaunting the Tunisian "economic miracle." (Hibou, 2011: xv)

A good example of "bread race" strategies is provided by the account of Walid, an unemployed bricklayer from Kasserine, described to "get by selling scrap iron one day, fruits another day and then maybe oil smuggled from Algeria" (Missaoui and Khalfaoui, 2011: 111).

With the fall of the Ben Ali regime, the margins of the "bread race" were dramatically altered. Police forces no longer controlled the borders—either because of the political uncertainty or maybe because migration was employed as a sort of relief valve for the social unrest. Therefore, an estimated 21,519 Tunisians set sail for Europe between January and April 2011 according to the Italian Interior Ministry.

This way many of those who had previously taken part in the revolution were suddenly transformed into "illegal migrants" for the Western public. Yet in the imaginary of the Maghreb, they had always been identified as *harraga*. "Literally, *harga* means 'to burn' and *harraga* in the Maghreb indicated 'those who burn,' meaning both young people who 'burn' frontiers as they migrate across the Mediterranean Sea and those who are ready to burn their documents (but also their past and eventually their lives) in order to reach Europe" (Garelli et al., 2013: 14). The *harraga* are literally the other soul of the Tunisian revolution. They are the same unemployed young citizens from the internal areas who triggered the change in 2010 and who have taken with them the revolutionary practices of contestation, which animated the migrants' struggle in Europe in 2011 and 2012.

Eventually, another strategy of "bread race" in the post-revolutionary setting had been the involvement in religiously inspired organizations. More than 1,700 associations were established between January and October 2011. Some of them were part of what Fabio Merone has called the "Islamic social movement," which focused on welfare and charity activities in the poorest areas of the country and of its cities, while finally being able to openly preach (Soli and Merone, 2013). Those same poor areas, such as the western cities or the urban suburbs, have become the basin of recruitment for a massive number of young Tunisians traveling abroad for the armed struggle after 2012. American sources have stated that more than 7,000 Tunisian citizens have joined the army of the Islamic State (between 2013 and 2015), with 3,000 traveling to Syria and Iraq and 4,000 to Libya (Zarocostas, 2015). Moreover, hundreds of young Tunisian women have reached these countries pursuing the *al jihad al nikah* or the "marriage jihad," which allows the fighters to temporarily marry for one night and sexually engage with their wives without disrespecting the religious rules (Kilani, 2014: 305). Although the Islamic militancy might seem to have a weaker connection to the "bread race," it partially indicates the frustration and poverty of many of its subscribers. In fact, most (but not all) of the fighters come from disenfranchised settings and are even willing to pay in order to take part in the armed struggle abroad (Merone, 2013b). Their expectations are not only to make a stand against the enemies but also to achieve recognition and prestige, as well as one's livelihood and the possibility to be temporarily married.

3.2. AN ALTERNATIVE CHRONO-GEOGRAPHY? MAPPING THE FOUR FLOWS OF STRUGGLE

This section is intended to systematize some of the claims made so far. Namely, I have often referred to an intersection of flows of struggle on the Tunisian territory. I will frame who composed these flows and how they crossed the country, partially connected to the revolutionary events, as both a cause and their immediate effects. The flow is a productive term, which helps me to address a different chronology of the revolution. The analysis started with a series of personal accounts around the events, some of which I collected (in Italy and Tunisia) on informal occasions.[4] Others I have gained knowledge of thanks to instances of Tunisian self-representation of the revolution on the part of local artists.[5] All these accounts shared the reference to a range of events connected to the popular upheaval: some regarded previous examples of resistance, like the Gafsa uprising or the clashes in Ben Guerdane; others regarded instances of collective action in the immediate aftermath of Ben Ali's departure, like the two occupations of the Kasbah. A third type of events focused on connected experiences of resistance across the borders, pursued by the Tunisian "undocumented migrants" or enacted by non-Tunisians, like the protests of the refugees of the Choucha camp (in the south of Tunisia, close to the border with Libya). Eventually, after the victory of Ennahda in October 2011, the so-called Islamists also became an important component of the debate around the revolution and its subsequent emancipatory development. I decided to collect and rearrange all these events so as to give them a different organization opposed to the mainstream narrative, based on those happenings that many activists, participants, and critical observers found majorly significant. This experiment is in some ways an attempt of rebuilding a minor history of the grand narrative of the so-called Jasmine revolution and will be carried out through visual diagrams of the flows. The flow is composed of the geography and direction drawn across the borders by the movement or striving of those who compose these very flows. The flow starts off as a list of significant events, which can later be assigned with a direction and a political content. The flow itself holds a highly fluid and provisional nature, so this analysis will be dealing with a snapshot of it. The snapshot gives an account of some highlights of the 2008–2015 period. These flows are constituted by the people who animate them, and their object is always these people's struggle.

Initially, I simply followed the unfolding of these events and imagined them as *foci*, which I united in a provisionally unitary way. Their orientation was imagined based on the movement outlined by the network of events. What all these flows share is a constant pressure against the belated forms of power, whether national or global, such as the Tunisian government or the European enforcement bodies that police the borders. Their standpoint is that of a molecular, multi-polar force, incessantly on the move, able to build pragmatic cohesion when needed or to dive into invisibility and recompose again if the situation requires it.

In order to follow the flows, it became clear right away that the temporal and spatial focus had to go beyond the generic frame of the revolution, set between December 17, 2010, and January 14, 2011, mainly in the cities of Sidi Bouzid (where Mohamed Bouazizi set himself aflame on December 17) and Tunis (from where Ben Ali escaped on January 14). In fact, the flows cover a time frame starting with January 2008 and ending in March 2015. In terms of space, the diagrams regard mobility practices involving numerous countries of the Middle East and Europe. The four flows of struggle I came to identify as clearly related to the Tunisian events are animated by four collective provisional groups: the underclass from the poor internal areas, the Tunisian migrants in Europe, the non-Libyan refugees escaping from the civil war in Libya, and the Tunisian Islamists, some of whom have devoted to armed struggle inside and beyond the Tunisian borders. The idea of the flows does not imply a univocal relationship between the individuals or groups taking part in the struggles that make the flows and the flows themselves. In other words, one shouldn't exclude the possibility of the same individual taking part in more than one of these flows, first as a revolutionary, then as a struggling migrant in Europe, and possibly also joining the Islamic militancy.

This understanding of the Tunisian events in terms of flows—drawing a new chronology and geography of struggles—wouldn't have been possible without the inspiration provided by the counter-mapping attempt put forward by Glenda Garelli, Federica Sossi, and Martina Tazzioli in their collection *Spaces in Migration: Postcards of a Revolution* (2013: 170–71). In the "attempt to posit a counter-visibility" (Idem: 168), the authors engage in a "cartographic game" as opposed to the dominant representation regime. The result is not simply an overturned image of a de-bordered Euro-Africa, but one that tries to pierce "in between the folds of the upheaval," depicting the space of the events illustrated by the postcards mentioned in the title of the work. They focus on snapshots of practices that have been commonly disconnected from the revolutionary context but constitute, indeed, significant invisible layers of it: not only revolution but also departures, shipwrecks, crossings, popular solidarity chains, confinement policies, struggles/resistances/escapes, border enforcements, expulsions, insistences on space, occupations/squats, returns, and new states (Garelli et al., 2013: 168).

The Flow of the Underclass

The first flow is composed of what I provisionally called the "underclass." The term is employed in this thesis rather provocatively to draw attention to the fact that the revolution was animated neither by the middle class, as the "Facebook revolution" paradigm would have it, nor by the working class, in the strictly industrial understanding of the term. On the contrary, the struggle was enacted by that large category of unemployed or underemployed Tunisians (graduates or not), whom some have been called the "Lumpenprecariat" (Rizk, 2014). In other words, by all those concerned with the daily "bread race."

At this point, it is important to briefly specify how "underclass" and other connected terms will be employed throughout this work. When referring to class composition in relation to the Tunisian revolution (and the Arab

Spring), it is crucial to keep in mind that the most common narratives depicted bloggers/social media activists/artists as the protagonists of the mobilizations. These people are associable to the middle class (El Mahdi, 2011). Therefore, it is in this sense that many observers—like the Egyptian activist Philip Rizk that I've drawn from—have stressed the role of the impoverished citizens using terms like "underclass" or "Lumpenprecariat."

These terms, in fact, describe common socioeconomic conditions of urban and suburban inhabitants marked by precarious subsistence. In this sense, the use of the term "underclass" here is in no way related to liberal theorizations of it, such as the ones promoted by scholars like Charles Murray (Murray, 1999). Rather, I use the term because Rizk uses it, alongside "Lumpenprecariat," in order to draw attention to the fact that the people who have sparked the revolution are not the middle class and that they appear to occupy a social space beneath that of the working class, if by working class one could refer to all those who in Tunisia (and Egypt) hold stable employment (mainly as public servants).

In this sense, and keeping in mind the Tunisian case, I will refer to the underclass with different terms. Each of the terms will emphasize one particular feature of the impoverished urban inhabitants. In this third chapter I will use the redefinition of the term "mob" (Aradau and Huysmans, 2009) in order to account for the relevance of mobility and of the criminalization that this group is subjected to by the state. In chapter 4, I will write about this same group in terms of "surplus population" (Clover, 2016) in order to stress its relationship with the informalization of labor and state abuse. I will argue that these two aspects—precarious informal labor and state violence—are what leads this category to become the vanguard of the mobilizations in 2010 and after.

The events of rupture that compose this first diagram show that the underclass is sometimes supported by activists with political experience (such as the representatives of the Union Générale Tunisienne du Travail [UGTT] trade union or the graduated unemployed trade union), as well as by the high school and university students, the more guaranteed workers (such as teachers and lawyers), and their own kin. Consequently, there is a trans-generational participation to the mobilizations, which involves both men and women.

The most violent precedent of the revolution—which the underclass was a protagonist of in the recent Tunisian history—was registered in the Gafsa mining basin between January and June 2008. In the past hundred years, the region had hosted the industry of phosphate exploitation, which turned most of its nomadic Bedouin population sedentary. Of the initial 15,000 miners, only 5,000 still held jobs with the Gafsa Phosphate Company (GPC) in 2008, after the progressive deindustrialization. A massive rebellion was triggered by the January 5, 2008, announcement of the results of the hiring contest for 380 workers, technicians, and managerial staff (Gobe, 2010). Thousands had applied for those positions, and the impression was that the results followed nepotistic criteria. The protest spread to the neighboring cities of Redeyef, Moularès, M'Dilla, and Métlaoui, employing tactics such as hunger strikes, demonstrations, sit-ins, and riots. Long-lasting sit-ins and tents were set up in the strategic sites in order to slow down the economic and commercial activity of the phosphate extraction company. Camps were set up in front of the iron ore washing plants or along railway tracks (Gobe, 2010: 2). The protest tent of the "Eleven Widows" became the symbol of the movement, organized by the widows of workers who died in work accidents in the GPC, demanding that their sons be hired as due reparation for the loss of their husbands.

The repressive answer was massive. More than 6,000 policemen were sent to siege and occupy the aforementioned cities, and frequent raids were operated in the homes of the rebel unemployed. Hundreds of protesters were arrested and many subjected to torture (Missaoui and Khalfaoui, 2011: 127–28). The local trade union delegate, Adnan Hajiji, was sentenced to ten years in prison. Four people were killed during the clashes with the police. Despite the solidarity from the neighboring cities, the regime managed to obstruct the propagation of these protests. The "mining basin rebellion" or the "Intifada of Gafsa" was pursued both against *and* alongside the UGTT trade union. On the one side, some representatives of the "trade union aristocracy attached to the *status quo*" (Gobe, 2010: 8) directly managed the outsourced staff of the GPC and were consequently ousted by the population; on the other side, other representatives disobeyed the directives of their leaders and fully engaged in the struggle. This is an interesting example of how activists have collaborated with the less-experienced unemployed rioters, creating a synergy of strategies of contestation. In fact, for most of the time, the motor of contestation was the people with no previous political experience. As such, Gafsa is commonly considered the "general rehearsal" for the 2011 Tunisian revolution.

In August 2010, another rebellion occurred at the border with Libya, in Ben Guerdane, after the Libyan authorities blocked the passage of Tunisian citizens in the process of introducing imported goods. Many of the inhabitants of the city got by thanks to the small trade with Libya, so the border block was met with broad clashes.

Later that year, on December 17, local municipal agent Fadia Hamdi dispossessed Mohamed Bouazizi of that which allowed him to maintain his family. He was, like many, a street fruit vendor without a license, and that day his merchandise and cart got confiscated for the nth time. He tried to negotiate in vain—allegedly the policewoman even slapped him in public (Tlili [film], 2013).[6] Eventually, Bouazizi chose to set himself on fire in front of the local governor's headquarters after asking in vain for his belongings. He was taken to the hospital, where he would die in January, but his gesture ignited a series of protests across the region. Brigades of public order were called in from Kasserine, Kairouan, and Sfax to sedate the unrests, but this time the mobilization spread. The protestors of Menzel Bouzaiane, Meknassy, Gafsa, and Regueb marched in solidarity with Sidi Bouzid and clashed with the police, often attacking the centers of the local governors or the police stations. On the other side, the state forces shot at the protestors, raided their houses at night, and made arrests. The following months, two other people killed themselves in Sidi Bouzid as a sign of protest against hopeless unemployment.

On December 24, the police of Menzel Bouzaiane killed two people, the first "martyrs" of the revolution. By the end of December, the unrest reached the coastal cities of Gabès and Sousse, as well as the capital. On December 30, 2010, the lawyers' movement organized a thousand-person march and sit-in in front of the Interior Ministry in solidarity with Sidi Bouzid. In less than two weeks, the cry of peripheral Tunisia had reached the capital, becoming the catalyst of a long-suppressed discontent. On December 28, 2010, Ben Ali held a televised speech promising to take into account the requests of the protesters but threatening to repress those continuing the protests.

After the speech, the most aggressive repression occurred in the city of Kasserine, where sixty people were killed in three days between January 8 and 11, 2010 (Cantaloube, 2011). The city dived into massive riots. Several buildings of local authorities were burned down, alongside three bank centers, the police station, and the centers of the government's party, the RCD (*Rassemblement Constitutionelle Démocratique*—the Constitutional Democratic Party). The police shot from the roofs and employed buckshot bullets. Children and burial marches were also shot at. The slogans chanted *Bread and water, but Ben Ali no! Bread and oil, Ben Ali against the wall!* (Missaoui and Khalfaoui, 2011: 114). This is a very significant episode because it marked the moment when all protests allied against Ben Ali and his authoritarian rule. After the events in Kasserine, even the UGTT trade union, the strongest and most represented union of state workers, decided to support the protesters. More riots enflamed the cities of Thala and Regueb, but also touched upon Tunis's suburbs, while police surrounded the El Manar University of the capital because of the students' support to the rioters. The regime announced the liberation of all the arrestees, and on January 13 Ben Ali held his last speech, proclaiming the freedom of press and the lowering of the prices of some food products. He publicly asked the police not to shoot the protesters and assured he would no longer be a candidate in the future elections. Only on January 14, 2011, when the Internet censorship—colloquially labeled as "Erreur 404"—fell, did the media activism, which was highly repressed before, start playing a fundamental role in spreading the insurrection. Nevertheless, it is crucial to point out that "the central role of the web has been to create proximity between the spaces inside Tunisia and the spaces outside it and to create real—not virtual—spaces for practices of resistance" (Garelli et al., 2013: 180).

On January 14, a general strike was declared by the UGTT, and thousands rallied in front of its headquarters joining others in front of the Interior Ministry on Avenue Habib Bourguiba in the center of the capital. The police charged and shot tear gas, while a curfew and an emergency state were announced. Nevertheless, Ben Ali eventually left the country that night, fleeing to Saudi Arabia (Missaoui and Khalfaoui, 2011: 151–82). January 15 was a night of heavy looting and destruction in Tunis, some believe by the hand of Ben Ali's militias—the *baltaghias*—interested to seed chaos and legitimate the return of the president. The protesters' self-organized committees of defense of the neighborhoods collaborated with the *Garde Nationale* and the army, who, at this point, had started to publicly support the rioters.

On January 17, a provisional government under Ben Ali's prime minister, Mohamed Ghannouchi, was announced. Many were outraged by the continuity with Ben Ali's regime and took the streets to ask for Ghannouchi's resignation. Right after Ben Ali's last speech on January 13, a "Liberation Caravan" was initiated in Menzel Bouzaiane, the city of the first "martyrs," situated in the center-south of the country. The Liberation Caravan was determined to march toward the capital for its demands of social justice and ask the resignation of Ghannouchi.[7] Around 4,000 people joined the caravan, which crossed the cities of Meknassy, Regueb, and Saida (Missaoui and Khalfaoui, 2011: 88). The crowd left their means of transportation at the outskirts of the capital and reached the square of the Kasbah,[8] the ancient residence of the Bey, now inhabited by the prime minister and considered the governmental center of the capital. This crucial occupation of the central administrative headquarters in Tunis is historically referred to as the "First Kasbah" and took place between January 23 and 28, 2011. People reached it from Sidi Bouzid, El Kef, Siliana, and Kasserine. They set up a Bedouin tent and, despite the curfew, slept in the square putting pressure on Ghannouchi to resign and leave the power to a new political class not connected with the previous regime.

A conflict soon emerged between the temporary inhabitants of the Kasbah and the well-off neighborhoods of the capital. The revolutionaries' presence at the heart of the administrative center was a reminder of the historical inequalities that the western and internal areas had always been subjected to. But for many of Tunis's inhabitants, the block imposed by the occupiers' presence was perceived as a danger for the urban routine and, most importantly, for their property. They gathered at the Qobba sports complex, the same space that Ben Ali would employ for his party's gatherings, in the rich neighborhood of Menzah to show their support to the Ghannouchi government.

> While the *Kasbah* protests were held in the name of the people united behind the slogan: "We took down the dictator, now let's take down the dictatorship," at *Qobba*, slogans were in the name of the "silent majority" and called for a return to work. Work and property were considered symbols, creating a mirror image of the young political revolutionaries that were unemployed and cared very little about property, portraying them as lazy and dirty. (Dakhli, 2013)

The first occupation of the Kasbah was forcefully cleared after six days. It was followed by a second occupation of the Kasbah square between February 22 and 25, 2011, which included the participation of many trade union and Leftist activists, who reemerged in the public sphere after the interruption of state repression.[9] The second Kasbah's demands were the resignation of the old guard of Benalist politicians alongside the formation of a constituent assembly. The police killed two people during the violent eviction of the second Kasbah. But in the end, the Kasbahs achieved their goal. On February 27, Ghannouchi resigned and was substituted by the ministry of Habib Bourguiba, Béji Caid Essebsi, known for his opposition to Ben Ali yet part of the old establishment. Some activists have criticized this return to gerontocracy, but for most Tunisians, this was lived as a victory.

The Kasbahs represent the most important moment of the Tunisian revolution, although they are set beyond the common revolutionary time frame, after the fall of the regime. While the previous moments were marked by an audacious constellation of contagious riots, what happened after Ben Ali's departure is just as impressive. Thousands of revolutionary disenfranchised Tunisians took the center of the capital, imposing their troublesome presence to a political establishment that had always ignored them, therefore making themselves visible to their governors and also to their fellow citizens. The Kasbah was the place of class alliances, where the poverty of the rest of the country became visible to the inhabitants of the capital. Those moments fostered significant practices of solidarity and literally inaugurated Tunisia's new public space, leaving behind the terror imposed by censorship and repression.

From the accounts of its participants, the Kasbahs are the experimental space of a revolutionary sociality, one where classes and languages crossed in one safe, common space. A participant in one of the occupations of the Kasbah compared the gathering to the reincarnation of the Greek *agora*:

I spent one entire week debating and protesting! There were tents and knots of people discussing everywhere. I even saw some Salafists debating with some feminists. If you walked around the second Kasbah you could choose the topic you were more interested in and easily make an intervention in the debate. It was like the Greek *agora*, only that we had to defend it from the police and the attempted evictions. (Massarelli, 2012: 62, my translation)

After the moment of the two Kasbahs, the front of struggle was subjected to a sort of decomposition, which put an end to the cathartic alliance of most of the Tunisian society behind the revolutionary claims. The social demands kept being the main focus of the underclass. After their electoral victory, on October 23, 2011, the liberal Islamists of Ennahda became the new interlocutor of the people who had initiated the revolution. Occasional riots and self-immolations still continued to touch upon the poor regions. After the massive migration of many young Tunisians toward Europe, a new significant struggle was animated by the mothers of the young Tunisians dispersed in the Mediterranean Sea, who sought truth and justice for their sons (Garelli et al., 2013: 154).

Despite the alleged achievement of freedom of speech, between 2011 and 2014 the dissent put forward by politicized activists like video-makers, bloggers, and independent journalists was often met with state repression and detention. Sometimes the state employed the excuse of the fight against the use of cannabis according to the infamous "Law 52," which was invoked in the case of the arrest and detention of several activists (Bayoudh [film], 2014). Massive international campaigns helped release some of the arrestees (El Hammi, 2011).

An important last date of the "Tunisian permanent upheaval" (Alba Rico, 2012) and of the struggle of the unified Tunisian underclass at home, as I will be depicting it in the diagram of the flows, happened on November 28, 2012. On that date, a massive march was organized in Siliana, a city south of Tunis, demanding new policies of investment able to create jobs and the resignation of the local governor. The march was supported by the trade union and the Leftist party of the Popular Front and was also meant to put pressure on the Islamist government, both local and national, which had refused any negotiation with the trade unions. The protestors were shot at with Italian buckshot bullets, which explode a series of metallic spheres and are usually employed for wild boar hunts. More than 250 people were injured and twenty protestors lost their sight after being hit by the buckshot bullets. Because the city was put under siege by the police and as a protest against the governor's rule, the people decided to symbolically abandon it, marching for five kilometers in the direction of Tunis. The city's governor eventually resigned, and the blinded protestors of Siliana became the new symbol of the struggle of the underclass, depicted in graffiti art as a new expression of the revolutionary energy and indignation.

In conclusion, the flow of the struggles of the underclass—as selected in the diagram of the flows (Figure 3.1)—started in 2008 in Gafsa and unfolded as a contagious riot against state oppression and for social justice across many of the internal as well as southern cities before spreading on the coast and eventually reaching the capital. The culminating point of this flow was the double occupation of the central Kasbah in January and February 2011, which succeeded in pressuring Ben Ali's prime minister, Ghannouchi, to resign. The mobilization of Siliana was the last significant collective episode related to this flow.

The Flow of the *Harraga*

The flow of struggle of the *harraga*[10] is a consequential articulation of the Tunisian underclass. As mentioned above, when the border control was loosened many unemployed revolutionaries identified migration as a finally viable solution to the "bread race." Significant sums were paid to the smugglers or *passeurs*, and while defying the visa and anti-immigration policies of "fortress Europe," thousands set sail for Italy. The island of Lampedusa, south of Sicily, not far from the Tunisian coast, became the symbol of this flow. The first one hundred Tunisians reached Lampedusa only one night after the departure of Ben Ali, on January 15, 2011. This flow of struggles witnessed the transformation of the much-praised Tunisian revolutionary into the troublesome illegal migrant scornfully entering the West. The boats departed from the coast, from Zarzis, Djerba, Sfax, Mahdia, Monastir, Sousse, and Tunis (Garelli et al., 2013). In February, the channel of Sicily started being patrolled by the Italian authorities joined by Frontex (European Border and Coast Guard Agency), while the ones who survived the crossing were often detained in numerous detention centers in Italy. Soon, these centers were enflamed by massive riots and rebellions, as well as collective escapes. Many Tunisian migrants wanted to reach their friends and family in France. But France employed *ad hoc* measures to impede their access, invoking that they had to prove to be economically self-sustained in order to cross the border from Italy. In the first months of 2011, this measure unilaterally and temporarily suspended the Schengen Treaty, which regulated the freedom of movement between Italy and France. In less than a month (March 2011), 1,800 Tunisians were "pushed back" by the French authorities. The flow of the *harraga* is symbolized by three instances related to the crossing: the massive shipwrecks (the *Fortress Europe* monitoring website estimated around 1,822 deaths in shipwrecks in 2011); the fight for freedom in detention; and

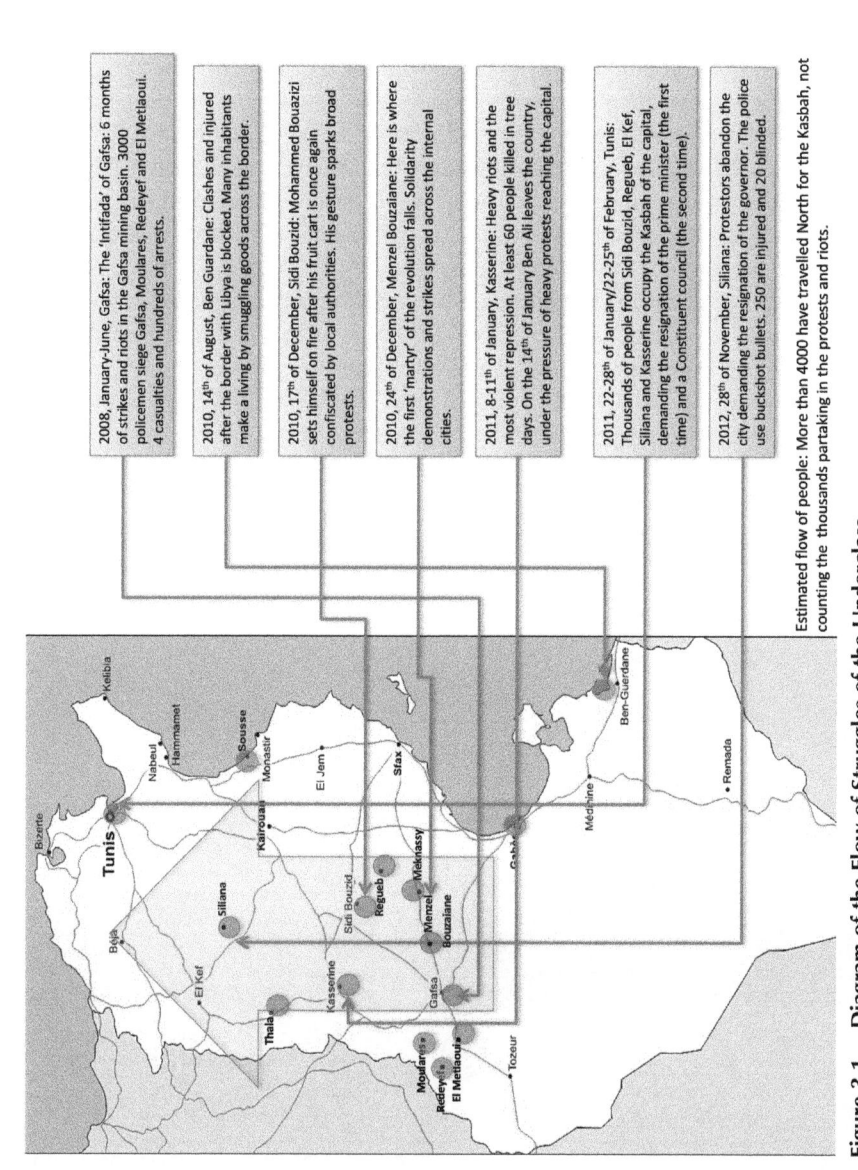

Figure 3.1. Diagram of the Flow of Struggles of the Underclass.

the fight for dignity and the right to stay once they reached the European cities as "undocumented migrants." Between January and April 2011, the Italian Interior Ministry registered 21,519 arrivals from Tunisia by boat. Since the Italian territory became a crucial passing country toward France for thousands of Tunisians, the government was faced with the dilemma of whether to stop or ignore the flow of migrants. Eventually, the Italian authorities granted a temporary travel permit to the ones who reached Europe until April 5. At the same time, Italy signed a repatriation agreement with the provisional Tunisian government for the migrants who had or would reach the peninsula after April 5. The prospect of deportation ignited an infinite series of riots in the Italian detention centers, accompanied by hunger strikes, self-harm, fires, and collective escapes. The protests culminated with the Sicilian Lampedusa detention center being set aflame on September 20, 2011, which also involved violent clashes with the police and some local inhabitants (Garelli et al., 2013: 199).

Meanwhile, on May 1, 2011, a group of Tunisians organized under the name of the Collective of Tunisians from Lampedusa in Paris had already reached Paris and carried out an occupation of a building in 51 Simon Bolivar

Figure 3.2. The short occupation of the Collective of Tunisians from Lampedusa in Paris: "Neither police, nor charity, but a place to organize." *Source: juralibertaire.over-blog.com (May 4, 2011).*

Avenue. Their demands were clearly stated on the banner exposed on the building: "Neither police, nor charity, but a place to organize" (see Figure 3.2, *Archives du Jura Libertaire*, 2011). They had chosen to come out of the invisibility that illegal migrants are forced into, claiming, "We made the *democratic revolution*" and "We are here to help you do the same" (*Archives du Jura Libertaire*, 2011).

In the meantime, Italy employed extraterritorial detention measures against the rioting Tunisians (Garelli et al., 2013: 195–99). More precisely, it detained the migrants directly on ships, with four of them "charged" with more than 700 migrants, which eventually completed their deportation. By October 2011, 3,385 Tunisians had been deported.

The flow of the *harraga* (Figure 3.3) exemplifies the circulation of the resistance strategies of the Tunisian underclass, such as riot, hunger strikes, sit-ins, occupations, and self-harm, already practiced during the revolution. However, the addressee of the protesters now is a different one. This time, the rioters were no longer contesting the local repressive state but the European anti-immigration policies enforced through detention and repression. In this context, migration worked as a massive relief valve, allowing the mobility of precisely those young unemployed who inhabited the poor areas and who had ignited the revolution in the first place.

The Flow of Refugees

The flow of struggles of the refugees on the Tunisian territory might seem disconnected from the revolution, yet it constitutes a fundamental challenge for the post-revolutionary Tunisian society, which many activists—both secular and religious—will find significant. Partially, this flow of events will follow the path of the struggles of the *harraga*, while a very resilient part of it will enact extreme strategies of "insistence in space" at the risk of their very lives (Tazzioli, 2014). In other words, many refugees moved along the same paths of the *harraga*—both in terms of routes to reach Europe (through Lampedusa) and in terms of locations of struggles for the right to stay (Paris, for example). There were, nonetheless, a few extraordinary exceptions.

This flow was started after the so-called Libyan crisis occurred between February 20 and November 3, 2011, triggered by the bloody civil war before and after the fall of Muammar Gaddafi. The neighboring country of Libya was, thus, devastated by three deadly forces: the anti-Gaddafi rebel groups, who targeted Sub-Saharan Africans for their alleged support to Gaddafi, and eventually the bombings on behalf of both the government and the allied Western countries. In the period between February 20 and November 3, 2011, more than 200,000 African (including the Libyans) and Asian refugees

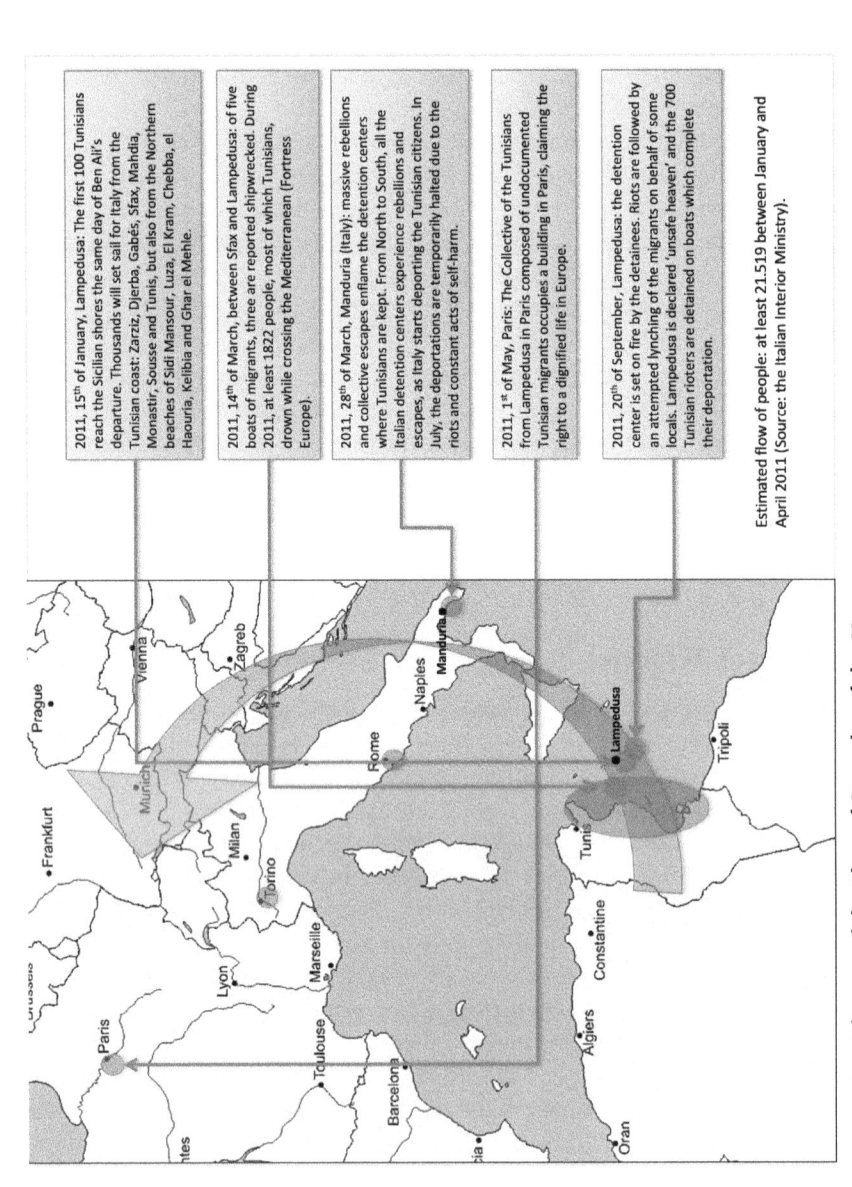

2011, 15th of January, Lampedusa: The first 100 Tunisians reach the Sicilian shores the same day of Ben Ali's departure. Thousands will set sail for Italy from the Tunisian coast: Zarzis, Djerba, Gabés, Sfax, Mahdia, Monastir, Sousse and Tunis, but also from the Northern beaches of Sidi Mansour, Luza, El Kram, Chebba, el Haouria, Kelibia and Ghar el Mehle.

2011, 14th of March, between Sfax and Lampedusa: of five boats of migrants, three are reported shipwrecked. During 2011, at least 1822 people, most of which Tunisians, drown while crossing the Mediterranean (Fortress Europe).

2011, 28th of March, Manduria (Italy): massive rebellions and collective escapes enflame the detention centers where Tunisians are kept. From North to South, all the Italian detention centers experience rebellions and escapes, as Italy starts deporting the Tunisian citizens. In July, the deportations are temporarily halted due to the riots and constant acts of self-harm.

2011, 1st of May, Paris: The Collective of the Tunisians from Lampedusa in Paris composed of undocumented Tunisian migrants occupies a building in Paris, claiming the right to a dignified life in Europe.

2011, 20th of September, Lampedusa: the detention center is set on fire by the detainees. Riots are followed by an attempted lynching of the migrants on behalf of some locals. Lampedusa is declared 'unsafe heaven' and the 700 Tunisian rioters are detained on boats which complete their deportation.

Estimated flow of people: at least 21.519 between January and April 2011 (Source: the Italian Interior Ministry).

Figure 3.3. Diagram of the Flow of Struggles of the *Harraga*.

crossed the border toward Tunisia through Ras Ajdir and Dehiba (International Organization of Migration). On that occasion, the Tunisian population of the south of the country, some of which had just returned from the experience of the Kasbah, enacted one of the most remarkable examples of collective solidarity and organization, the so-called *gifle tunisienne*, literally the "Tunisian slap in the face," an implicit reference to the government and the humanitarian organizations (Garelli et al., 2013: 193–94). Tunisian families hosted 160,000 refugees in two cities of the south: Tataouine and Djerba. The *gifle tunisienne* was a significant moment of mass self-organization and solidarity, but it also marked the limits of the Tunisian revolution. In fact, many Tunisians mainly focused on welcoming the Libyan citizens, who they perceived as wealthy and "non-African," which meant that they left the destiny of the refugees of color in the hands of the humanitarian organizations. Revealing a racial bias inherent, at least, in the local community, Tunisians ignored the "Africans," as Tunisians call them, who had been Libyan residents mainly coming from Sub-Saharan countries and who had migrated and resided in Libya for work, where they escaped from due to the anti-Gaddafi persecutions alongside the governmental and Western bombings. These people were now instead sheltered in refugee camps run by humanitarian agencies (Garelli et al., 2013: 194). On February 23, 2011, the United Nations High Commissioner for Refugees (UNHCR) opened the Choucha camp in the middle of the desert, seven kilometers away from the border with Libya, close to Ras Ajdir. The next month, the camp reached 22,000 inhabitants.

Like Lampedusa for the *harraga*, Choucha was the symbol of the struggles of the refugees escaping from Libya. Many of them hoped to receive asylum in Europe since they were unable to return either to Libya, where they had emigrated for work, or to their countries of origin. Some were willing to be repatriated; others were lucky enough to be relocated to Europe with an asylum status. But there remained a large group of people, mainly with Sub-Saharan African citizenships, not recognized as liable for asylum and thus rejected and eventually abandoned by the UNHCR. In fact, the agency declared the camp closed in the summer of 2013. Unable to integrate into an already economically challenged society such as the Tunisian one, and to have access to the—even informal—labor market as people of color, many "rejected refugees" decided to cross the Mediterranean. "Between the spring and summer of 2012, migrants coming from Libya substitute[d] those from Tunisia at Lampedusa" (Garelli et al., 2013: 183). On the other hand, a part of the remaining "rejected" refugees decided to stay in Tunisia fighting for their recognition as refugees by a European country, since Tunisia doesn't have an asylum law. Most importantly, despite the injunction to leave and the unlivable conditions at Choucha—set in the desert, with no water or electricity after its "closure"—many decided to stay in the camp and pursue their struggle also in this way, exposing the deadly effect of the asylum laws on their lives and refusing to silently vanish in the nth shipwreck in the Mediterranean.

The flow of struggle of the "Libyan" refugees is the most indicative of the complexity of resistance mechanisms and power apparatuses in the contemporary global world (Figure 3.4). In fact, the refugees found themselves having to struggle in an inhospitable, often racist, territory—the Tunisian one—allied to other African and Asian citizens in their attempt to challenge the conservative notion of asylum based on the country of origin, enforced by the highest Western institutions such as the UNHCR. In doing so, they've employed extreme strategies of an almost progressive suicide by means of "insistence on the space" (Tazzioli, 2014).[11] In the Tunisian context and for its connections with the West and the rest of the African continent, the struggle of Choucha represents one of the most extraordinary examples of political contestation.

The Flow of Islamic Militants

It appears paradoxical to include the flow of the Islamic militants, so very connected to the notion of "terrorism,"[12] among the other flows of struggle. As Santiago Alba Rico explains in the aftermath of the 2015 Sousse attack, "The post-revolutionary Jihadism cannot be defined as a radicalization of Islam, but on the contrary, as an Islamisation of radicality. The youth of this region (not to mention the European youth!) is radical, and if it won't be allowed to be radically democratic, then it will be radically un-democratic" (Alba Rico, 2015). In this sense, the problems arising, or rather obscured by, the nexus revolution-terrorism is crucial to discuss but is not the point of this specific section, yet it will be addressed in different ways in chapter 4.

The number of Tunisians involved in this phenomenon is the reason for this reflection on the Islamic militants. American sources estimate that around 7,000 young Tunisians have joined the army of the Islamic State, fighting in Libya, Syria, and Iraq (Zarocostas, 2015). What drives these Tunisian citizens toward armed struggle and martyrdom? And what does that have to do with the Tunisian revolution? First of all, it was the Tunisian revolution that reopened the public space for two categories that had been heavily persecuted by the Ben Ali regime: the Leftist and Islamist activists. As a consequence of the fall of the regime, an "Islamic bloc" had emerged in the post-revolutionary civil society, with a specific class stratification (Soli and Merone, 2013). The middle class rallied to the Islamic moderate camp, represented by the Ennahda party and the scriptural Salafis, interested in studying the *sharia*

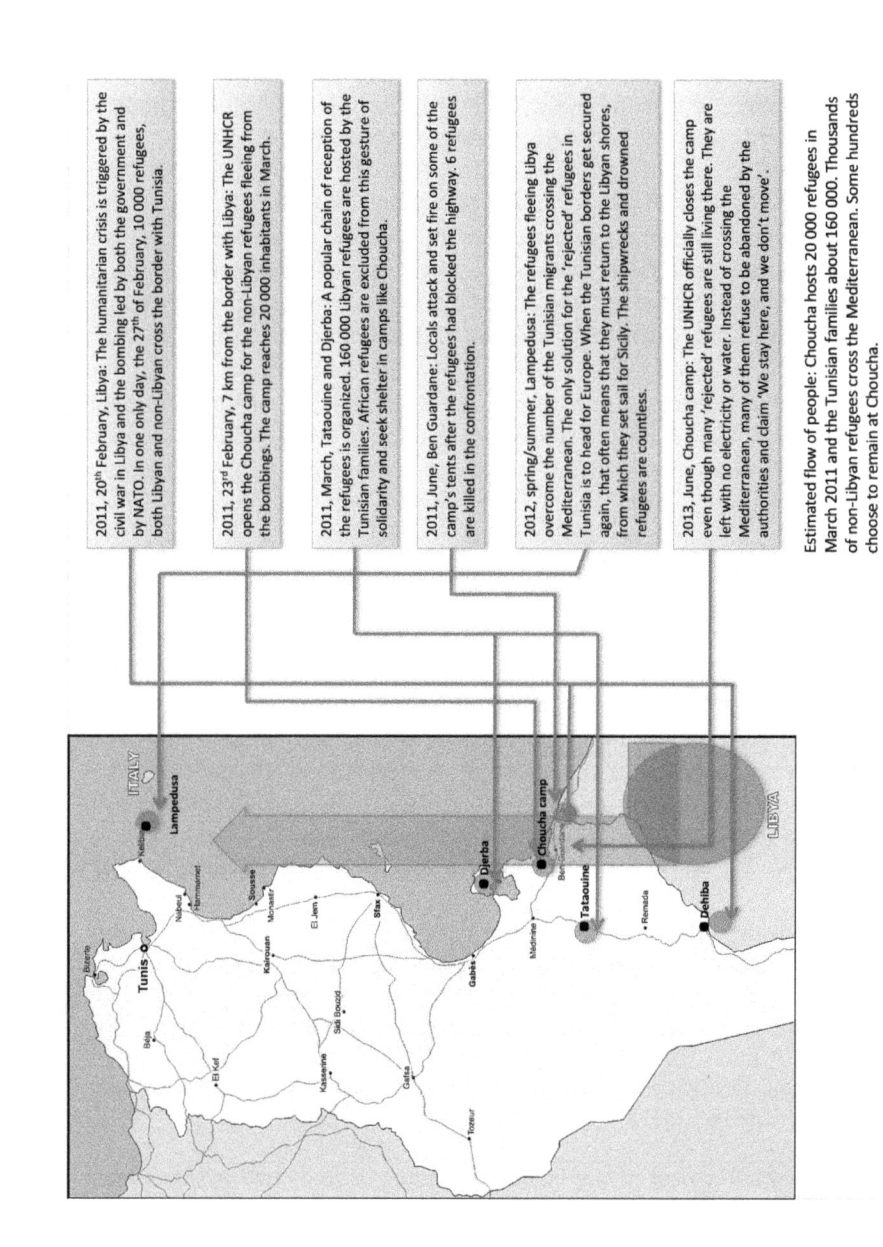

2011, 20th February, Libya: The humanitarian crisis is triggered by the civil war in Libya and the bombing led by both the government and by NATO. In one only day, the 27th of February, 10 000 refugees, both Libyan and non-Libyan cross the border with Tunisia.

2011, 23rd February, 7 km from the border with Libya: The UNHCR opens the Choucha camp for the non-Libyan refugees fleeing from the bombings. The camp reaches 20 000 inhabitants in March.

2011, March, Tataouine and Djerba: A popular chain of reception of the refugees is organized. 160 000 Libyan refugees are hosted by the Tunisian families. African refugees are excluded from this gesture of solidarity and seek shelter in camps like Choucha.

2011, June, Ben Guardane: Locals attack and set fire on some of the camp's tents after the refugees had blocked the highway. 6 refugees are killed in the confrontation.

2012, spring/summer, Lampedusa: The refugees fleeing Libya overcome the number of the Tunisian migrants crossing the Mediterranean. The only solution for the 'rejected' refugees in Tunisia is to head for Europe. When the Tunisian borders get secured again, that often means that they must return to the Libyan shores, from which they set sail for Sicily. The shipwrecks and drowned refugees are countless.

2013, June, Choucha camp: The UNHCR officially closes the camp even though many 'rejected' refugees are still living there. They are left with no electricity or water. Instead of crossing the Mediterranean, many of them refuse to be abandoned by the authorities and claim 'We stay here, and we don't move'.

Estimated flow of people: Choucha hosts 20 000 refugees in March 2011 and the Tunisian families about 160 000. Thousands of non-Libyan refugees cross the Mediterranean. Some hundreds choose to remain at Choucha.

Figure 3.4. Diagram of the Flow of Struggles of the Refugees.

law rather than doing politics; the lower social classes emerged on the public scene thanks to organizations such as Ansar al-Sharia Tunisia (AST), literally "the partisans of the *sharia*," the Islam-inspired law system born in April 2011. As Merone explains, "The particular function of Ansar al-Sharia was to act as a social movement, looking at how to form a consensus between the disenfranchised masses [. . .] focused on preaching and charity. [. . .] This group was interested in forming an alternative to the disastrous social conditions of large swathes of the Tunisian population" (Merone, 2015a).[13]

On September 12, 2012, a protest in front of the American embassy in Tunis against the desecrating movie *The Innocence of the Muslims* led to the killing of two protesters, with two others left to die in prison after a prolonged hunger strike. In the meanwhile, a series of deadly attacks at the border with Algeria, in the region of the mountain Chaambi, started regularly targeting Tunisian military forces. Furthermore, the assassinations of the Communist leaders Chokri Belaid and Mohammed Brahmi in 2013 were also associated with Islamist groups. At this point, the government initiated a massive repressive campaign, very much in continuity with the pre-revolutionary techniques, yet this time pursued in the name of the "war on terrorism." Over 6,500 people considered connected to political Islam were detained—more than the ones imprisoned during the Ben Ali period.

With the Ansar al-Sharia group blacklisted as a terrorist organization in 2013, no political solution had been provided for the "institutionalization of a significant part of Tunisia's Salafist movement" (Merone, 2015a), which fueled the departures toward *jihadi* fronts abroad or the radicalization of attacks inside the borders, as the shooting at the National Bardo Museum in 2015 proved. On that occasion, the *Okba Ibn Nafaa* Brigade (a splinter group of al-Qaeda in the Islamic Maghreb) killed twenty foreign tourists and two Tunisians. As Merone explains, after the repressive campaign started in 2013:

> A large Salafist radical constituency remained in existence. One part of it went to Syria-Iraq and Libya; another stayed inactive, fearing repression, and rejecting the reaction for political and practical reasons. Yet another faction tried to join those who wanted to mount some reaction against the government (most likely Okba Ibn Nafaa). Okba Ibn Nafaa has indeed been evolving in this context of radicalization, which encourages a confrontation between Salafists and the State. (Merone, 2015a)

The important aspect of the Islamic militancy flow is that it stems out of the same disenfranchised youth that the revolutionaries and the *harraga* also originated from (Figure 3.5). It is yet again a cry of frustration, and it can be argued that its radicalization has been partially conditioned by the largely repressive answer of the post-revolutionary Tunisian state. As Merone claims,

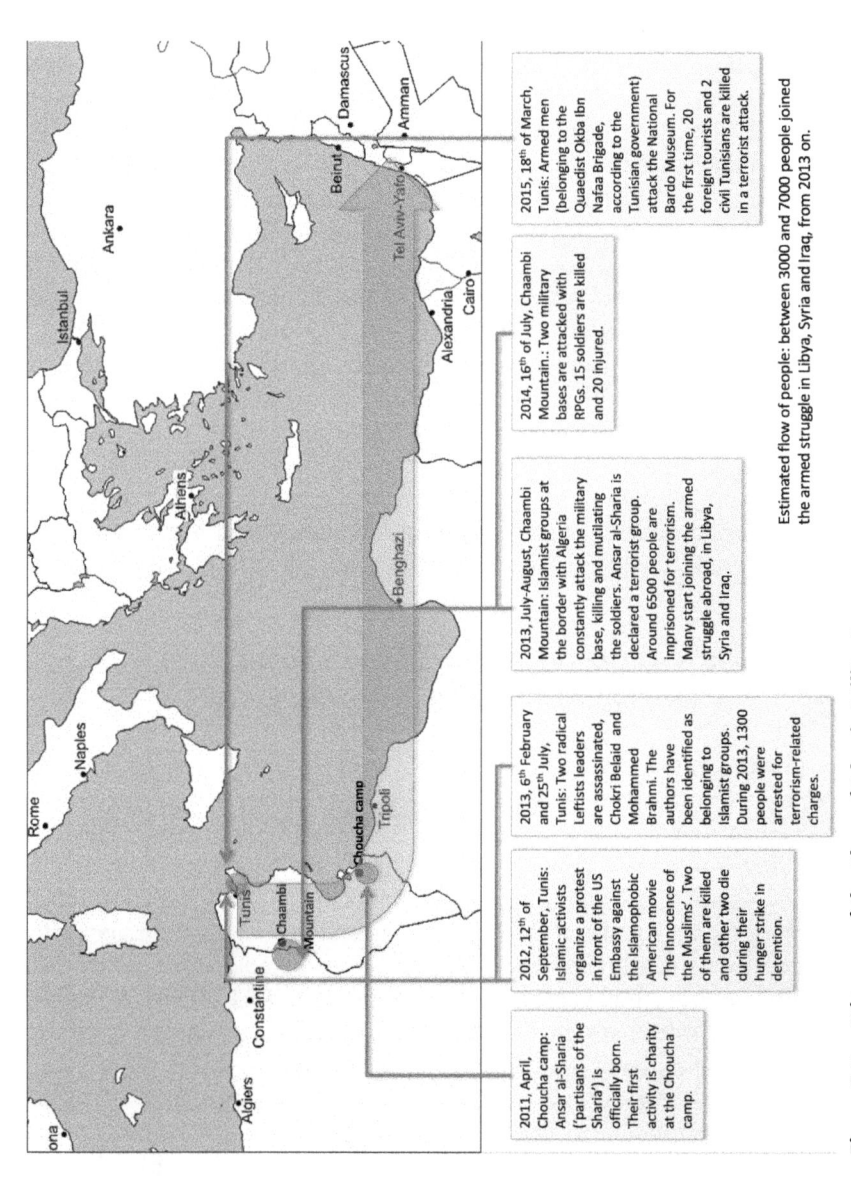

Figure 3.5. Diagram of the Flow of Islamic Militants.

besides the *jihadi* international dynamics, Tunisian political Islam cannot be reduced to a "generic and abstract 'terroristic threat' [. . .] instead cries out for a political solution" (Merone, 2015a).

The intention of the counter-mapping of the Tunisian revolution was that of allowing the events of resistance to mold the geography and draw the chronology of contestation. In so doing, the diagrams proved to be both a practice and a result by virtue of their non-discursive nature. In this sense, rather than building a new narrative, they allowed to simply follow the "red line" of different examples of resistance and other significant actions.

At the same time, the diagrams made it possible to dig deep into the invisible layers of the Tunisian revolution in terms of the events that triggered it and the events it caused. My claim is not that these four flows have composed the unitary revolutionary effect, but rather that it is through the flows' intersections that the most interesting aspects of the revolution are revealed. In fact, when the struggles create alliances or interrogate each other, it becomes clear how the territory of reference they relate to is much more complex and expands far beyond the Tunisian borders. At the same time, taking into account the geography drawn by the flows also gives the chance to look at different apparatuses of power, both local and global, and at how extreme strategies of resistance have managed to challenge them.

3.3. THE EMERGENCE OF THE "MOB" AND THE EXPANSION OF THE POLITICAL

In this research, the interest in the class aspect emerged when reading the analysis pursued by Rizk, a member of the Egyptian Mosireen collective,[14] who claimed that the "Lumpenprecariat have become the radical element within the revolutionary struggle" (Rizk, 2014). By "Lumpenprecariat," he referred to "those most suppressed, most exploited and most desperate under the former regime's political system," "the underclass without the luxury to attain an education, with no fixed jobs and thus vulnerable to the reality that police officers and employers existed above the law" (Rizk, 2014). Although his analysis regarded the Egyptian revolution, it is also applicable to Tunisia. In fact, many observers have pointed out that, related to this mass of occasional workers and graduate unemployed, the Tunisian working class—made of the ones who hold a permanent working contract and are therefore more "guaranteed"—assumed the role of a pseudo-"working class aristocracy." This group, mainly represented by civil servants, often avoided participation in the various mobilizations for fear of jeopardizing their positions (Gobe, 2010: 6). To this trend, the 2011 revolution was an obvious exception.

Along the same lines, Mohammed Ltaief of the Tunisian Ahl Al Kahf collective stresses the protagonism of the disenfranchised citizens of the internal areas as opposed to a narrative focused on the artists and intellectuals[15] as the agents of change:

> The same people who made the revolution are the poor people of Sidi Bouzid, of Regueb, of Thala and Kasserine. These are the people who want to achieve the goals of the revolution. People think it's the artists or the intellectuals who have come out to take pictures next to the tanks, who might be able to continue the revolution. These are the people who only come out during the celebrations, who arrive once the others have achieved the revolution. Their interests are not necessarily opposed to those of the oppressors. (Ltaief quoted in the film by Tlili, 2011, my translation)

I have previously referred to this group of people as the "underclass,"[16] mainly to stress their distance from what could be called the "working class," assigned to an "aristocratic" condition due to their stable jobs. The Tunisian underclass is the result of the massive contraction of the labor force, polarized around nepotism, due to deindustrialization and the unequal regional development. It mainly regards the majority of the youth, both graduate and not, from Tunisia's less developed areas, like the poor internal cities and the outskirts of the larger, richer ones. The underclass occupies an intermediary space between the urban working class with stable jobs and the rural precarious workers: men, but mostly women, whose living conditions have hardly been challenged by the revolution and who continue being the poorest of the society (as documented in the film by Alberti, Clementi, and Magoni, 2013).

The underclass is marked by a continuous and anxious activity focused on providing its livelihood, the so-called bread race, constantly threatened by the various agents of power such as the local authorities, the police, or the employers. It includes the significant population of the suburbs of the richer cities, whose inhabitants are commonly called *houmani*, literally "those attached to their neighborhood." The *houmani* are largely present in the capital's poor neighborhoods, like Hay Ettadhamen. These are the same neighborhoods that have been marked by the first revolutionary confrontations in the capital and which have self-managed their defense against Ben Ali's militias.

This large category of the Tunisian population, "concerned with day-to-day realities" and "frustrated because of the deterioration of their standard of living," operates outside the realm of the political, mainly monopolized by a small political elite, even after the revolution. As Merone observes, "A generation of apolitical, but nonetheless actively youth engaged in what has been called 'street politics'" (Merone, 2013a). In the Tunisian context, the most popular instances of large-scale organized "street politics" enacted by the disenfranchised youth are the Ultras movement of the football supporters and the *jihadi*-Salafi movement, initially focused on preaching and proselytism (Merone, 2013a). The Ultras movement, similarly to Egypt, has been and remains an important element in the confrontation with the police forces, since it "never misses an occasion to confront the police and to be a destabilizing element in an open conflict between the two political blocs," alternatively supporting the one identified as more "anti-system" (Merone, 2013a).

It is important to also point out that this large underclass category, which expresses its frustration with particularly risky and conflictual practices, is not considered part of the political arena. In fact, "what is being analysed in terms of 'political events' is largely down to the narrow categorization of a small political elite," "reliant on the same middle class" (Merone, 2013a). In addition, the national authorities also indistinctly criminalize this category. As Merone has referred after the March 18 (2015) terroristic shooting at the Bardo Museum in Tunis: "The Interior Minister is convinced that no difference exists between *this large disenfranchised population*, Ansar al-Sharia [the Tunisian Salafi social movement] and Okba Ibn Nafaa [the Quaedist brigade]: they are all 'terrorists'" (Merone, 2015a, my emphasis).

This is the reason why I have chosen to rename what I provisionally and generically called "underclass" as "mob." This is a term revisited by Aradau and Huysmans following Baruch Spinoza and Étienne Balibar's reflection on the notion of mass (Aradau and Huysmans, 2009). Their work emerges as a critique to the notion of "rights," which produces a separation between citizens (*demos*) and masses, depicted as "being denied rights or with limited capacity to claim rights" (Aradau and Huysmans, 2009: 595). Aradau and Huysmans's claim is that forms of mobility—such as those of the migrants—open up new political terrains, while they challenge the global power structures and allow "excluded social groups to enter the political process and accede to equality" (Aradau and Huysmans, 2009: 592). In this way, these political actors question who is a subject of rights as well as invent democratic practices (Aradau and Huysmans, 2009: 603).

The "mob," a derivation of the Latin *mobile vulgus*, literally the "moving riffraff," classically described a category that emerged in the eighteenth-century urban setting of London, that of the "citizens-discontents marshalled by the Whigs for political processions and rallies." "Not just rioters but everyone in London's lower classes who was present in the streets"; "politically motivated groups who are represented as numerous, mobile and an urban phenomenon" (Aradau and Huysmans, 2009: 596). By its very definition, the contemporary mob stands outside of the realms of politics, democracy, and citizenship, or it could be said that it represents the "constitutive limit" of these very categories, *qua* "disorderly force, whose actions are depoliticized either as economically determined—e.g., by hunger—or as socially irrational" (Aradau and Huysmans, 2009: 597).

As opposed to terms such as "underclass" or "mass," the "mob" contains an inherent depreciatory note, which I find very significant because it represents the common reactions of dismissal, but mostly of heavy criminalization that the "politics of the underclass" is generally met with. As a matter of fact, the Tunisian revolution is a perfect example of this category's practices being completely overshadowed by the activity of actors coming from the middle class, or the "working class aristocracy," such as bloggers, artists, or trade unionists. Instead, the latter have only been temporarily allied with a phenomenon triggered by the underclass of the internal cities and the metropolitan peripheries of the country. In this sense, the "mob" is the main—yet invisible—actor of the revolution, both in Tunisia and abroad when struggling as a migrant.

However, the process of "mob-ization" itself—intended as the process of criminalization/moralization/de-politicization carried out by the authorities, both institutional and intellectual, around the practices of the disenfranchised citizenship—is the best indication that a process of subjectivation has taken place. In this sense, the "mob" can be regarded as indicating the space of visibility and political protagonism that the disenfranchised majority is banned from. Once this space is occupied and a large category emerges from its invisibility due to intolerable governance conditions, the space of their political contestation is promptly neutralized through "mob-ization." This basically exorcises the government's fear of the "mob's" radical demands, asserting instead its incontestable irrationality and need to be repressed. The "mob's politics" is the substantial expression of a political will, by virtue of its "rejection of the price of being a subject," by enacting a "collective and physical refusal to be governed that way in all the realms of existence" (Tazzioli, 2015). The Tunisian "mob" has enacted this type of rejection toward the regime, eventually bringing it down. This is why I claim that the "mob" politics constitutes an indication of both an attempt of erasure, of the already excluded categories renegotiating their subject position, alongside the attempt of a fundamental expansion or extension of the political terrain. This expansion questions who can be the subject of rights and operates a resignification of the political, indicating its priorities, such as less precarious livelihood, less abuse from the state, while also devising new strategies of struggle to achieve them.[17]

CONCLUSION

In addressing the consistency of this event in a different manner, I have chosen to follow the accounts of the participants both in terms of the temporality and of the spatiality they redraw. I have interpreted the resulting series of events of resistance visually as diagrams of flows. It became clear right away that the revolution had its historical precedents and political emergence in the poor internal areas, rather than in the capital. Moreover, after weeks of protests, repression, and the departure of the president, those same streams of contestation coming from the internal areas had also spread across Europe, thanks to the unexpected possibility that allowed the Tunisian citizens to cross the border, even if illegally. This temporary opening up of the borders determined the arrival of thousands of ex-revolutionaries in Europe, where another series of struggles unfolded, mainly set in the detention centers and the Western cities. Along the lines of the previous theorization of the network of events of resistance and of its implicit contagious dimension, all these layers of struggle have been interpreted as "flows," since they inherently imply the circulation and mobility of their practices of contestation. The spreading of unrests and the mobility of large masses of people characterize these flows. The Tunisian territory has been marked by at least four flows: the first one saw the people from the internal areas spread the uprising toward the north; the second regarded the *harraga*, the undocumented migrants crossing the Mediterranean; the third gathered the mostly Sub-Saharan African refugees fleeing the civil war and the bombings in Libya who lived in the refugee camps with no prospect of asylum; while the last flow was that of the young Tunisians who had chosen to devote their lives to the Islamic militancy in Tunisia but mostly abroad, traveling for the *jihad* in countries like Syria, Iraq, or Libya.

Borrowing Aradau and Huysmans's reflection, I have referred to the agents of the revolution as the "mob" because of their constant criminalization and depoliticization on behalf of the authorities, whether they were rioting in their town demanding "Bread, freedom, dignity!," occupying the capital's Kasbah claiming the resignation of the post–Ben Ali government, or burning down the Italian detention centers.

In this sense, my claim is that the emancipatory potential of the Tunisian events stems precisely from the conditions of possibility of the intersection of these streams of struggle. In this sense, the "mob" could be the political agent of the future, with its radical demands and tactics, its constant challenge posed to the border system, and its ability to implement contestation in hostile and foreign environments. One of the most significant tasks of the future becomes that of building patterns of transversal support and solidarity with the struggles of the disenfranchised, the unemployed. That's why accounting for them and acknowledging their push to expand the notion of the political is a first step toward the alliances of the future.

This chapter is an attempt to transform into practice the claims that I have developed in the previous chapters. For example, here I engage in a detailed manner with the *singularity* of the Tunisian revolution, in that I seek to show the specificity of the different struggles and mobility practices connected to it. The diagrams of the flows of struggle are the concrete application of the *network of events of resistance* and address in a visual way the contagious dimension of resistance, especially in the case of the flow of the underclass. In other words, the diagrams are one of this work's attempts to counter the practices of representation that capture the event, by showing how it continues to develop its potential, by acknowledging its virtual dimension.

Chapter Four

Histories of Dispossession and Contemporary Vanguards

> Only the act of resistance can resist death: either in the form of an artwork or in the form of the human struggle.
>
> —Gilles Deleuze, "What Is the Act of Creation?," 1987

THE INAUDIBLE VANGUARDS OF ART AND POLITICS

In the previous chapter, I laid out an alternative chronology and geography of the Tunisian revolution by focusing on the flows drawn across the territory by the events of resistance, both within and beyond the Tunisian national borders. I have, therefore, drawn the attention to how this event is to be regarded as an intersection of flows of struggle, of which I provided a snapshot with the help of diagrams. The protagonists of these flows—drawn by a series of events of resistance that emerged as significant—were mainly Tunisian nationals, alongside which I've signaled the fierce struggle of the Sub-Saharan refugees from Libya in Choucha.

In the view of this research, the symbolic triad figure of the "revolutionary," the "undocumented" migrant/*harraga*, and the "terrorist"/*irhabi* are all connected to a category of people marked by existential precarity and a great sense of striving. I chose to call this category "mob," drawing from the resignification of this term operated by Claudia Aradau and Jef Huysmans. In fact, the term "mob" makes visible two fundamental aspects that the previous term I employed—underclass—was suggesting to a lesser extent. First, it inevitably points to a process of stigmatization. Second, by virtue of its re-signified version, it indicates how practices of mobility work toward expanding and transforming the field of the political.

This chapter will develop some of these conclusions, taking them one step further. The inquiry will place the year 2011 within a wider context of lineages of both dispossession and resistance that have touched upon the Tunisian territory, starting with the period of the French colonial rule until the 2016 protests in Kasserine. In this sense, I will argue that the peasants (alongside the indigenous Amazigh communities) represent the constitutive absence of the Tunisian revolution since the poor cities and suburbs (*hwem*) that the revolution started from are one of the physical consequences of the historical rural dispossession. In fact, in terms of "economy of dispossession" (Ayeb, 2011), the richer Tunisia, the Sahel region where capital was and still is accumulated, has traditionally exploited the west, center, and south, the "Tunisia of the resources" (Ibidem).

Furthermore, I will trace a relation between what I refer to in terms of two types of "vanguard." On the one hand, I will explore the practices of minor art enacted by the Tunisian Ahl Al Kahf street art collective (between 2011 and 2013). On the other hand, I will introduce the reflection on practices of minor politics (which I'll further discuss in chapter 5) enacted by the Tunisian "relative surplus population," who in 2011 "entered the world of politics through riots" (Lamloum, 2016: 9). Against the argument that many impoverished Tunisians are inexorably destined to work on the battlefields of the Islamic State, I will bring the example of the 2016 mobilization of the unemployed in Kasserine, originated by the public suicide of Ridha Yahyaoui. Reflecting on the significance of this episode, I will address the political subjectivity of the revolution in terms of "vanguard" (after having previously thought about it through terms such as "underclass" and "mob") in order to acknowledge the affirmative determination of this group of people. The members of this Tunisian vanguard, I will argue, enact the political also by weaponizing "bare life," by paradoxically demanding for their life to be valued while they risk it with gestures of self-harm or public suicides. These gestures, that I will describe as necroresistant practices of the vanguard—especially given the centrality of the body as a political arsenal—will be further discussed in relation to the importance of the gesture as a mediator of circulation of dissent (chapter 5).

4.1. LOOKING AT THE REVOLUTION FROM THE "BLIND" SPOT: THE PEASANTS AND THE IMAZIGHEN

This parallel journey of imagining perspectives of the revolution that aren't immediately apparent started with the work of Habib Ayeb, the critical geographer, and his 2013 article titled "The Rural in the Tunisian Revolution:

The Inaudible Voices." Analyzing an event from a perspective that appears to be external to it, that of the peasants and the Amazigh community, in this case has proven to be productive because it made visible a series of layers that were mostly effaced from the common discourse or deemed irrelevant.

This is what Ayeb alludes to when he writes about "inaudible voices." Inaudible is maybe the keyword for the Tunisian revolution. It indicates an entire tradition of interaction between governed and governing bodies. It tells the story of a category that would repeatedly speak and not simply remain unheard, but rather confirm its constitutive inaudibility! It also draws attention to a particular distribution of the sensible, and of disposability, that has evolved with a certain continuity throughout the colonial and the post-independence period until the years prior to the revolution—namely, from 1956 to 2011.

The social and economic marginalization is "the main cause of the invisibility and inaudibility of the small peasantry," since the debate around the revolution was often limited to "the only space of politics/politicians and the usual dominant issues around identity, religion, political rights and individual liberties," thereby avoiding to address economic and social issues. As a consequence, the "unpleasant question around the social classes (wa)s disregarded in the political, media and even academic analyses." In other words "the classes nobody knows how to look at" were being hidden (Ayeb, 2013).

Upon a closer look, in fact, the rural dimension appears to be the very motor of the revolution. Peasants are in fact a constitutive absence of the event itself. More precisely, they inhabit the very roots of the revolution and are a crucial component of the lives of the men and women who have inflamed the poor cities and suburbs of Tunisia in a way that I will try to unpack as follows.

Ayeb's research is focused on agriculture and food policies in post-colonial Tunisia. His analyses show how the French colonists have targeted the extensive subsistence agriculture of the Tunisian peasants. He argues that the post-independence governments enacted the same attack with their cooperativist agricultural projects (Ibidem). Eventually, the final blow to the rural economy was inflicted by the liberalization processes, also known as "structural adjustments," which targeted the state-subsidized agriculture at the beginning of the 1990s and succeeded in massively impoverishing the rural population by 2007, a year that was marked by an agricultural commodities crisis (Elloumi, 2015).

Under the pressure of the international financial organizations, the Tunisian government initiated a process of public divestment and liberalization of resources such as land and water in the rural environment—namely, the majority of the Tunisian territory. These policies progressively crippled the subsistence activity of most of the population, especially given the harsh desertlike climate that most of the country is affected by and the centrality of family farming. In 2006, for example, 43 percent of the families lived on and of farmlands with an extension of less than 5 hectares (Ibidem).

To put it in a simple manner, the Tunisian state initiated a process of public divestment, decreasing its presence on the internal agricultural market in a very particular way. Whereas immediately after independence the state had invested in the internal market empowering the autonomy of small family farms, from the 1980 to the '90s the state was conditioned to increasingly withdraw or rather only provide support to large agribusinesses, therefore pushing the subsistence and the extensive agriculture into a progressive and disastrous decay. This is particularly visible, Ayeb argues, in the state's actions vis-à-vis one of Tunisia's most important resources: water.

In fact, the state continued to subsidize the irrigation network, but only the one necessary for the so-called big investors, the big agricultural companies whose products are exported and mainly managed by the entrepreneurs of the north, who benefit from their collusions with the government and the Western economic interests. Irrigation is a litmus test for the increasing gap between what some have called the "two Tunisias." It is, in fact, omnipresent in the documented discourses of the "inaudible" voices of the rural population (Ibidem). Most of the peasants interviewed by Ayeb explained that they have no access to running water, neither for their households nor for their farmlands. This is even more dramatic, considering that desertification is an increasing phenomenon on the Tunisian territory.

The uneven access to water further exemplifies the widening of the gap initiated with the "Franco-Sfaxian colonization," intended as the economic domination of the north and the coast and developed into what Ayeb calls the "economy of dispossession." What he refers to is the national labor division between rich Tunisia, centered on the capital and the coast, with pioneer cities like Sfax and Sousse, and the "Tunisia of rich resources" (Ibidem). As Amel Rahbi from the League of Human Rights explains, "Ever since the colonial period, the country has been built upon the illusion of a useful Tunisia concentrated on the coast. This model continued after independence. The rest of the country is therefore abandoned, impoverished, discriminated" (Moussaoui, 2016).

On the one side, rich Tunisia is the financial center of the gains derived from the agricultural, mining, textile, and tourist industries. On the other side, the rest of the country is subjected to a constant extraction of its natural resources, such as "water, agricultural lands, oases, ores (like phosphate, iron), gas and oil" (Ayeb, 2011). At the same time, the poorer areas of Tunisia (namely, the south, center, and west) are being pushed into a "spiral of exclusion" (Elloumi, 2015) that sees them drifting away from the national project itself.[1]

In this case, the Tunisian underprivileged areas were subjected to a double dispossession, from both the state and, most importantly, the international market. More precisely, the state pushed them toward the expropriative international competition, which was focused on enforcing and legitimizing the power of the already dominant monopolies, mainly through financial strategies.

In this way, the "accumulation by dispossession" (Harvey, 2007) radicalized by the liberalization policies deepened the gap between the two Tunisias: "one, the Tunisia of power, money, comfort and 'development,' which covers the coastal areas, particularly the capital city and its upper-class suburbs and the Sahel (including the gulf of Nabeul, Sousse and Monastir) and, second, the marginalized, poor, submissive and dependent Tunisia (of the South, the centre and the West)" (Ayeb, 2011: 470). In this direction, at least from the '80s to the '90s, the state supported the interests of a particular minoritarian political community, that of the "*baldi*-Sahel[2] which is *francisant* and bourgeois" (Larbi Sadiki in Zoubir and Amirah-Fernández, 2008: 115), to such an extent that some have called Tunisia the "bourgeois republic" (Ibidem; Zubaida, 1993: 3).

This process of territorial differentiation was partially initiated by the colonists, who invested in the development of the capital in general as a sign of the "colonial triumph" (Liauzu, 1976), while actively hindering the food sovereignty of the rest of the country and destroying the pre-colonial networks of subsistence exchange between sedentary and nomadic groups. This tendency, to concentrate all the wealth and production in the north, continued after independence. The gap in terms of access to the resources was only briefly interrupted in the '60s and '70s (Elloumi, 2015), when the state focused more on supporting the internal market by making it easy for all its citizens to develop subsistence strategies, mostly within agriculture, and the mining industry, whose dismantlement started later.

The wider the gap between the Sahel and the rest of the country grew—given that the demographic growth was not absorbed by the labor market—the more these areas started implementing a series of ever-changing survival strategies connected to the "race for bread" (Meddeb, 2011). In pre- and post-revolutionary Tunisia, survival depended on monoculture family agriculture (mostly worked by the women), the men's poly-activity, and the internal migration, alongside many activities of informal economy such as smuggling and street vending. These are the subsistence activities of the poor Tunisians. To these, the revolution added a temporary alternative (from January 14 to April 5) by disturbing the system of borders control put in place by Ben Ali, in that it gave the opportunity to many Tunisians to set sail for Europe in the search of a financial fulfillment. At least 20,000 left immediately after the fall of the regime, and many perished in the Mediterranean.

It is in this sense that Ayeb has identified the "spatial, economic, social and political marginalization of one part of the country and society in favour of another" as being the "direct cause of the revolutionary process that ended the mafia dictatorship of Ben Ali-Trabelsi" (Ayeb, 2011: 467). Moreover, the fact that a popular movement has succeeded in short-circuiting the patterns of power, both internal and external, was "due to an *ad hoc* and conjunctural alliance of the middle classes and the popular classes around a common demand: dignity, a major condition for the ability to be and to do" (Ibidem).

My argument is that the revolutionary outcry came mainly from the *hwem*, which are nothing but the physical extension of a rural space that represents the majority of the Tunisian territory, deprived of its own subsistence by a stratification of oppressive interests. These interests are both local and global and include the local organized crime, the national interests of the main families, alongside the liberalization policies imposed by the foreign countries in their interest, which the state implemented under financial pressure. Following the works of Claude Liauzu (1976) and Mohamed Elloumi (2015), it is easy to reconstruct the genealogy of accumulation by dispossession, which the Tunisian territory has been subjected to.

In fact, this has started in the recent period—if one is to look back only to the nineteenth century—with the territorial reorganization operated by the French colonists, once the so-called French Protectorate had been established in 1881. This is when the self-regulating sustainable interdependence between the Tunisian communities had been violently severed in order to deprive the colonized people of their autonomy and subdue them to the colonial mode of production.

In the following section, I will be taking consequent steps back in history in the attempt to identify the recent genealogy of this process of accumulation by dispossession that was questioned by the 2011 revolution. First, it is crucial to follow the genealogy of the *hwem*, the Tunisian *banlieus* and to point out that they descend from an initial urban development of the colonial capital. Tunis became, in fact, at least from the 1930s an emigration target for thousands of *fellaga* (Tunisian peasants), animal breeders, alongside the poor European settlers. These people, described as *corteges de déracinés*, "cohorts of uprooted people," were compelled to move mostly because their agricultural or breeding activity no longer allowed them to survive, let alone to pay the French taxes or credits. As Liauzu explains, "The climatic and capitalist calamities push(ed) entire sections of the rural society into becoming a subproletariat" (Liauzu, 1976). This process was initiated by the colonial system through the destruction of the pre-colonial subsistence networks and through debt, which also hit the poor European settlers. Most significantly, the French researcher points out that "it is not possible to have clear figures of the selling of land in the tribunals, but what is certain is that the suspension of the repossessions for debt in 1934 has avoided the dispossession of the biggest section of French and Tunisian peasants" (Liauzu, 1976: 611).

According to the official numbers, the precarious *bidonvilles*, or *gourbivilles* (shantytowns), at the outskirts of the capital hosted 2,000 people in 1935; 1,500 in 1936; 5,000 in 1938; and already 10,000 in 1941. The inhabitants of the *bidonvilles* were associated with the *lumpen*proletariat. They got by with petty crimes, reselling objects and food they found in the garbage, small robberies, begging, or practicing open or clandestine sex work (Idem: 615). The local beylical authority[3] tried to hinder their settlement in numerous ways: by disciplining their mobility either with detailed mobility permits for both human and animals or by repeatedly deporting, fining, and detaining them. By 1946, the *bidonvilles* were inhabited by 50,000 people. It became clear that these settlements wouldn't disappear and that they needed to be provided with decent housing. This idea was only implemented in the '70s, when the main peripheral neighborhoods of the capital, such as Ettadhamen (literally "solidarity") and Mnihla, turned from informal settlements to being part of the administrative organization. These are today's *hwem*.

Moreover, when looking even further back, it is possible to identify more significant gestures that have determined the destructuration of the rural subsistence economy. In connection to that, contemporary internal migration seems to have been in place from the '30s until today with a short break in the '80s.

When the French colonists took hold of the Tunisian territory in 1881, the survival of the peoples who inhabited it was based on a symbiotic relationship between the nomadic and the sedentary groups, distributed throughout the mostly arid land, centered on the oases for agriculture and the desert for the breeding of animals, such as the camel. This interaction was based on collective ownership of lands and on the occasional exchange between crops and animal-derived products or tools, in addition to a protection tax (*saliab*) that sedentary groups paid to the warrior nomadic tribes. The French colonists have, instead, prohibited the *saliab* tax, that was supporting the nomads, and imposed their own taxes, while forcing nomads to sedentarization. In addition, the inhabitants of the Tunisian territory were also subjected to taxes, and a process of privatization of the commonly owned land was initiated. The forced sedentarization, the privatization of lands, and the imposition of taxes resulted in a progressive proletarization, and erosion of autonomy, of all those peoples who supported one another in the past. The following is an illuminating passage of how the French described their endeavor in 1911, evaluating the "improvements" they had brought to what they called the "indigenous agriculture." This description also makes visible how credits were introduced in a way that would eventually cripple the peasants and dispossess them of their lands.

> We must act with much attention and patience in this matter of collective lands, especially since it particularly interests the nomads—i.e.—those of our citizens who had seen with the worst eye our installation in the country, since as from our arrival we suppressed one of their resources: the tributes paid by the Djebalia people (a sedentary tribe living in the mountains). [. . .]
>
> Moreover, in a country where one has a good harvest only every five or six years, while the rest of the time the indigenous peoples hardly collect the seeds they've planted; where the crops and livestock are the main resources of the tribes, discouragement threatens to seize people at any moment and cause their migration towards Northern cities. Therefore, the military authority had to provide for the reduction of the taxes. The reduction is put in place every time the harvest is lacking and it exempts the indigenous to pay back the seeds because often, after several bad harvests, the natives have no grain at the time of ploughing, to sow and it is necessary to make them benefit from the Insurance Society.
>
> *L'Agriculture indigene en Tunisie: Rapport general de la commission d'amélioration de l'agriculture indigene constituée par le décret du 13 mai 1911.* (Saliba, 1911: 668–69, my translation)

As far as the forced sedentarization of the nomads is concerned, it is chilling to read the way the French military authority invoked the people's well-being—with a very biopolitical undertone, one would say today—also alluded to in the title, with the reference to the *amélioration* or improvement of the "indigenous" agriculture.

> While the military authority has worked to improve the lives of nomads, always respecting their wandering habits, it hasn't renounced fixing them in certain points and making them adopt more regular habits. But the military authority wanted this to be the work of time and of their well-being. She has thought that the most effective measures to create and enhance the well-being were the following: settling an absolute security in the country, allowing the workers to peacefully enjoy, in a guaranteed manner, the products of their labor.
>
> The insecurity that has prevailed in the country since the end of the Roman occupation until the coming of the French, was, more certainly, the cause of its ruin. (Idem: 669–70, my translation)

What I wanted to show with these snapshots of the genealogy of dispossession that has afflicted the Tunisian territory is that the 2011 revolutionaries have a long lineage, at least as long as this short history of dispossession stretches upon. Every power apparatus that has imposed a certain regime of dispossession—either by limiting people's mobility or collective ownership, or simply by suppressing their subsistence activities and therefore their very existential sovereignty—was met with resistance. Many of these stories of resistance have been circulated only within local oral histories. Some have left traces in the known historiography, such as the 1906 rebellions of Thala and Kasserine or the 1911 events of the al-Jallaz cemetery, alongside the much-celebrated 1938 anti-colonial riots, which are commemorated as the national Day of the Martyrs on April 9.

In the post-independence period, the most explosive protests erupted on January 26, 1978 ("Black Thursday") and in 1984 with the "bread riots." Both dates were connected to the worsening of the economic crisis in Tunisia and were met with a violent response from the state. More recently, the 2008–2015 period has been a constellation of protests and riots, which I've detailed in the previous chapter. My understanding is that this last season of post-independence protests is a reaction to a renewed wave of accumulation by dispossession, similar to the colonial one. By virtue of which, local interests of the Sahel families, such as the infamous Ben Ali and Trabelsis, in charge of the government are interwoven with those of the global market of debt, alongside the water and land grabbing. In this sense, the revolution—started from Tunisia's agricultural regions and the *hwem* of the northern cities—is the cry of an entire generation against further dispossession.

As follows, I will discuss an additional layer that many debates around the revolution have made invisible but that, I believe, bears an important role in the unfolding of the event and should be acknowledged as such. Before its Arabization, Tunisia, as much of Northern Africa, has traditionally been the land of the Amazigh nomadic peoples, also known as Berbers. Today, it is generally known that Morocco, Algeria, and Tunisia are populated by Berbers, although these countries' populations are often deemed "Arab." These indigenous peoples call themselves *Amazigh—Tamazight* for the women, *Imazighen* for the plural. The term literally means "free and noble humans."

The Amazigh and their language have survived their many conquerors—the Phoenicians, the Byzantines, and the Romans—but initiated a still ongoing process of assimilation ever since the Arabs started conquering and inhabiting their lands in the seventh century AD. The Amazigh language was progressively substituted with Arabic and their worship of the sun and moon substituted with Islam. When the French colonized the Tunisian territory in 1881, the peoples living on it were mainly of Amazigh origins, either from Iberian-Numidian or Libyan descent and were classified according to their level of Arabization and sedentarity (Berger-Levrault, 1896). Most commonly, the Imazighen, also described by the famous scholar Ibn Khaldun (Khaldun,

[1377] 1969), are nomadic peoples who inhabit the desert. Ibn Khaldun describes them as camel breeders and valuable warriors who also mastered the craft of working with metals and produced tools, weapons, and jewelry.

Throughout history, until their self-determination struggle of the current days, the Imazighen have maintained a self-awareness of their identity and kept claiming that it be respected by the central government. Paradoxically, the Imazighen and the *fellaga* (the peasants) played a crucial role in the anti-colonial movement that pushed the French out of what then became Tunisia. And yet, the Amazigh peoples have been perceived as a threat by the post-independence Tunisian state. The case of Lazhar Chraiti, executed in 1963, is indicative in this sense. Engaged in the anti-colonial fight, Chraiti was then tried and executed by the first Tunisian government alongside other anti-colonial fighters as "conspirators" (Tlili [film], 2013).

Tunisia is therefore not only a state built around the political community of the Sahel but also one marked by the domination of the Arab-Islamic culture, which has historically "denied the Amazigh identity of the country" (*Organisation Non Gouvernamentale de défense des droits des Imazighen*, 2003), by prescribing Arabic as the official language in the Constitution and adding that "the state belongs to the Arab family" (Ibidem). Moreover, in the words of the Tunisian Imazighen, "all the individual and the collective attempt of expressing the Berberity and a will to take charge of the Berber culture was repressed. The expression of Berberity is considered an attack on the interest and the integrity of the state" (Ibidem).

The Tunisian Imazighen are a relevant presence in Tunisia today because, just like in the case of the peasants, although they seem to be external to the revolutionary process, they indicate a certain accumulation by dispossession, which is often the trigger for collective action. In fact, although they are made invisible—their identity is not explicitly mentioned—the Imazighen still speak their language today in many regions such as on the Djerba island, in the central regions, Gafsa, and in the southeast around Tataouine and Matmata. The so-called Berberophone regions are the poorest ones, lacking development possibilities, infrastructure, and opportunities, which is why their populations are compelled to a continuous exodus toward the richer cities of the north, where their customs and language are subjected to an inexorable Arabization. As a consequence, the Imazighen inhabit those same spaces of poverty and dispossession, especially in the deep desert south, both rural and urban that have fueled the revolution. Because of the traditional repression of "expressions of Berberity," and since the revolution contained no claims of their recognition, it is difficult to evaluate what the Amazigh presence among the revolutionaries was. But it is, nonetheless, crucial to account for this layer of oppression, be it even only to make clear the implications of calling an entire nation "Arab," when the Arab identity constitutes for many the active and state legitimate denial of their own identity, especially in terms of how the Tunisian state has been set.

With these apparently unrelated focuses on aspects of the Tunisian history and conflicts, my goal was to suggest a different manner of reading the recent history of the revolution, while simultaneously tying it to the long lineage of resistance, which has inflamed the Tunisian territory. The next section will engage in more detail with the artistic production that I've referred to so far, with the intention to show how useful it has been in order to account for this event's singularity but also with the aim to frame the work of the Ahl Al Kahf collective as an example of minor art.

4.2. THE AHL AL KAHF COLLECTIVE: THE EXILED BELIEVERS AND THE SEEDS OF REVOLUTION

Ahl Al Kahf is probably one of the most important and well-known Tunisian street art collectives born out of the Dignity revolution, but it is certainly not the only one. The members are part of a large, highly politicized street art movement that includes other relevant collectives such as Zwewla and Molotov (Lacquaniti, 2015). The reason art on the streets and graffiti became such a powerful and political tool after the revolution is precisely because of the harsh system of censorship and occupation of the public space enacted by the Ben Ali regime. The Ahl Al Kahf collective is connected to the capital's Academy of Arts and gathers young artists belonging to the Leftist underground, active in the student trade unions during the regime, therefore holding a strongly political awareness. On their Facebook profile, they describe themselves as a "movement of young artists from Tunisia, anti-Globalization & anti-Orientalism, born inside the revolutionary process." They promote "'aesthetic terrorism' and 'revolutionary art' as opposed to the art 'of the revolution,' namely against the celebratory *façade* aesthetics, subtending the narrative of the 'Jasmine revolution' or of the 'Arab Spring' (which are Western definitions, in any case)" (Lacquaniti, 2014: 132–33). In fact, their activity starts with the coverage of the Sidi Bouzid riots in December 2010 and later on, after the toppling of Ben Ali, with the participation in the occupations of the Kasbah (1 and 2). They get their inspiration from Banksy, the Situationists, the classical street artist Ernest Pignon-Ernest, and the ones they call the "philosophers of resistance": Gilles Deleuze, Antonio Negri, Edward Said. While the revolutionaries take the streets, Ahl Al Kahf participates in the taking of the walls, filling them with political messages. The group's art weaves together European and Middle Eastern theory and resistance histories, with Dada and no-global visuals, while harshly critiquing the political transition and, *de facto*, making available forms of counter-information on one of the most democratic urban platforms: the city's walls. With its manifesto, the collective is also the first to make explicit the question around identity and signature in the art industry and beyond. In fact, members encourage anyone to take on their signature and create, add, or destroy their ephemeral artworks—of which only virtual photographic albums trace the existence.

In this sense, the Tunisian walls, "the non-Western walls, in the postcolonial sense of the term, have succeeded in becoming the memory of resistance" (Ltaief in Lacquaniti, 2015: 173–74). Like the work of the Mosireen collective in Egypt, this group's critiques and practices constitute an archive of political reflection on the Tunisian revolution, built in an inclusive, collective, anonymous, and often humor-led manner, where contemporary public art is conceived as a means of education and liberation. In this sense, their artwork is a very good expression of many "seeds" of the Tunisian revolution, in terms of all those meanings that that event was able to reactivate and propel toward the rest of the world, both "Arab" and non-"Arab."

Before its artistic manifesto was made public on December 27, 2011, on the social media profile, the group was already alluding to a particular type of aesthetics with its name. Ahl Al Kahf (أهل الكهف) can be literally translated as "the people underground." The name actually refers to the "Pious Long-Sleepers" myth, which exists in Greek, Jewish, and Christian antiquity, known as the "Seven Sleepers of Ephesus" in Christian martyrology. In its Muslim version, it is developed in the Qu'ran in the 8 Sura, verses 9–26, and it doesn't specify the number of the sleepers. The legend goes that a certain number of young believers, who weren't willing to submit to the dominant faith, hid from persecution in a cave, where they fell asleep for a very long period of time (the Qu'ran speaks of 300 solar years). They woke up in a different epoch, in which their faith was recognized, but they died soon after. The cave that different countries claim as local is surrounded by religious celebrations of the Sleepers' martyrdom.

> All the elements are perfect to name a movement of anonymous members, whose number is to remain unknown, forced by circumstances to operate underground, not limited to one particular country but aspiring to universality. A movement able to deal with contemporary art, which, in Félix Guattari's definition—one of the group's cultural references—is articulated as a "non-temporal art." (Lacquaniti, 2014: 132, my translation)

In this sense, the name suggests the practice of an anonymous, potentially threatened, untimely artistic group aspiring to a universal production. In fact, the collective is adamant about declining its sense of belonging in terms of a universality coming from the marginal spaces of society. Members explain that

> the people underground are [. . .] those ones living underneath the rubble [. . .] the ones working underneath the rubble. Those ones working illegally and who belong at the same time to a culture and to the world. There are some Tunisian citizens and some other citizens who belong to a universal culture. This is the principle of the People Underground movement. (Tlili [film], 2011, my translation)

On the issue of "culture," they specify their anti-essentialist position, quoting the practice of Said in the United States, in the sense that "the issue has nothing to do with geography or borders" and that "culture is in a constant process of development. I take it with me wherever I go" (Ibidem).

It is important to understand that alongside its capacity as an anonymous, underground, universal group, Ahl Al Kahf functions like a signature available to everyone. In other words, the main goal is to open up a space of expression in the public sphere, which had been previously cluttered by the regime-led rhetoric and art. That's why the group is fond of the idea of public art and stresses the necessary access to expressing oneself. In this sense, the name, the signature itself is a liberating practice. In their manifesto, the artists exhort their public to use their identity: "If you walk down a street and you happen to find on a wall one of Ahl Al Kahf's works, put your signature. The artistic work is said to derive its value and price from the signature it bears" (Ahl Al Kahf, 2012a).

Their art is born out of the absence of any freedom within the art circuits funded by the state, or the foreign countries, which commission productions that confirm their Orientalist expectations. This is why the privileged space of their art is the street, rather than the gallery or the museum. At the same time, the street allows Ahl Al Kahf to explore the collective practice of co-authorship and to make "revolutionary art" accessible to all.

Eventually, this collective is a signature and its signature works as a reappropriative practice, open to all. The artists make this very clear when they address a Facebook comment on them being *Banksy à la tunisienne*, "the Tunisian version of Banksy." Banksy is undoubtedly a source of inspiration for them, insofar as he is considered a "reference." "In the visual arts that is called a 'reference' (like when you reference a text in another text)." In fact, they explain, "it needs to be known that Banksy is not an individual, rather a signature. Everywhere in the world, there are young people employing these motifs. Just in the same way, Ahl Al Kahf is a signature and many young people work using it."

The group's main goal is that of making visible the abuses of authority by means of "infecting" the most agglomerated public spaces, such as beaches, train or metro stations, high streets, and squares with their viral messages. The artists, therefore, re-signify these spaces through ephemeral artworks produced thanks to a close organic relation with the surrounding environment, both human and non-human.

The collective employs various media. Not only street and online art, but also video, projections on the city's walls, performances, occasionally long pluri-language reflection texts, and even online radio, which they employed temporarily in 2011 to broadcast poetry. As concerns the street art, its media are mixed. Production started off in the form of digital posters, so-called revolution posters, used to promote the cause of the rebellion in Sidi Bouzid. These initial artworks (see Figure 4.1) were spread online in an attempt to counter the censorship of information and make the rebellion known to the public.

After the escape of Ben Ali, the group was invited to support the "14th of January Front" as its "artistic brigade" (Lacquaniti, 2015: 127). Members took part in the occupations of the Kasbah (January–February 2011), where they started using the walls as canvases. Their initial approach was that of

Figure 4.1. A collage of some of Ahl Al Kahf's digital affiches de la révolution, "revolution posters." *Source: Ahl Al Kahf Facebook Profile*

employing stencils, alongside occasional collages of rather extensive paper images or preprinted posters. Sometimes they sprayed additional writings, other times they subverted already existing advertisements with their written messages. Most of their interventions are a complex of all these media and represent each time a unique recombination of preexisting highly reproducible elements, such as stencil matrixes. On other occasions, they instead produce special street art projects, in which they employ massive stencil-based street painting. The production is always location-specific, temporary, and unique.

As follows, I will attempt to provide a temporal and spatial dimension of the evolution of the collective's work, as far as I was able to trace it based on the public resources I've had access to, the main one being the group's Facebook archive (Figure 4.2). This means that I could be missing many of their interventions and that this can only be a provisional understanding of the extension of their work.

The titles of the following works are mine; they are only indicative and aimed to identify the works. When the date is uncertain, it is signaled in the title with a question mark, whereas the reference date is mainly based on the date of the online upload of the relative album of works. When I refer to "stencil-based street painting," it is to indicate projects of large dimensions produced employing the stencil technique.

Two preliminary observations will help to frame their production. The first one is a brief consideration of the group's geographical sensibility. The second provides an outline of its main theoretical, political, and artistic references.

First, although the collective is based in the capital, it goes to great lengths to decentralize its practice. When in the capital, the artists focus on very agglomerated spaces, like the Kasbah, bus stations, squares, tax office, and the surroundings of the Internal Affairs Ministry. Their ephemeral works are intended to target as many Tunisians as possible. In fact, they are not interested in touristic spaces such as the Medina, the Bardo Museum, or the elitist Sidi Bou Said neighborhood, or at least there isn't any record of their works in these areas. This indicates that their target audience is the average Tunisian citizen holding no particularly privileged social status. This is even clearer given that the artists focus some of their most significant projects on suburban neighborhoods of the capital, such as El Gorjani, Ettadhamen, and Djebel Lahmar, the latter being a former shantytown. Moreover, the artists have actively made an effort to reach many cities beyond the capital. This is particularly relevant since, as I have tried to make clear so far, the revolutionary process was accelerated and promoted mostly in the poor areas of the south and the center of the country. Finally, they have also operated abroad in the last period of their production, mainly in Germany. Changing the setting

Indicative Title	Date	Media	Location
Les affiches de la révolution	December 2010	Digital art	Virtual Space
Kasbah 1	January 2011	Street art (stencil)	Tunis, the Kasbah
The Listening Rats	February 2011	Street art (stencil, collage)	Tunis, Place Barcelone
Kasbah 2	22-25 February 2011	Street art (stencil)	Tunis, the Kasbah
The Zarzis Arches	(?) April 2011	Street art (stencil, street painting, collage)	Zarzis
The Day of the Martyrs	10 April 2011	Street art (stencil, street painting)	Tunis, Djebel Lahmar
Farhat Hachad in El Kairouan	(?) April 2011	Street art (stencil)	El Kairouan
The center of Tunis	(?) 24 April 2011	Street art (stencil, collage)	Tunis, Avenue Bourguiba/National Theatre
Bibliography (Deleuze, Negri, Said, Choukri)	(?) April 2011	Street art (stencil-based street painting)	Tunis, Bab Sadoun
Art in an abandoned factory	(?) 6 May 2011	Street art (stencil, collage, street painting)	Tunis, Rue Carthage
The teaching of a fighter in a wheelchair	21 June 2011	Street art (stencil, stencil-based street painting)	Mezzouna, Sidi Bouzid
Said, Deleuze and the activist Mouda Mhadheb Sboui	(?) June 2011	Street art (stencil-based street painting)	Jbenyana, Sfax
Deleuze and the tanks	July/August 2011	Street art (stencil)	The island of Djerba
Darwish and the children	October 2011	Street art (stencil, street painting)	Tunis, Hay Ettadhamen
Occupy Tunis	11 November 2011	Digital art	Virtual Space
Sidi Bouzid/Palestine	17 December 2011	Street art (stencil, collage, street painting)	Sidi Bouzid
Collaboration with a homeless street artist	(?) December 2011	Street art (stencil)	Ksar Hellal, Monastir

Figure 4.2. List of the artistic interventions of the Al Ahl Kahf collective (2010–2013).

Manifeste Fondateur	27 December 2011	Text	Virtual Space
Vienna Performance	January 2012	Performance	Vienna, Austria
Mahdi Amel and the Anti-Oedipus at school	February 2012	Street art (stencil, collage, 3d collage)	El Gorjani, Tunis
Projections on the walls of Tunis	(?) March 2012	Street art (projections)	Tunis
Projections on the walls of Bizerte	(?) May 2012	Street art (projections)	Bizerte
Solidarity with Fadwa Suleiman	16 May 2012	Street art (stencil)	Tax office, Tunis
"Dogma"	10 November 2012	Video	Virtual Space
Resistance vs. Power	January 2013	Street art (stencil, stencil-based street painting)	Thala, Kasserine
"The Interpretation of Exile"	October/November 2013	Street art (stencil, collage) Video, Text	Tunis/Berlin

Figure 4.2. *(continued)*

of their work has stimulated a new thread of reflection on mobility and the anti-immigration policies of "fortress Europe."

One can imagine the collective's intervention organized in concentrically arranged circles, starting from the heart of Tunis, spreading across its suburbs, followed by the cities in the center and the south, all the way to the northern European cities of Vienna and Berlin. This, of course, only applies to their material production, since their virtual archives and works have a far wider circulation.

Second, in order to make an additional step within the Ahl Al Kahf universe, it is worth listing some of the references that the artists have incorporated into their artwork and texts, both in terms of politics and in terms of art. For the artists, practice and reflection are constantly reciprocally generative since "they have always merged the improvisation in the artistic practice with a conscious reflection on their goals, forming a virtuous circle in which one originated the other" (Lacquaniti, 2015: 132).

On a political level, the Ahl Al Kahf collective refers to Tunisian martyrs, such as

- Mohamed Bouazizi, the young man who sparked the revolution with his self-immolation;
- Hafnaoui Maghzawi, the first martyr of the 2008 "Gafsa Intifada";
- Mouda Mhadheb Sboui, a philosophy teacher and activist in a wheelchair of Mezzouna, active against the regime; and
- Farhat Hachad, the assassinated founder of the Tunisian trade union.

These names appear alongside icons of symbolic past and ongoing struggles such as Fadwa Suleiman, the Syrian actress and activist involved in the 2011 Syrian revolution; Ernesto "Che" Guevara, the Argentinian revolutionary; *Subcomandante* Marcos, the Mexican Zapatista revolutionary; and Mahdi Amel, the assassinated radical Lebanese theorist and activist, also known as the "Arab Gramsci" (Prashad, 2014).

In terms of artistic practice, the British graffiti artist Banksy and the French classical street artist Ernest Pignon-Pignon are the collective's more visible influences, alongside the Dada and the Situationist movement. They also name the French performer and theorist Antonin Artaud, the Palestinian cartoonist Naji al-Ali, the Lebanese musician Marcel Khalife, the Black American jazz composer Miles Davis, as well as the Moroccan painter Jilali Gharbaoui.

The philosophical and literary references stretch all the way from what the artists call the "philosophical movement of resistance," in which they include French theorists like Deleuze and Michel Foucault, alongside Said, to important names of the Arab literature, such as the Palestinian poets Mahmoud

Darwish and Mu'in Bseiso, the Tuareg poet Ibrahim al-Koni, and the Moroccan novelist Mohamed Choukri. They also occasionally quote significant French thinkers of the twentieth century such as the novelist Louis-Ferdinand Céline, the poet Jean Cocteau, and the filmmaker Jean-Luc Godard.

The type of culture and history the collective is a promoter of, through its works and texts, is somehow a declination of that global, universal, common set of practices and theories it declares to be part of. It expands from the Palestinian struggle and the Amazigh poetry to the experimentations of the French Surrealist movement and the way Deleuze, Foucault, and Said were reading resistance in the second half of the twentieth century.

One of Ahl Al Kahf's artists main achievements is that they make authority visible, while they challenge it. In fact, some of the group's most used and popular stencils regard the portraits of the Tunisian politicians that the revolution fought against, accompanied by ironic captions. The ousted president, el-Abidine Ben Ali, is depicted above a sentence stating, "Those who induced him in error are still there." This is an extremely incisive historical connection as it references not only the president's last speech but, most importantly, the fact that this expression was borrowed from the French president Charles de Gaulle while he was addressing the Algerian people fighting against France for their independence (Lacquaniti, 2015: 128). By choosing this sentence, the artists are underlining the continuity between the French colonialism and the post-independence Tunisian rule. Most significantly, Ben Ali's stencil is often articulated within a performatively iconoclast spatiality, in the sense that the artists locate it on the pavement for it to be stepped over, or in dirty corners. The same devaluative operations influence the iconography of the Libyan president, Muammar Gaddafi, whose head is depicted on top of a rat body; sometimes the stencil is sprayed on top of a real dead rat.

Another frequent target of the group is Béji Caid Essebsi, a member of the governmental old guard (born 1926) nominated prime minister at the end of 2011 after a series of protests forced the resignation of the Benalist prime minister. Essebsi's political protagonism gives the artists the opportunity to address the dangerous gerontocratic structure of institutional politics and the extent to which no new actor was allowed to take part in the political decisions, even after the revolution. The caption clearly states: "I cannot dream with my grandfather!" Another version of the same anti-gerontocratic message is the collage of a dinosaur with the caption "No to the rule of the dinosaurs!" Their critique of an active governing politician explains the need for anonymity since Tunisia was and is well known for being very intolerant toward political critique and opposition.

The most dangerous oppositional message that the Ahl Al Kahf engaged in was the one that exposed police brutality. As mentioned before, a strong repressive apparatus managed by the Ministry of Internal Affairs supported the Ben Ali rule. The police forces frequently employed violence, unlawful detention, and torture against dissidents. Unfortunately, these practices continued after 2011 (Human Rights Watch, 2016). With their stencils, the group addressed three levels of state violence: (1) the unlawful surveillance, alluded to with Banksy's sonic rat followed by the caption: "No to political police!"; (2) the constant police brutality; and (3) the mysterious impunity of the operatives who killed the revolution's martyrs and who were still mentioned in the public discourse as unknown "snipers." To tackle the aspect of the justice for the martyrs, the artists used one of Banksy's stencils again: the little girl with the floating red balloon. Yet the artists turned the balloon into a haunting question: "Where are the snipers?" (see Figure 4.3).

The collective was also critical of the global governing authorities such as the United States represented by President Obama, whom they chose to depict above a set of tibiae, alluding to his deadly foreign policy, possibly referring to the American War on Terror and security campaign.

With these examples, I wanted to show how important stencil-related art was for the collective. This medium was so suitable for its practice for various reasons. First of all, the employment of stencil matrixes facilitated a high rate

Figure 4.3.   Zarzis/Tunis, 2011. *Source: Ahl Al Kahf Facebook profile*

of adaptability and speed of intervention on the walls. The relatively small matrixes were easy to transport and hide and allowed a fast composition between various elements, resulting in rapid original and modulable assemblages. The same matrixes could be organized geometrically and chromatically in a different manner, therefore changing their impact every time they were "uttered."

The small stencil matrix was the ultimate "revolutionary art" dispositive in post-2011 Tunis, which was still under serious surveillance. The stencils functioned as memes by virtue of their high reproducibility and circulation.

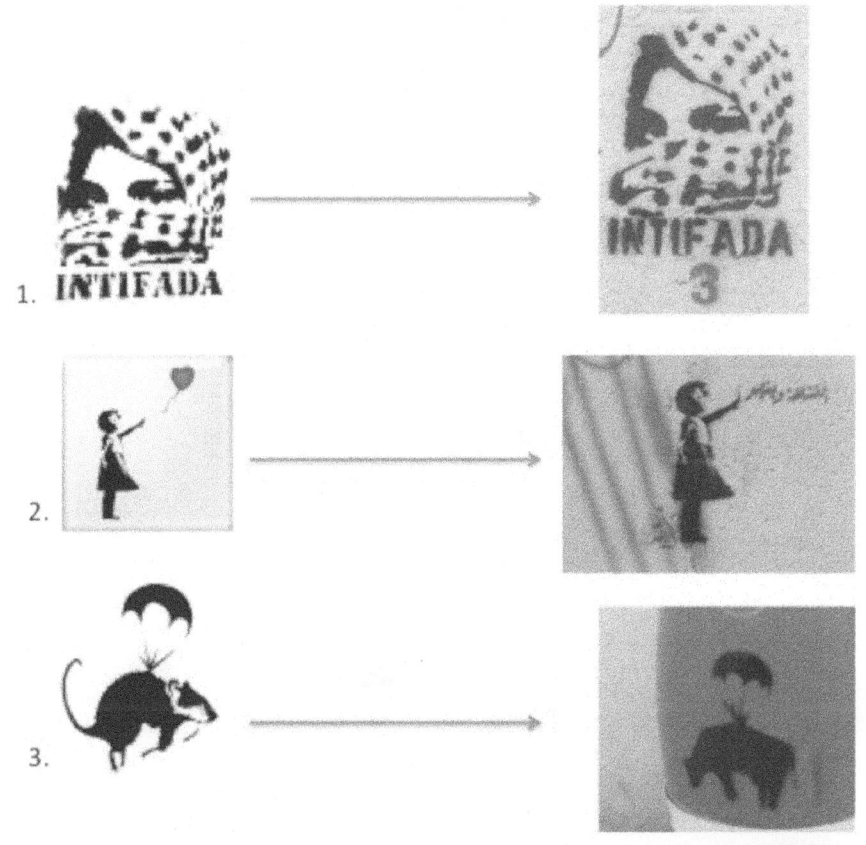

Figure 4.4. The group's adapted stencils: 1. To the Intifada stencil, they added the number 3, alluding to a third uprising, either to their own or a new Palestinian one; 2. They substituted the balloons from Banksy's stencil with the question alluding to the people who have been killed during the revolution: "Where are the snipers?"; 3. Instead of Banksy's parachuted rat, they used a cow, given that the word is pronounced similarly to the Arabic "revolution," to allude to a subtracted, stolen revolution. *Source: Ahl Al Kahf Facebook profile*

These elements focused on local contagion and defiance, but they also contained different degrees of connectivity to the rest of the global stencil language. In fact, Ahl Al Kahf's stencil language could be divided between: (1) classic, already existing matrixes (mostly of no-global tradition); (2) matrixes that have been adapted to the Tunisian context (see Figure 4.4); and (3) completely original matrixes (see Figure 4.5).

In terms of speed of intervention, one could imagine a scale going from the handwritten graffiti to the small stencil to the collage and ending with the massive stencil-based painting on the wall, which required the most continuous physical presence of the artists and which I will be looking into later in this section.

The adoption of popular anti-capitalist stencils, also employed by their fellow street artists in other corners of the world, seems to suggest the alignment to a sort of graffiti *koiné*, a common language with reference to a critique of power, especially since graffiti artists operate, by their very nature, within a

Figure 4.5. Some of the group's original stencils: 1. Mohamed Bouazizi; 2. Mhadheb Sboui; 3. Farhat Hachad; 4. Mahdi Amel; 5. Mahmoud Darwish; 6. Mohamed Choukri; 7. Fadwa Suleiman; 8. Antonio Negri; 9. Gilles Deleuze; 10. Edward Said; 11. a human with a clock head with the caption: "revolution under 5 minutes"; 12. Muammar Gaddafi; 13. Béji Caid Essebsi with caption: "I cannot dream with my grandfather"; 14. Zine el-Abidine Ben Ali. *Source: Ahl Al Kahf Facebook profile*

criminalized anti-authoritarian space. When they adapt the already existing stencils, Ahl Al Kahf artists are adding creativity to a common, recognizable set of elements, therefore increasing their contagious reach. Furthermore, their original stencils and collages are developed to add the Tunisian specificity to that language. In their production, they are always plugged to an anti-Orientalist sensibility as they declare from the beginning.

As can be seen from their most used stencils (see Figures 4.4 and 4.5), their messages are focused on some general themes. First, they promote a strong anti-capitalist critique, influenced by anti-globalization aesthetics and informed by global instances of resistance, such as the Zapatista but mostly the Palestinian struggle. Second, they harshly expose and dismiss the media propaganda that claims that the Dignity revolution is over and in which state violence is ignored. Finally, they show a passionate solidarity with the uprisings in the neighboring countries, Syria and Libya, which, at that time, were still pioneered by a popular movement.

One of the most frequent points made by the group, which partially explains its activity in the streets, is a violent critique of the system of production, institutionalization, and commodification of art, as well as of the regimes of appropriation and ownership that condition and regulate the circulation of art, images, and information. Art and information, or rather counter-information—in a country with a long tradition of censorship and comprador media—are never separated domains in the group's practice. And both of them are practiced with the intention to foster liberation and, where it is most needed, education. As such, the Ahl Al Kahf collective is born out of the rejection of any space for art production granted and controlled by the state, the market, or foreign donors.

Its texts express their distance from any institutionally sanctioned art dimension:

> Any resemblance that may be perceived between Ahl Al Kahf's actions and art is a mere product of the viewer's imagination. Thus, Ahl Al Kahf refuses to accept any responsibility for it. [. . .]
> One of Ahl Al Kahf's members might enter an art gallery if he feels an urgent need to crap or to pee (even if it is better to pee in front of a wall). (Ahl Al Kahf, 2012)

One of the collective's most famous projects was strongly focused on the critique of the artistic establishment. It was located in an abandoned industrial ruin near Rue Carthage in Tunis and completed in June 2011. The intervention's photographic album is significantly titled "Art in the Rubble before Institutions Take Over"; in the manifesto was written "Art doesn't blossom but in rubble and ruins." One of the main walls of the building chosen to "attack" is filled with the multilayered portrait of the Italian Autonomia theorist Negri above the caption "Power can somewhere be broken," alongside an explosion of the word *Intifada*—"uprising" in Arabic—and the portraits of Farhat Hachad, the assassinated Communist founder of the Tunisian trade union, and "Che" Guevara. In the corner of the wall, a television bears the statement "I lie to you every day," while on the opposite side Obama's face appears placed above two skull tibiae as a deadly warning.

The reason why the artists prefer to work within the public space is because galleries and museums are perceived as classist and hierarchical institutions that rather separate the artists from their fellow citizens. Ahl Al Kahf makes it clear that there is no separation between the producers and consumers of art, that they are part of the margins where the art blossoms. Members argue, "We would rather paint with children, mad people, tramps, crooks, and drunkards of the street . . . since these people are Ahl Al Kahf" (Ahl Al Kahf, 2012).

It should be specified at this point that the collective's manifesto was published in December 2011, approximately one year after the group had already started its activity. That is to say that nearly every sentence in it is a direct reference to at least one particular project or practice and not the other way around. As explained in the manifesto: "Art isn't issued by theories, but gives birth to them."

For example, in terms of "painting with children," the group has several projects to support this particular aesthetic assertion. The artists are very fond of creating in collaboration with children, especially children from the poor cities or the capital's suburbs, the largest majority of the Tunisian children. On these occasions, the artists bring in their knowledge and skills, which they transmit to their co-workers and whoever witnesses their practice and its results. What the Ahl Al Kahf achieved on these occasions were instances of radical collaborative education in the most underprivileged corners of the country where art and certain cultural expressions are unlikely to be accessed.

The most significant example in this sense is the project the artists put in place in Hay Ettadhamen, one of the capital's poorest suburbs, in October 2011. They provided the local children with painting colors and with the help of a big stencil matrix, they impressed the portrait of the Palestinian poet Mahmoud Darwish on the wall, alongside a quote from his poem *A State of Siege* (I quote the entire stanza and *italicize* the quoted section):

Here, by the downslope of hills, facing the sunset
And time's muzzle,

Figure 4.6. Hay Ettadhamen, Tunis, 2011. *Source: Ahl Al Kahf Facebook profile*

Near gardens with severed shadows,
We do what the prisoners do,
And what the unemployed do;
We nurture hope. (Darwish, 2007: 120)

The presence and collaboration with local young people were widely documented in the photographic album of the project published on the collective's social media profile (Figure 4.6). In their comments, this is how the artists described the encounter between the children and Darwish's poetry: "Unhappy because of their impoverished education system. Mahmoud Darwish was discovered through what we have done together."[4]

Another educational project was completed by the group upon the commissioning on behalf of a secondary school in El Gorjani, another suburb of the capital. On this occasion, the artists chose to merge the tradition of four very significant characters (see Figure 4.7). The gigantic multilayered stenciled portrait of Hassan Abdullah Hamdan—more commonly known by his pseudonym Mahdi Amel—was the main presence on the school's wall.

In fact, the album is called "Amel No"; the word and symbol No, *la* in Arabic, is also the symbol for anarchy in the Arab world. Mahdi Amel (1936–1987) was one of the most influential Marxist theorists and activists in the Arab world and was assassinated in his native Lebanon. His work hasn't entirely been translated from Arabic, but he is known for his "Marx in Edward Said's Orientalism" and for his poetry. The group often quotes his line: "You shall not be defeated as long as you resist," which they employed in a digital poster supporting the Syrian revolution.[5]

126　　　　　　　　　　*Chapter Four*

Figure 4.7. The images of Mahdi Amel (top) and Mhadheb Sboui. El Gorjani Secondary School, Tunis, 2011. *Source: Ahl Al Kahf Facebook profile*

Alongside Amel, the work also promoted the image of Mhadheb Sboui, a Tunisian philosophy teacher and activist, known to have been very involved in protests and strikes in his wheelchair, and whose memory the collective had extensively worked on during their project in Mezzouna, which I will expand on shortly. The portraits of Amel and Sboui are joined by a rain of Arabic words and interjections alluding to the 1972 work of Deleuze and Guattari, *The Anti-Oedipus*, which is also present with its English title, bouncing inside, or outside, a basketball hoop.

Thanks to the brief series of works I have outlined so far, it is more visible how the group's universality is significantly constituted out of the

Figure 4.8. Bab Sadoun, Tunis, 2011. *Source: Ahl Al Kahf Facebook profile*

interweaving of Western and Arab cultural and political references. One of the most obvious declinations of their universal references is the project they've completed at Bab Sadoun, one of the city's gates, situated next to an agglomerated tram station in Tunis, most probably in the spring of 2011 (see Figure 4.8). It is constituted of multilayered gigantic stenciled portraits of four thinkers: the Moroccan novelist Mohamed Choukri, the Italian Autonomist Antonio Negri, the Palestinian scholar Edward Said, and the French philosopher Gilles Deleuze. Each of their portraits is accompanied by a significant quote easily relatable to the Tunisian situation: "I write in order to be banned" (Choukri); "Power is everywhere. It can be broken" (Negri); "The intellectuals must be witnesses of the bad use of history" (Said); and, one of the group's favorite mantras, of course, "To create is to resist" (Deleuze).

The "bibliography" is accompanied by a sarcastic composition on its left side, ironizing upon the Arabic word *irhab*, "terrorism," and advertising it as an Activia-like digestion yogurt (Lacquaniti, 2015).

Almost more important than the portraits of the quoted thinkers is the black hole on their left side, out of which dozens of stenciled ants and flies make their way out. The hole is easily associable with the "crack in the wall," which the artists mention in their manifesto: "Ahl Al Kahf members may leave under a spot or a crack in the wall the movement's signature. And this may not be deemed as desecration or blasphemy but as one of the pagan rites of the movement" (Ahl Al Kahf, 2012). In this case, the crack in the wall is also a direct reference to a Tunisian dialectal expression: "all those ants that went in that hole." It is an informal way of saying, "I was saying something, and you weren't listening" (Lacquaniti, 2015: 133). It can be argued that the inaudible voices could, at this point, belong to either the artists fighting to express themselves in the Tunisian society or, more likely, to the Tunisian disenfranchised people who brought about the revolution that made this art possible in the first place. Ahl Al Kahf's ants are coming out of the hole. Could this mean that the inaudible voices are no longer wasting their breath to be heard? This return to the dimension of the "inaudible" voices links back to the beginning of this chapter and the discussion on the importance of considering the constitutive absence of the peasants and the Amazigh communities from the most common narrative of the revolution. The collective is certainly aware of the way certain communities are disregarded, and this is proven by their frequent references to the peasants and the Imazighen. In fact, the narratives they have propagated through their practice have been determinant for this research.

There is also an instance—arguably one of the group's most influential experiences—in which the collective actively contributed to transferring the knowledge from a local oral history into a global memory of resistance, thanks to the online exposure of its work. It is the case of a project in Mezzouna, a small city in the rather impoverished governorate of Sidi Bouzid, the region where the 2011 revolution originated. This time, instead of stenciled portraits, the walls of the downtown café are filled with the silhouettes of local children who participated in the project (see Figure 4.9). They are photographed and their figures inspire the stencils on the walls, but they also participated in the coloring. They are both the objects and the subjects of the work. In the album's description, the artists point out that the "children of Mezzouna were not present in this work as images only, but also as actors."

The texts impressed on the wall belong to Sboui, the late philosophy teacher of the city who, despite being in a wheelchair, had always been at the forefront of the local protests. This is how the collective celebrates him in its manifesto:

Mhadheb Sboui got up and took part in protests, strikes, and marches, being at the same time in his wheelchair. And he tells you: "No one has any longer the right of guardianship on our reason and our perspicacity under the pretext of a

Figure 4.9. "This body will be victorious!," Mezzouna, 2011. *Source: Ahl Al Kahf Facebook profile*

permanent paternity and maternity, that does not realize that we were weaned a long time ago. We no longer need the sermons of preachers nor the advice of chaplains. We are neither ignorant nor minors." (Ahl Al Kahf, 2011)

These sentences are a direct critique of the patronizing attitude of the dictatorship and of the ousted president who promoted himself as the "father" of the nation. But they also symbolize the struggle for self-determination of the Tunisian people who strongly assert their independence and autonomy against attempts to submit or make them feel inferior. Thanks to the art project, Sboui's quotes enrich the city's walls; the children's stenciled climbing bodies are joined by his affirmation: "This body will be victorious!"

Sboui's teachings left a deep trace in the collective's production. His words are present in its manifesto, as well as the projects completed in Jbenyana, El Gorjani (Tunis), and Sidi Bouzid. In Sboui's case, the collective is actively building a minor history made of stories, comments, quotes, and his portrait, all of which are intended to be virally accessible, locally on the walls and globally, thanks to their photographic archive.

If the group's Tunisian production was mainly focused around the notion of resistance and on its relationship with art, with their last project in Berlin the Ahl Al Kahf came full circle, explicating the condition of exile and connecting it precisely to the reason they chose to be named after the myth of the Cave Sleepers. Their Berlin project made it clear that exile goes beyond a geographical displacement and is rather a state of unhomeliness that can only be fully embraced through creativity. In fact, one of the quotes, from Victor Hugo, that they impress on the wall is: "The exile is a sort of long insomnia." To that, they added a broader explanation of the relationship between exile and creativity in the text accompanying their street art (in Arabic): "The Ahl Al Kahf's movement idea is to *enact creativity and resistance from within the exile.* The story of the people of the cave, according to the religious mythology, is the story of a group escaped from the unfair sultan into exile to Hiljaoa, namely in a cave" (Ahl Al Kahf, 2012b, my emphasis).

I have so far attempted to provide just *some* hints as to the reason I consider them one of the most influential artistic movements of post-revolutionary Tunisia. They are undoubtedly an artistic *avant-garde*, not only a very sophisticated street art project. The type of art the members promote comes from a space of marginality, of silence, and develops untimely reflections, which is also why their identity is centered upon the idea of exile, alluded to by the choice of their name. In this sense, I propose that the Ahl Al Kahf practice resonates very much with Deleuze and Guattari's understanding of "minor literature," which they developed in their reflection on the practice of Franz Kafka against the backdrop of the Jewish literature in German-speaking Prague (Deleuze and Guattari, 1986). "A minor literature doesn't come from a minor language; it is rather that which a minority constructs within a major language. But the first characteristic of a minor literature is that in it language is affected with a high coefficient of deterritorialization" (Idem: 16).

According to Deleuze and Guattari, minor literature holds three main characteristics. First, it deterritorializes language, bringing about a "neutralization of sense" (Idem: 21) and short-circuiting its symbolic, significant usage, making it "vibrate with a new intensity" (Idem: 19). Second, it connects the individual to a political immediacy. And finally, it results in a collective assemblage of enunciation, therefore making visible that "the most individual enunciation is a particular case of collective enunciation" (Idem: 83). Just like Ahl Al Kahf's practice, minor art is not dialectic as such but it rather "produc(es) movement from within the major." Most significantly, movement is the very constitutive feature of becoming minor, since the major or molar basically refers to an instance of "immobilization of becoming."[6] In fact, Simon O'Sullivan points out, "becoming minor art is deterritorializing forms that have become fixed" (Ibidem), such as political and artistic institutions.

The practice of the Tunisian artists abandons the canvas and escapes into the streets, which it attempts to contaminate with their "aesthetic terrorism." The group's work resonates significantly with O'Sullivan's understanding of minor art. First, the collective focuses mainly on the interventions within the local, like in its Mezzouna project, in which artists drew upon Sboui's work. Second, they use not specifically artistic materials and may include any object present on site. They resist commodification by making their ephemeral art available to their poorest fellow citizens. The works often concentrate on the level of affects, which they try to stir up and make viral, rather than conveying a highly articulated discursive message. Finally, they push against the edges of representation by often employing humor as a strategy of both propelling dissent and pushing toward the invention of new behaviors.

The most important feature of minor art is that it both negates *and* creates since it is "involved in the production of new subjectivities as well as in turning away those already in place." It, therefore, puts in practice both a politics of dissent as well as a politics of affirmation, both critique and creativity. "It might well speak to an already constituted audience (no doubt a small one) but at the same time it speaks from a future place in order to draw forth from its audience subjectivity still to come (a subjectivity in progress)," "always at a different speed to those discourses of disciplines that attempt to track it" (Ibidem).

The collective's practice has been crucial for this research for two reasons. First, because it provided an interaction with, rather than a representation of, the revolution that made visible a whole range of assemblages and conflicts most of the narratives would conceal. Second, because it thematized the strong coalition that some artists had articulated with the group of marginalized Tunisian citizens who pioneered the 2011 Dignity revolution. As I will explain in chapter 5, the revolution itself resulted out of the alliance between two very courageous and productive vanguards, one of which is represented by the likes of the Ahl Al Kahf collective. In the following section, I will continue the reflection on the political subjectivity brought to fore by the revolutionary event, hypothesizing some of the ways in which identity is formed in the context of the Tunisian underclass, but also suggesting the concept of "vanguard" as a suitable way to account for how this political subjectivity enacts forms of transformative politics.

4.3. THE VANGUARD: THE BODY THAT QUESTIONS THE TERRITORY, OR THE MUTINY OF THE RESERVE ARMY

In the previous chapter, I attempted to approach the class aspect of the Tunisian revolution closer. I started from the assumption that the event was *neither* the result of the mobilization of the Internet-savvy, middle-class bloggers and artists *nor* of a depoliticized generic "youth" using peaceful methods to achieve Western-like democracy. The revolution was anything but peaceful, and its initiators anything but depoliticized, although most of them had grown up in a country where any political expression was met with instant state repression.

I have also referred to them as the underclass, "Lumpenprecariat" (Rizk, 2014), or "mob" (Aradau and Huysmans, 2009), while describing how they have altered their identity through mobility practices, some of them becoming either *harraga* in Europe or Islamic militants fighting in Syria and Iraq. The class-based frame struggles to embrace their fluidity, but it is important to point out that these people live beneath the proletarian living standards, if the proletariat were to be identified as people with a job. The "underclass" or the "mob," therefore, gets by thanks to small family farming, informal economy, and illegalized migration. Here I mostly refer to the under- and unemployed people, most of whom are very young, living in the poor cities of the west, south, and center and in the suburbs of the rich cities, mostly the capital.

Although written in the nineteenth century, Karl Marx's words easily resonate with the systematic dispossession enacted by the French colonists who forcibly pulverized the Tunisian *fellaga*'s subsistence, but also with the way the neoliberal and post-independence appropriation drive have later produced poverty by either imposing "structural adjustments" or through the extensive system of bribes inflicted upon all the economic activities, both formal and informal, in the name of the *halibat al-dawla*, the "prestige of the state" (Marzouki and Aliriza, 2015). Marx stresses the centrality of dispossession—here referred to the colonial primitive accumulation—insofar as:

> The development of the social productive power of labour, co-operation, division of labour, use of machinery on a large scale, are impossible without the expropriation of the labourers, and the corresponding transformation of their means of production into capital. In the interest of the so-called national wealth, he seeks for artificial means to ensure the poverty of the people. (Marx, [1867] 2015: 549)

What the German thinker calls the "industrial reserve army" is precisely the result of this crucial process of dispossession or expropriation, one that deprived people of their subsistence and tied them irreducibly to their relationship with capital, under the form of a salary and some retributed activity. As such, the industrial reserve army is a "mass of human material always ready for exploitation [. . .] that belongs to capital quite as absolutely as if the latter had bred it at its own cost" (Idem: 444). The starving reserve army of unemployed people is, therefore, not a calamity or the "collateral damage" of an economic system, but its very essence, since "the whole form of modern history depends [. . .] upon the constant transformation of a part of the labouring population into unemployed or half-employed hands" (Idem: 445). This is also a necessary condition of the general movements of wages. As a consequence,

> during the periods of stagnation and average prosperity, (it) weights down the active labour-army; during the periods of over-production and paroxysm, it holds its pretensions in check. The relative surplus population is, therefore, the pivot upon which the law of demand and supply of labour works. It confines the field of action of this law within the limits absolutely convenient to the activity of exploitation and the domination of capital. (Idem: 447–48)

In Marx's vision, the way to counter this productive impoverishment and reciprocally conditioning exploitation—of the overworked workers threatened to become jobless and of the jobless relegated to "forced idleness"—is through the organization of a "regular *co-operation between employed and unemployed*" (Idem: 448, my emphasis). This is a very spot-on description of what the Tunisian Dignity revolution managed to achieve, temporarily nullifying the barriers between two types of workers: the ones bearing a recognized labor status and the ones being exploited by the informal circuits and, from a certain perspective, deemed unemployed.

In fact, even after the revolution, the industrial reserve army has gone back to its everyday battle for survival, this time exploring two new exploitative destinations as an addition to the traditional internal migration toward the capital for work. First, the migration to Europe for those lucky enough to survive the trip and escape deportation. Second, the migration toward the Islamic battlefronts in Syria and Iraq. In this sense, the Tunisian disenfranchised continued to engage in nonrecognized forms of labor, including smuggling, substance trade, and military labor, alongside sex and care work in highly risky environments such as the militarized Islamic communities in Syria and Iraq.

This suggests a historical stratification of expropriation technologies, which have preyed upon the territory and the people's resources throughout the past more than two centuries. It started with the French colonization that severed the symbiotic survival relationship between the sedentary and the nomad groups and ended with the contemporary regime of Ben Ali, who was only the last example of a deadly "negotiation between international oligarchy and national plutocracy" (Marzouki and Aliriza, 2015), with all its implications.

As I have suggested with the diagrams, this research not only reflects where this surplus population has come from but also where it chose to move toward in the legitimate attempt to gain its dignified livelihood. In what follows, I want to briefly reflect on two of the reserve army's destinations; namely, the urban peripheries of the capital and the battlefields in Iraq and Syria.

Olfa Lamloum, a Tunisian sociologist who looked into the political processes crossing the country's suburbs, argues for the "emergence of the working-class neighbourhood as the *main platform for collective action* among poor people," since "with the erosion of the social bonds formed by work, territory is now the main factor that creates bonds between young people and shapes their social identity" (Lamloum, 2016: 27, my emphasis). Funded by the British charity and NGO International Alert, Lamloum developed an extensive ethnographic research in 2014 (39 semi-structured interviews, 6 focus groups, 714 questionnaires) in the capital's most populated suburbs, Douar Hicher and Hay Ettadhamen, also called *houma* (plural *hwem*), inhabited by around 180,000 Tunisians. Her research focused on understanding the young inhabitants' sensibility toward the revolution, politics, and the Salafist phenomenon.

The findings have made visible the multiple-layered inequalities that the suburban youth are subjected to. The first inequality is in terms of social exclusion, because coming from a *houma* automatically means being exposed to precarity and unemployment. The second is in urban terms, since the inhabitants have "unequal access to the available resources (e.g., leisure, culture, eating/drinking establishments, places where social groups and genders can mix) in these side-lined urban territories," and, finally, by means of the stigmatization and discrimination that these citizens are subjected to (Lamloum, 2016: 7). For the inhabitants of these neighborhoods, the revolution has constituted an explosively inclusive moment. "From the 9th of January 2011, onwards, it was through riots that hundreds of these young people entered the world of politics" (Lamloum, 2016: 9). On that occasion, "a mixture of left-wing activist, Islamists, *clochard* Salafists and *zabrata* [literally partygoer, can be referred to people smoking cannabis] all came together and joined forces to confront the police and attack symbols of authority" (Lamloum, 2016: 9). After the riots that chased the police out of the neighborhood and the toppling of the dictatorship, "young people, even minors, set up self-defence committees, an embryonic form of power structure, which ended up being the only real source of authority in the two neighborhoods for over five months" (Lamloum, 2016: 10).

This proves how intense the social cohesion of the inhabitants of the *houma* was and how it managed to not only destitute a form of organization but also create a new one. This resistance to state authorities was also alimented by the high rate of police brutality in these territories, with police allegedly even sealing off the neighborhoods during the weekend preemptively, against "potential resurgence of juvenile delinquency," therefore preventing the *houmani* from reaching the center of their city (Idem: 11). Even after the revolution, the *houma* remained "excluded from all the benefits of social citizenship (such as health insurance, social protection, community facilities), and deprived of access to cultural or leisure infrastructures" (Idem: 12).

As an answer to this political and social marginalization, the *hwem* have often organized around religion. The *Movement de la tendence islamique*, a predecessor of the moderate Islamic party Ennahda, was in fact born in Douar Hicher and Ettadhamen in the 1980s (Idem: 16). Moreover, the revolution has also seen the rise of a radically conservatory type of Islamic activism, that of the Salafist movement, who literally advocate for the return to original Islam practices, to the *salaf*, the "predecessors," the "ancestors." The Salafis organized in associations such as Ansar al-Sharia, literally "the partisans of the Sharia law," declaredly involved in charity work and preaching.

But, unlike the state, which put the organization on the national terrorist list in 2013 after attacks that they were allegedly connected to, the inhabitants of the suburbs don't perceive Salafists as a threat. On the contrary, they occasionally accept being advised and oriented by these young people when violent conflicts arise between rival groups or tribes within the *houma* because many *houmani* see the Salafists as devoted to moral integrity as a religious mission (Idem: 22). The inhabitants draw a line between the "bad" Salafists, represented by the *mutashaddid* (the "extremists") or the *irhabi* ("terrorists"), and the *awlad al-salafiyya* (the "children of Salafism"), who they see as *ouled houma*, "kids from the suburbs." Most importantly, they are perceived as sharing their same "daily existence full of obstacles, difficulties, hardship and uncertainty" (Idem: 20–21). In fact, 64 percent of the respondents rejected the idea that Salafism wants to impose the Sharia law (Idem: 20). Nevertheless, 80 percent of those same people knew somebody in their neighborhood who went to Syria. This suggests that the majority of the 7,000 to 8,000 foreign fighters of the Islamic State are actually coming from those same marginalized suburbs (Idem: 24).

This brings me to the second destination of the Tunisian reserve army. It can be suggested that this paramilitary organization can be regarded as an instance of "corporate terrorism,"[7] which has absorbed vital unemployed labor force in the region while neutralizing the radical potential unleashed by the revolutionary process.

Adam Hanieh, among others, explains the relationship between the Arab revolutions and the consolidation of the Islamist groups, as the latter stepping into the vacuum created by the former, therefore as an ultra-conservatory militarism suffocating the new Arab Left. Rather than seeing the 2011 Arab revolutions as a mere opposition of democracy vs. dictatorship, their causes are "deeply connected to forms of capitalism in the region: decades of neoliberal economic restructuring, the impact of global crises, and the ways in which Arab countries were governed by autocratic police and military regimes long backed by Western powers" (Hanieh, 2015).

Beyond the Islamic State's eschatology, based on utopic religious authenticity and the employment of the brutality meme as a deterrent (Ibidem), the radical Sunni organization is the result of a complex assemblage of responsibilities of foreign states. Examples include the American de-Baathification of Iraq in 2003, with the imposition of the Shia rule (backed by Iran), the repression and exclusion of the Sunnis (many of the Islamic State's generals having met in the American camps of Abu Ghraib and Bucca), alongside the sympathy of important states such as Saudi Arabia and Turkey, which occasionally facilitated the smuggling of oil and foreign fighters across the borders (Burke, 2016). In addition, the historical roots of the Islamic fundamentalism can be traced back to the "alliance between the US and the Gulf States, particularly Saudi Arabia, through the 1960s and the 1970s" (Hanieh, 2015).

Moreover, it must be said that religious ultra-conservatism and sectarianism[8] have been largely promoted by Western and Arab powers as a counterweight against the progressive emancipatory popular movements. In fact,

> faced with growing left-wing and nationalist political movements in the region, the sponsorship of Islamism was seen as an effective and disarming counterweight. By the 1980s, this policy was applied most systematically through the US and Saudi support for Arab Islamist fighters in Afghanistan. It was here that preparations for armed *jihad* received their first practical boost. (Ibidem)

There's a complex weaving of rivalries, both sectarian and not, that Tunisian fighters are exposed to when reaching the front. How can one place the same underprivileged subjectivities I've previously spoken about, the young unemployed men coming from the capital's *hwem* or poorer cities of the country,[9] within this overlayered sectarian conflict? How can people from the same spaces who have initiated the toppling down of a dictatorship or who fight for their dignity in Europe (despite their deportability) also become involved in such a deadly military occupation?

The answers can only be approximated and are largely similar to what could be argued around Western military service engaged in fighting operations in general, be they under Western or Islamic management. The Islamic State organization holds one of the most successful propaganda outlets, controlling over 100,000 Twitter accounts, with 50,000 tweets per day selling the "Islamic dream" (Ibidem). This system is fueled by an extensive and ever-growing wealth: It owns nine oil fields in Syria and Iraq worth $1.5 million per day alongside the money coming in from the control of the access and supply routes and from kidnappings, extortions, the sale of antiquities, smuggling, and various taxes the organization imposes (Ibidem).

Therefore, part of the answer is connected to the well-spread propaganda of a proposed justice mission against Syria's Assad and his crimes, but also with the promise of a Golden Age return to a Muslim-dominated caliphate blessed with prosperity and peace, which the region hasn't been enjoying for a long time. As Hanieh puts it, "In a moment of deep crisis, the promise of some level of security is part of what makes ISIS attractive (or, at the very least, a less-worse option)" (Hanieh, 2015).

Moreover, it must be noted that the pay for an IS fighter is $300–400 per month, which is double the amount paid by the Iraqi army and way more than any Tunisian *houmani* could hope to earn with some continuity (Ibidem). Paradoxically to the mainstream discourse, some thinkers suggest that "without the political integration of Islamism, the people of the region will never free themselves from the dictatorships that promote themselves to counter it, nor from the Islamism itself which finds legitimation against them" (Alba Rico, 2016b).

In my understanding, corporate terrorism is a way of conserving and accelerating the movement of dissent, which emerged in the Tunisian Dignity revolution and in the other popular movements in the region. The goal of this capture is not only that of blocking the movement toward emancipation of the poorer categories, but, on the contrary, that of possibly increasing their discontent and frustration in order to be able to extract value out of their affective energy by using the frustration linked to impoverishment and marginalization as a leverage for military labor. Essentially, the military system capitalizes upon the frustration and the desire for freedom and independence. In this case, corporate terrorism has both contributed to providing a relief valve for much of the dissent of the disenfranchised while simultaneously supporting the marvelous functioning of a million-dollar economic enterprise based on low salaries.

And yet, despite the emigration toward Europe and the IS fronts,[10] in 2015 alone the country was inflamed by 4,288 social protests, most of which have had their epicenter in the center-west of the country (Alba Rico, 2016b).

There was one particular event that has made me reflect on the egalitarian vocation of the disenfranchised and their choice to fight for dignity at home. This event was the protest that broke out in the western city of Kasserine on January 16, 2016, when a young unemployed man named Ridha Yahyaoui protested alongside other fellow citizens against their blacklisting and erasure from the employment lists due to their activism in the student trade union. Yahyaoui climbed on a light pillar and committed suicide by exposing himself to the high-voltage electricity.

What follow[ed] can be seen as the copy of the class-based mapping of the 2011 protests: following the same paths of contagion, with differential speeds, the rebellion spread out, first around Kasserine and then in the neighbouring regions (Sidi Bouzid, Thala, El Kef, Jendouba, then Kairouan) until it reached the suburbs of the capital, Hay Ettadhamen and Intilaka on Thursday night [the suicide happened on Saturday]. (Ibidem)

Yet there were several differences in comparison to the 2011 revolutionary process. This time, after five years, unemployment and corruption had increased. In addition, the authorities had learned the lesson on violent repression and mostly focused on low-intensity repression, such as arrests, fines, and detention, accusing the protestors of terrorist infiltrations and of "forming gangs and inciting to disorder," rather than shooting at them like the Benalist state had done five years before. Unfortunately, few local and global observers recognized the authenticity of the protests for fear of the terrorist threat. This also worked as the government's legitimation for not addressing the protestors' demands but rather for limiting their mobility and for detaining them.

Finally, the most important difference was that this time the Tunisian trade union didn't express solidarity and didn't join the popular movement, destining it to fade away, while its members got individually pursued and worn off by state repression.

After Yahyaoui's suicide and the expansion of the protests in other cities and the capital's suburbs, one of the collective actions that was taken was the occupation with tents of the *wilaya*, the Prefecture of the city of Kasserine, carried out by two hundred unemployed citizens (Sana, 2016).

Thirteen of the occupiers of the *wilaya* chose to start a hunger strike for employment. To show their determination, they sewed their lips and demanded public employment. They were called the "Kasserine 13." As Nawfel Nasralli, one of the protesters—who had been unemployed for five years— explains, employment is a luxury few can afford: "In order to work, one has to pay the corrupt men and prove one's loyalty toward the State. They talk about freedom. Which freedom? Does freedom feed anyone? The animals, in Europe, are better treated than we are. We want work, a dignified life, that things finally change" (Moussaoui, 2016).

I see these protests as a paradox, the *Kasserine paradox*, because they challenge the thesis of the political ambiguity of the "mob," according to which the unemployed could easily be revolutionaries one day and oppressive military forces at home or abroad the next day as Islamic militants.

The Kasserine paradox has helped me understand that the term "mob" should be substituted with a more affirmative term, able to recognize this group's devotion to emancipation politics, and that the Tunisian disenfranchised can only push for a revolutionary change if they are joined by more protected sectors of the society.

On the other side, the state continues to ignore the vast majority of the rural and ex-industrial settlements and areas of the center, west, and south, whose inhabitants focus on subsistence and an informal economy for survival. In other words, it can be argued that the Tunisian state is only based on a minoritarian citizenship and does not include within its project the dignified existence of the majority of its territory, both rural and suburban.

As explained by Ali, a young inhabitant of the *houma* interviewed by Lamloum, "Whether you're a *zatal* (someone who smokes joints), a Salafist, a bricklayer, a painter . . . no one is relying on the country any more, everyone has to make their own way of life" (Lamloum, 2016: 21). The "two Tunisias," of which the revolution is but the most recent expression, are the index of a profoundly exclusionary national project.

The Kasserine paradox and another significant event, namely, the killing of Mabrouk Soltani in November 2015,[11] have pointed out that not all the disenfranchised Tunisians—whether they've taken part in the revolution or not—are attracted by Islamic militancy or other forms of violence upon others.

This is why, based on these recent events, I wanted to substitute the term of "mob" with one that would leave less doubt as to the conscious radicality of its members' politics. So, I have chosen to call these people the "vanguard." My notion of vanguard is emancipated from vanguardism, and although it refers to a group of people, it is inspired by what Rodrigo Nunes has called "vanguard-function": "opening a new direction that, after it has communicated to others, can become something to follow, divert, resist" (Nunes, 2014: 39). The vanguard is a highly mobile political subjectivity driven by an internal contradiction. It challenges the regime of governmentality by claiming its life to be valued, while at the same time employing that same organic life as a political weapon.

I don't intend to draw from the tradition of "revolutionary vanguards" literature nor affirm a hierarchy of the revolutionary movement based on political education or class-consciousness. On the contrary, my understanding derives directly from the reflection around the Tunisian revolution where a radical change—the official end of the Ben Ali era—was achieved thanks to an alliance between popular and middle-class groups. In this alliance, the popular groups, the disenfranchised, unemployed of the poor cities and suburbs were the vanguard. Without their courage and action, nothing would have changed. By using the notion of vanguard, I am acknowledging that these people consciously challenged the most dangerous forms of power and that, rather than any type of superiority, their being vanguard implied the highest risk in the front line against state repression, especially by virtue of their highly disposable existential condition.

The vanguard constituted by the Tunisian revolutionaries is one that continuously puts forward techniques of "unruly mobility," while inhabiting a space marked by destitution, "illegalism and criminalized conducts" (Tazzioli, 2016). It is the result of a constitutive excess or surplus of the neoliberal post-independence economy, but by virtue of its very existential precarity, it is also a haunting promise of sedition.

It has a particular relationship with its people's bodies and the way they claim recognition, two interconnected aspects on which I will be now focusing.[12] The Tunisian vanguard's claims are marked by self-burnt bodies, suicides, and sewn lips and eyelids, alongside the contagious riot fire devouring the headquarters of authority and the detention centers.

Banu Bargu is a Turkish scholar who has worked on the techniques of protest enacted by the Turkish socialist activists in the 1990s against the repression, mainly in the high-security prison. She has mostly focused on the hunger strike, which led to the death of 122 activists in that period, and her work aims to counter the assumption that hunger strikes and self-harm are inferiorly respectable political practices. This is also in relation to the Agambenian distinction between *bios* and *zoe*, which Bargu critiques. The debate here unfolds around the interweaving of the political and the biological (like in Esposito, 2013), reflecting on the potentiality of using "bare life" as a political weapon (Ziarek, 2012; Landzelius, 1999; Aradau, 2004).

Bargu develops Achille Mbembe's notion of necropolitics as opposed to biopolitics and, by looking at the practices of the Turkish activists, she theorizes the notion of *necroresistance* against the neoliberal biosovereign assemblage. "Necroresistance transforms the body from a site of subjection to a site of insurgency, which by self-destruction presents death as a counter conduct to the administration of life. Practices of necroresistance are thus both creative and destructive lines of flight that constantly escape being co-opted into the biosovereign assemblage and destabilize the assemblage itself" (Bargu, 2014: 85).

The "biosovereign assemblage" refers to a particular interweaving of sovereignty and discipline in which the "administration of life" is overtaken by "sovereign decision, while the power of life and death is marshalled in support of life and well-being" (Idem: 52). This is why self-harm and suicidal violence become a practice of delegitimizing the power of a state, with "bodies deny(ing) their state-sponsored mutation into colonial subjects, obedient nationals" (Dabashi, 2012b: 9). Not only is the body a significant political tool, but its necroresistance rearticulates the order of the political and an appropriation of agency precisely and paradoxically around biological disposability. "Necroresistance presents an embodied form of radical critique. Embodied because the biopolitical management of bodies needs resistance from the points of its application. Bodies have become sites of contestation and the vessels of a political intervention" (Bargu, 2015).

It is noteworthy to point out that bodies have been largely and tragically at the forefront of the political activity of the Tunisian vanguard. "According to the Forum for Economic and Social Rights there have been 4,288 protests and 498 succeeded or attempted suicides in 2015" (Alba Rico, 2016a). The Kasserine 13, namely, the group of unemployed men who joined the occupation of the Kasserine Prefecture—after the protests sparked by Yahyaoui's suicide—and who started a hunger strike for public employment, is one of the most recent examples of Tunisian necroresistance. They took their protest form one step further: sewing their lips, a practice also enacted by Tunisians in the Italian detention centers for migrants in 2011. This is a very significant gesture since it tacitly implies that those they wanted to reach—the authorities, the politicians—wouldn't take their protest seriously. Their sewn lips represent a metaphor of the "inaudible" voice, but also enforce the causality relation of their potential deaths, suggesting "if we die, there must be no doubt on who is responsible."

In her discussion around Mohamed Bouazizi's gesture of self-immolation, Bargu briefly illustrates the reasons why necroresistance can be associated to counter-hegemonic political practices or counter conducts (to use the Foucauldian term she employs) aimed at emancipation, which is the case with the aforementioned Kasserine 13. Necroresistance actively works against the "individual good, self-preservation and the value of life," which the biosovereign administration of lives is based on. Moreover, suicides, self-immolations, or practices of self-harm are attempts to "make a dent in a *status quo* that appears unchangeable" and occasionally initiate a process of mutation when the practice spreads to other sectors of the society. But eventually, since necroresistance is mainly individual, it is "upon the collective to decline it according to a progressive emancipatory politics" (Bargu, 2015). This reflection on the necropolitical modalities of the vanguard ties into the reflection on the underclass and the "mob" in chapter 3, in the sense that it's an attempt to reflect on how the political is enacted in settings of high disposability.

CONCLUSION

This ambitious chapter has attempted to keep together three different lines of thought originated by three crucial research questions. The first question regarded the absent or "inaudible" voices of the revolution, which I identified as rural Tunisia (thanks to Habib Ayeb's work) and the Imazighen. Both the peasants and Tunisia's indigenous population, the Imazighen, shed light on the lineage of dispossession—both colonial and post-independence—that the revolution was a response to. In fact, I argue that the 2011 revolution was a cry against a historical sequence of expropriative and impoverishing gestures from above, the last of which was marked by a convergence between neoliberalism and local oligarchy, both supported by a growing regional inequality.

Moreover, this framework allowed me to acknowledge the importance of the contemporary metropolitan suburb—the *houma*—as a direct result of historical dispossession but also as the location of a new sense of belonging and of emancipatory politics.

The second question regarded the practice of the Ahl Al Kahf collective, which I've read in terms of minor art. With the artists' interventions—which I've provisionally listed, both chronologically and geographically—they provided an example of the risks and achievements of a type of contemporary minor art. With their opposition to and exposure of the Tunisian police state; their recognition of the revolution as enacted by the disenfranchised; and their "untimely" devotion to the condition of exile (both at home and when they became diasporic artists), the Ahl Al Kahf showed how, at a given time, it was possible to push against art commodification and stay profoundly "respectful when a singularity revolts, intransigent when power violates the universal" (Foucault, 1979).

Finally, this chapter marks my passage from the term "mob" to the term "vanguard," which I've chosen with the intention of acknowledging the affirmative dimension of the political commitment of the Tunisians who pioneered the revolution, in the light of the Kasserine protests. In this sense, the vanguard appears as the contemporary manifestation of a lineage of resistance, whose roots include the resilience of the Imazighen against Arabization and the anticolonial *fellaga*.

In conclusion, thanks to the valuable work of Bargu, this chapter also establishes the link between the practices of the vanguard and the employment of the body as political terrain and tool, able to weaponize "bare life" in terms of *necroresistance* (Bargu, 2014, 2015). With this term, I intend to argue for the political validity of the practices of the vanguard, while bearing in mind the way this group's resistance functions as a possibility of contagion for all those who share conditions of marginalization. In fact, the next chapter is devoted to the aspect of propagation of protests. I will reflect both on how communication occurs alongside the corporate media outlets (including the corporate social media ones), and on how the revolution and the following struggles of the Tunisian brought to light counter-hegemonic ways of organizing meaning and affects while moving them across the Mediterranean.

Finally, I am interested to show what explains certain patterns of contagion of protest, such as the similar propagation of mobilizations in Tunisia, which occurred with very similar geographies both in 2011 and 2016. What do these modalities of political composition show in terms of how the contemporary transformative politics can be imagined? And also, how could the necroresistant drive be captured?

Chapter Five

Mediation of an Event

Circulation of Cultures and Practices of Resistance

Until some gang succeeds in putting the world in a straitjacket, its definition is possibility.

—Ralph Ellison, *The Invisible Man*, 1952

There will be no pictures of you and Willie Mays
Pushing that shopping cart down the block on the dead run
Or trying to slide that colour television into a stolen ambulance
NBC will not be able to predict the winner at 8:32
Or report from 29 districts
The revolution will not be televised.

—Gil Scott-Heron, "The Revolution Will Not Be Televised," 1971

The virtual that proliferates around each and every knot of the real constitutes the chaosmic background based on which every event and every reality define their own consistency.

—Introduction to the Italian edition of Félix Guattari, *Chaosmosis*, 1966[1]

MEDIATION AND POLITICS FROM WITHIN CONTAINMENT

In the previous chapter, I looked at the lineage of dispossession that touched upon the Tunisian territory after 1881 and at some of the ways in which it developed until the 2011 revolution. This historical outline made visible the long history of oppression of the populations inhabiting the area, but also how resistance was always present, enacted by groups such as the Imazighen or the anti-colonial *fellaga*. I have, therefore, tried to identify some ways in which dispossession and resistance unfolded before and after the 2011 revolutionary climax. It became clear how crucial the impoverishment of rural Tunisia was for the current situation, and how much it conditioned the agglomeration of the dispossessed in the metropolitan suburb, the *houma*. At the same time, the *houmani* and the *harraga* emerged as some of the categories that resisted and fought the ongoing process of dispossession and consequent segregation. Their struggle has been thematized and supported by the critical practices of the Ahl Al Kahf collective, whose work I've chosen to describe as a remarkable example of minor art. Finally, I returned to the discussion around the terms able to name the political subject of the revolution. In the light of the 2015 protests after the killing of Mabrouk Soltani and after Ridha Yahyaoui's suicide in 2016, to the revisited term "mob" I substituted the term "vanguard" in recognition of the pioneering and affirmative vocation of so many of the most disenfranchised Tunisians.

This chapter will develop along two lines of inquiry more or less connected to the aspect of communication related to the Tunisian revolution. In the first section, I will interrogate what concretely lies beyond and alongside the much-praised social media presence connected to the protests. By drawing from examples of struggles inspired by the "Arab" revolutions in Italy, I will reflect on the circulation of practices and cultures of resistance, investigating the role of technology and connectedness. The reflection will articulate how the struggle circulates within an informational culture in which technology seems to be increasingly embodied.

I will explore how the notion of mediation can be intended in an oppositional manner; namely, as working against hegemonic forms of organization of meaning and affects. Thinking beyond the "technofetishism" connected to the Arab Spring, I will draw from the previously described practices of the Tunisian rioters, of the *harraga*, and from the way languages of resistance born in Tunisia were taken up in the struggles of migrant porters in Italy in 2013. To account for these types of organization of meanings and affects, I will use the notion of mediation (drawing from Braidotti, 2014; Griziotti, 2016; Massumi, 2002; Munster, 2001; Terranova, 2004, 2007, 2016; Kember and Zylinska, 2012) that I will complexify in accordance with issues raised by my case study. The main aspect of this understanding of mediation is that when it is faced with a breaking point, such as the accumulation of dissent that leads to a generalized mobilization, it operates as an agent of plurification rather than one of containment of dissent, as is the case of hegemonic representation and of modulation of affects.

Secondly, this chapter is also intended to address the question around the propagation of protests in more depth, describing how protests spread across the social field within different communities. Aware of the uneven distribution of digital connectivity in many of the sites of politics I describe, I will stress that propagation of dissent is based on the commonality of an embodied experience rather than on the digital connectedness or on mere contagion/contamination, a paradigm I've relied on previously but of which I identify the limits here. The notion of "resonance" (that I borrow from Clover, 2016) will address this aspect of embodied commonality that I make a declination of in terms of sense of space (the suburban "internal colony," Cowen and Lewis, 2016), of time ("weaponisation of waiting time," Povinelli, 2011), and of illegalized forms of mobility.

As an arrival point of the previous chapters, here I will show what lies alongside the capture of the event (that I address in chapter 2) and how a revolution is defined in terms of addition of resonances and alliance between different groups, drawing from the Tunisian example.

5.1. MEDIATION AND THE CIRCULATION OF STRUGGLES

I am using the concept of "mediation" because the Tunisian revolution is strongly attached to a particular narrative of technological mediation in the mainstream media, mainly through the lens of "technological optimism" or "technologies of liberation" (Mejias, 2012). What is alluded to by these descriptions, alongside expressions such as "Twitter/Facebook revolution," is that the "Arab" people have accessed a space of much-awaited democracy and political "modernity"—that they have finally overcome the stigma of the "Arab exceptionalism"—mostly thanks to the use of Western-designed technologies of communication such as social media. In this chapter, I will use the term "mobility" to indicate the movement of bodies and use the term "circulation" to indicate the movement of affects and knowledges along different types of infrastructures: online, offline, but mostly hybrid ones combining both.

For the sake of clarity, I will not deal specifically with the interaction between the Tunisian revolution and the state and/or corporate media outlets, be they television or social media. Rather, my intention is to turn mediation on its head. It is not my intention to dismiss the role of social media within the techno-social articulation of the revolution. I am aware that social media stands for a sociality of a particular type (Terranova, 2016) and that it is relevant for aspects of contagion (and resonance) even in cases of discontinuous connectivity, which mark many of the struggles of the Tunisian vanguard. What I intend to reveal by exposing the limits of paradigms of technofetishism is that a focus on the technical (social media) as an agent of revolution and "democratization," such as in the Arab Spring narrative, silences the complex histories of this revolution. This doesn't mean that the revolution, and the struggles after its apex, has not been propagated through media, such as the necroresistant gestures, rumors, songs, and street art. It simply means that social media is just one aspect of this ecology and that it cannot be made to account for the event's complexity. This is why I choose to focus on aspects of mediation that I consider underrepresented and overshadowed by the focus on social media.

In this sense, I will look at the ecology of situated, embodied media used by the revolutionaries—as rioters, first, and as "illegal" migrants, later—while acknowledging the qualitative modifications that they have effected in the environments they have crossed with their cultures and practices of struggle. As I described in chapter 3, I see the Tunisian revolution as characterized by an intersection of flows of mobile categories. The three flows that directly regard the Tunisian population are the revolutionaries, the "undocumented" migrants, and the Islamist militants. Rather than considering the latter as the "proof" of the failure of the Tunisian revolution, I view their choice as the development of a "deadly line of flight" (mostly) addressing the historical marginalization that the revolution was an expression of in the first place. Yet, in this chapter, I will only focus on the mediation enacted by the first two groups: the revolutionaries and the migrants. The reason is that I have a particular interest in accounting for the circulation of resistance practices and because my previous experience has allowed me to come in contact with Tunisian revolutionaries who have emigrated to Europe.[2]

The Tunisian revolution was an important moment of disruption for a certain receptacle of powers (an assemblage of national and international interests), therefore it was connected to significant practices of perception management and affect modulation, enacted as attempts to capture the event's possible ramifications. The mediation that I am interested in goes beyond and against these practices. I am interested in reflecting on the interactions discontinuously interwoven with the plane of hyper-connectivity. What kind of mediation inhabits the offline space? Or what mediations are enacted when the connectivity is seriously compromised or inaccessible? In addition, while activating in a discontinuously connected space, the Tunisian revolution and the struggles in its aftermath have unfolded within a post-cybernetic control regime,[3] whose disciplinary face, in terms of a police state, was also very present. How can this aspect be acknowledged and reflected upon?

In this understanding, mediation is a particular type of circulation of affects and information, which bears the intentionality of the protesters; it is the transmission of tactic knowledge and affects. I have developed this understanding by asking what patterns of communication unfolded alongside the institutional ones, both in the political activity of the rioters and in that of the illegalized migrants.

As a response, I have thought mediation as a counterpart of representation. In this view, mediation and representation function as parallel and often antagonistic forms of organization of meaning and affects, especially when they are related to instances of mass dissent such as a revolution. Therefore, I have regarded representation as a large-scale, strategic operation of containment of dissent, exemplified by the "domination narrative" described in chapter 1. On the other hand, mediation is seen as an underground tactic and subversive operation of plurification of the sites of dissent. This plurification occurs, for example, when the news of Mohamed Bouazizi's immolation circulates, thus spreading the impulse to riot, but it also occurs with the transmission of information regarding safe passages toward Europe, for instance.

I have derived the notion of mediation from the work of authors such as Rosi Braidotti (2014), Paolo Griziotti (2016), Brian Massumi (2002), Anna Munster (2001), Tiziana Terranova (2004, 2007, 2016), and Sarah Kember and Joanna Zylinska (2012). The work of these thinkers has helped me craft a term that accounts for a transmission of meaning that runs parallel to the hegemonic functioning of representation. The term allows me to shift the focus toward the process and the becoming of mediation rather than on its stabilization in institutionalized forms (i.e., the media), while considering the intertwining between organic life and mediation as "an intrinsic condition of being-in, and becoming-with, the technological world" (Kember and Zylinska, 2012: 1).

Along the same lines, Terranova poignantly shows how "remembering and sharing by technological means produce both surplus value for netarchical capitalists but also an exceeding of affects, desires, and beliefs materializing a 'common ground'" (2016). This "common ground" represents an important precondition for the struggle. In fact, the possibility of transformation, Terranova argues, "depends not on interest, but on transferable social quantities" such as beliefs and desires (Ibidem). Although the mediation I will be analyzing benefits from a discontinuous access to connectivity, the focus is the "common ground" built upon the beliefs and desires by virtue of its importance for the revolutionary unfolding of the event.[4]

The Tunisian revolution—with its migratory ramifications—offers a unique instance of situated, embodied mediation of an event through the meanings and affects that its participants chose to circulate through their mobility practices. In this sense, bodies become primary mediators and circulators: unruly bodies, like those of the rioters and the protesters; dead bodies, like those of the martyrs; disappeared bodies, like those of the Tunisian *desaparecidos*, lost between the Mediterranean and Europe. The argument is that the same group that propelled the mobilization turned revolution in 2011 (i.e., the under- and unemployed Tunisians of the poor cities and suburbs) also enacted particular practices of mediation connected to this event. I regard as instances of mediation political gestures such as self-immolation, chants, protest tactics, as well as poetry, music, or both, as in the case of the famous hip-hop anthem of the *houma*, "Houmani" (Hamzaoui and Kafon, 2013).

At the same time, this idea of mediation brings into discussion not only the mediation involved in the "minor politics," the politics of the "mob," of the population produced as "surplus,"[5] but also the one brought into being by the "minor art," specifically the work of the Ahl Al Kahf collective. In this view, visual art, sound, and gestures are some of the means of mediating the revolutionary event.[6]

Mediation will be understood through its quality as an agent of plurification and as opposed to practices of containment of resistance such as Orientalist representations or divisive modulation of affects. This understanding of mediation can be linked to the way resistance has been discussed previously in terms of contagion, which will be developed in section 5.3 with a more detailed focus on patterns of resonance.

As I discuss in the following sections, in terms of the specificity of the Tunisian revolution, it was resonance between different disenfranchised communities that helped the riots spread according to a recognition between subaltern groups based on "structural similarities"; namely, on the shared experience of dispossession and constant abuse (Chouti, 2011). Moreover, this expression of dissent has managed to evolve into a revolutionary climax thanks to the alliance of these groups with other groups of Tunisian society; most importantly, with the unionized workforce (mostly state employed) but also with students and artists. Therefore, the event's singularity is built upon these two elements—the possibility of resonance and alliance—but these aspects are particular to each conjuncture, as I have shown in the maps of struggles punctuating the European trajectory of the Tunisian migrants, for example. "Structural similarities" and alliances are constantly undergoing reconfiguration. They remain possible both on the Tunisian territory as well as on any territory that the Tunisian citizens choose to inhabit. In this research, I have chosen to focus mostly on the suburban population, which played a significant role in the revolution. This is why I relate instances of resonance and alliance to this group of people and their mobility within and across borders. I also do this because drawing from the Tunisian case—as a *post factum* analysis—it can be argued that when both resonance and alliance occur, a revolutionary transformation is more probable. In this sense, the notion of mediation and the focus put on the gesture is intended to address the social production and circulation of meaning and affects involved in the process of resonance and alliance.

Before specifically addressing the differences and interactions between the practice of mediation and representation, I will engage with some relevant examples of circulation of struggles connected to the Tunisian revolution, which have been pivotal for this inquiry.

In 2012, I had the chance to take part in a national gathering in Rome of several activist groups who were working on housing rights, most significantly involved in housing occupations of empty private facilities alongside communities of evictees, both Italians and migrants.[7] While driving toward one of the occupations—a private facility housing more than 400 people—with A., a member of the Metropolitan Precarious Blocs,[8] he started telling others and me about what the arrival of the "Tunisian young men" had meant for him and his comrades. After the Tunisian revolution, the Italian Minister of the Interior, Roberto Maroni, had spectacularly declared that the "Maghreb wall had fallen," and thus Italy needed support in "managing" the migration "flow."[9] A. was talking about exactly the same people Maroni was desperately trying to police. And he was describing their impact on the housing rights struggle in Rome. "They are many, very young, courageous, and willing to take big risks, after the experience of struggle they come from. [. . .] There is something about the way they understand politics. We don't speak Arabic and they don't speak Italian, but we have a common language. They are attuned to our work."[10] This common language is arguably a determinant foundation for the "creolization" of practices of struggle or for the alliances that increment their traction, such as in the case of the Tunisian alliance between the unemployed and unionized workers in 2011.

What A. said made me reflect on the circulation of the cultures and practices of struggle, given how the Tunisian young suburban unemployed were attuned to the struggle strategies of the housing rights coalitions beyond a specifically verbal correspondence. In other words, it made me consider how different revolutionary assemblages communicate beyond words.

With A.'s words in mind, it is even more relevant to look at instances of circulation of cultures of resistance within the Mediterranean space, from the Middle East toward Italy and, surely, other European countries. Paying attention to the chants, the slogans, and the choreography of protests in Italy, for example, reveals how the promise and the language of dignity of the Tunisian revolution has been traveling from Sidi Bouzid to Granarolo, Italy. I refer here to the admirable struggle of the outsourced porters working in the dairy and logistics industry in Emilia-Romagna, a region in the center-north of Italy.

On May 15, 2013, a massive wildcat strike, supported by the porters of the SI-Cobas rank and file union, brought many logistics hubs throughout Italy to a standstill, calling for better working conditions for the porters employed by outsourced companies, commonly organized as "cooperatives" (*Infoaut*, 2013). The mobilization had also started at the Granarolo milk factory, in the Emilia-Romagna region, where forty porters had been suspended after having exposed the company's bad working conditions in a YouTube video (Stinco, 2013). While forming a picket line with the intention to block the flow of transportation of products, some of the porters had been run over by the trucks, which led to a further mobilization of groups of underpaid and precarious logistics workers all over Italy. The majority of these workers were migrants either coming from Arabic-speaking countries or from Bangladesh and Pakistan. Many of the mobilization's political practices, narratives, notions, and words were directly derived from the imaginary connected to the 2011 uprisings in Tunisia and Egypt.

Most strikingly, the Granarolo workers used a "Game Over" banner, similar to the ones that the Tunisian and Egyptian protesters had made internationally recognizable during their gatherings. It could be hypothesized that the "Arab" protesters had employed the "Game Over" expression in 2011 as a result of many of them being involved in gaming communities, alongside their attempt to project a widely comprehensible message toward the Western audiences. In this case, though, it was the migrant workers, alongside the Italian activists, from Granarolo, Italy, who picked up the message.

Moreover, the workers' banners also featured slogans in Arabic (see Figure 5.1), many of which linked their political claims to the notion of dignity, a crucial keyword of the Tunisian revolution. One of its most famous chants called for "Bread and Dignity," and many call the event itself "the Dignity revolution."

Bearing in mind this remarkable example of circulation of the language of struggle, it is important to address in which way the Tunisian case sheds light on the interaction between the circulation of revolution-related affective intensities and the work of corporate or state media. Is it fair to argue that the institutional media, both social media and television, attempt to not only contain, in some instances, but also quantify those affective intensities by extracting value out of them (drawing from Terranova, 2016)?[11]

In this sense, the mediation of dissent, which concerns this research, communicates the possibility of resistance and multiplies its sites by producing and circulating tactical knowledge. Also in this sense, the world of the revolutionaries, which corresponds to the world of the Tunisian disenfranchised suburban population, runs parallel to that of the Tunisian state or that of the European states and their respective media outlets. Within this world, there are

Figure 5.1. Demonstration of the porters during the 15th of May strike, in 2013, when the logistic hub of the Interporto (Bologna, Italy) was blocked. The banners read "The cooperative of porters = Slavery" and "Strike and Struggle for Dignity until we reach the Victory" in Italian, Urdu, and Arabic. *Source: http://www.infoaut.org/*

gestures of defiance that work as mediators of the interruption of traditional power relations. Outside this world, the organic artists, who enact their own mediating gestures, support this interruption. In this sense, mediation partially resonates with the political importance of instances of self-representation or self-affirmation.

5.2. REPRESENTATION VS. MEDIATION: "IT'S LIKE THE UNDERGROUND RAILROAD, ONLY THAT IT'S DIGITAL"

The sentence I've included in the title is a quote from Maurice Stierl, who works for the NGO Watch the Med. He refers to the way rumors and news about routes of passage spread among the migrants directed toward Europe (*Economist*, 2017). Stierl's parallelism between the Afro-American fugitive knowledges and the contemporary routes of migration is crucial for this section as it helps to frame the notion of "mediation."

In this sense, it's useful to state that the employment of the notion of "mediation" that will be made in this chapter goes strategically beyond the mere understanding of it in terms of technological mediation, mainly focused around the so-called bio-hyper-media (Griziotti, 2016). In other words, I have turned to mediation *as a counterpart to representation* in a sense that I will further explain. The understanding of the term, in this section, develops from a focus on its political and/or artistic nature, although such separations are only useful for the argument, and I don't consider the two natures distinct. The main aspect is that mediation operates as an *agent of plurification* opposed to the technologies of "containment of the virtuality of the social" (Terranova, 2004: 12) aimed at by the practices of representation. More precisely, the difference lies mainly in the attitude toward the dimension of virtuality held by the revolutionary assemblage. When I speak of mediation in this section, I focus on those operations whose main goal is *not* that of containing, harnessing, and directing the virtual nested within the unruly community that has started the revolution and continued the struggle across the borders.

I am making this argument drawing from the realization of how the contemporary informational environment organizes perception, especially when the dominant system is faced with significant events of disruption in those occasions in which it becomes more visible how informational dynamics work toward delimiting a "possible action that moulds and remoulds the social field." In such moments, power systems attempt to govern the relationship between the real, the probable, and the improbable (Terranova, 2004: 19).

Following the work of Henri Bergson, Terranova explains, "What lies beyond the possible and the real is thus the openness of the virtual, of the invention and the fluctuation, of what cannot be planned or even thought in advance, of what has no real permanence but only reverberations" (Idem: 27).

In this case study and section, the concept of the virtual helps to imagine what lies alongside the Orientalist narratives funneled by state and corporate media outlets, what lies alongside the famous "Arab" bloggers and the façade of the "Twitter/Facebook revolution." Terranova's work has been crucial precisely because of her refined understanding of the dynamics of the contemporary informational culture while not disregarding the political aspect; that is, the need to reflect critically on the distribution of power relations. In fact, as has been stated earlier, the event of the revolution occurred during a period in which the global state apparatuses reached a significant development in terms of societies of control and of spectacle, alongside the affirmation of an informational culture, though this does not, by any means, imply an even distribution of the access to connectivity.

The contemporary informational environment is characterized by features that necessarily need to be taken into consideration when looking at the unfolding of an event of disruption. First of all, rather than conceiving of communication in terms of meaning and signification, when looking at the functioning of informational cultures, information should be regarded as indicating the successful transmission of a signal once a contact is established and the noise is overcome. "The relation of signal to noise [. . .] is concerned not only with the successful transmission of messages, but also with the overall constitution of fields of possibilities" (Idem: 20). This understanding (based on Claude Shannon's information theory) stresses the importance of attention management, for example. In fact, "the manipulation of affects and signs is an essential part of the politics of communication in informational cultures" (Idem: 14). In this immersive informational space, the actions of a subject are "decomposed, recomposed and carried along" (Idem: 37) and even resistance is often welcomed and incorporated as difference by the network power (Idem: 62). But most importantly, in this system, each "movement (of information) is a modification of the overall topology: of the sender, the code, the channel, the signal and the receiver" (Idem: 51). The modification of the overall topology is significant in this case because it allows one to understand how cultures and practices of struggle have impacted the environments they have crossed, whether from the south to the north of Tunisia, from the *houma* to the center of a city, or from Tunisia to Europe.

In my understanding, mediation amplifies these cultures and practices of struggle, based on past meanings and affects as opposed to representation and modulation, which are constantly attempting to reduce and harness the disruptive fluctuations of the power system. The way mediation occurs is through a constant circulation of beliefs and desires connected to the everyday experiences of the people involved in these types of struggles. What circulates are stories of past resistances, tactical pieces of knowledge on how to dodge the system, but also the different levels to which certain systems—whether the Tunisian police or the European border police—render certain bodies disposable. But most importantly, what circulates is the acknowledgment that certain forms of resistance are possible. In this sense, resistance, as pointed out in chapter 2, holds a crucially contagious potentiality, which, as I discuss in section 5.3, is based on commonalities that determine patterns of resonance. The importance of the propagation of the message of possible resistance is why I pointed out the direct relation between the actions of the revolutionaries in Tunisia and the examples of their integration in the activist groups in Rome, Italy, after their emigration toward Europe. Every knowledge or experience of organization or collective action matters for the communities that choose to migrate, either toward the richer Tunisian cities or toward Europe. I have touched upon this aspect by focusing on the instances of the struggle of the Tunisians, both in the Italian detention centers and in the urban setting of Paris, which are just two of the most visible examples. In this sense, mediation regards the circulation of forms of counter-knowledge. It also involves the collective construction of strings of signs—narratives, symbols, aesthetics, embodied practices connected to sound, movement, visuality—which originate from a significant breaking point. It is noteworthy that this production from below does not come out of nowhere and is not spontaneous but rather connected to a consistent lineage of past meanings and affects.

In what follows, I will sketch the initial reasoning behind this section, the way this research has understood the mediation connected to the event of the revolution. The starting point is a particular localized affective accumulation, which indicates a level of excessive frustration that can no longer be absorbed by the system. That excessive affective accumulation is transformed or mediated through collective political gestures, which, thanks to propagation and solidarity, reach a revolutionary dimension; namely, the dimension of a mass mobilization that overthrows the power system. Faced with this snowball effect of affects and political gestures, the power system—or other systems, which this disruption could disturb—mobilizes its media outlets, themselves fighting to survive the revolutionary transformation in the attempt to incorporate the disruptive fluctuations. This corresponds to the representation of the event, which can be understood both in symbolic terms ("speaking *about*") as well as in political terms ("speaking *for*"). In political terms, certain categories (and I am here thinking about the former regime's media outlet) might attempt to harness the flows of dissent, often by becoming their most vocal spokesperson, while making sure to preserve their own power throughout and after the transformations forced by the revolution, enacting a sort of *gattopardismo* (according to which "everything changes, so that everything can stay the same" [Di Lampedusa, 1958]). This attempt to incorporate and limit the fields of possibility of the revolutionary assemblage are expressed through interventions as different as the "Jasmine revolution" or Arab Spring narratives, alongside the promotion of the fear of the Other, whether referred to as the poor, the Muslim, the "terrorist," or the generic "West."

In this sense, the operation of meaning organization can be divided into three directions: mediation, representation, and modulation. Mediation indicates how meaning is re-created within the uprising community; it overlaps with self-expression to some extent, and it also employs non-discursive ways of mediating, such as the gesture.[12] The main aspect of mediation as a form of meaning creation and organization is that it represents a positive feedback to the initial affective breaking point. In other words, it seeks to amplify it, and it essentially respects its virtual dimension, as far as the demand for dignity is concerned.

On the other hand, the negative feedback to the affective breaking point is constituted by representation on the logico-discursive level and by modulation on the affective level. In this model, the outlets of the challenged power calculate the implications of the breaking point and attempt to direct dissent either by neutralizing it, harnessing it, or incorporating it into the ongoing power relations system in such a way as to limit the transformation. I already addressed the representation and modulation of affects in chapter 2, where I showed how both strategies of containment of dissent have been employed in the Tunisian post-revolutionary period.

On the other hand, the operations that I catalogue as mediation seek to amplify the initial affective charge, to expose the abusive nature of the power outlets, and to push for their transformation. The resulting fluctuations are constantly reverberated in new and unpredictable directions of political gestures, as demonstrated by the resonance between the revolutions in Tunisia and Egypt and the struggle of the porters in Italy. While representation has a logico-discursive nature, in contemporary apparatuses of power that level is intertwined with a set of asignifying practices, which operate according to a logic of modulation, the most paradigmatic example of which is the emergent importance of the "affective fact" as a tool (addressed in Massumi, 2002).[13]

Going back to the work of Gayatri Spivak, "representation" carries two meanings, which she derives from the employment of two German terms by Karl Marx: (1) *vertreten*, translated as "speaking for," in the sense of political representation, and (2) *darstellen*, in the sense of "speaking about" or "re-presenting," in the sense of "making a portrait" (Spivak, 1988: 275–76; Kapoor, 2004: 628). This double reference—both political and symbolic—is relevant for the event of revolution because it draws the attention on two representational practices, both of which have attempted to contain the possibility of dissent.

On the one side, from the point of view of a political representation, the ones who started the revolution had little to no contact with molar political bodies, such as parties and trade unions, mainly because of their condition as informal laborers. The Tunisians who pioneered the revolution and the struggles in its aftermath have only been granted representation through their direct actions. Many organizations and individuals have claimed to be speaking *for* the martyrs of the revolution, but these declarations never went beyond electoral marketing.

On the other side, the symbolic representation of the event—with narratives such as the Arab Spring, the Jasmine revolution, the 14th of January revolution—promoted by both state and corporate communication outlets, has expressed a constant will to de-/immobilize the protest, reducing it to a standstill, employing both the tool of eulogy (the Arab "Awakening") as well as that of the stigma (the Arab "Winter"). In some cases, these narratives have conquered such depths that the participants themselves have interiorized these ideas, sometimes "performing the roles they thought were expected of them" (Kapoor, 2004: 636). I refer here to the extensive corpus of artistic and journalistic expressions produced in connection to the imperative of "performing the Arab Spring," which often resulted in practices in alignment with the "official story," prompted either by the state or the global media.

On the level of modulation, images instead function as real "bioweapons," which harness different orders of affects (Terranova, 2004: 141). When analyzing the affective technologies of the traditional media, mainly television, for how they react in moments when disruptive events unfold, some tendencies seem to be recurrent:

1. A focus on the politics of attention and the diversion of attention toward more appealing news used as smoke screens.
2. A focus on propagating fear by any means, by exacerbating clashes/threats/conflicts, an approach that has historically been the precursor of abusive power interventions since it legitimizes states of exception.[14]
3. An unexpected alignment of the media with the interests of the movements of disruption, which are disproportionally celebrated and met with an explosive euphoria; for example, by over-celebrating the "achievements of the revolution" and the "martyrs," while overlooking their demands or the outcomes of justice.

These few examples of modulation technologies resonate with the image of modulation given by Gilles Deleuze in 1990: "a self-deforming cast that will continuously change from one moment to the other, or like a sieve whose mesh will transmute from point to point" (Deleuze, 1992b).[15]

In order to discuss the third mode of organization of meaning and affects, that of mediation, I will start with the focus on the importance of its embodied nature. In fact, Griziotti has referred to this aspect with regards to the "bio-hyper-media technologies," linked to the employment of those

> devices, such as smartphone, tablet, ultrabook, reader and hybrids (which) are the physical tools of mediation of the *homo cognitivus* with regards to a space-time in a continuum in which the interaction involves living bodies, machines, codes, data and networks: the environment of bio-hypermedia, a term drawn from the assemblage of bios/biopolitics and hypermedia. (Griziotti, 2016: 35, my translation)

In this setting, "the whole body is connected to the networked devices so intimately that it enters in a symbiosis that determines reciprocal modifications and simulations" (Idem: 120). Furthermore, the mediation is not only informational but also biogenetic. In fact,

> the contemporary embodied subjectivities operate under a double imperative: they must be responsible for their surplus value, in their capacity of biogenetic containers, on the one side, and in their capacity of visible goods, on the other

side, which circulate in the global media circuit and in the global financial flow. Bodies today are met with a double mediation, both biogenetic and informational. (Braidotti, 2014: 128 in Griziotti, 2016: 96, my translation)

The aspects pointed out by Griziotti and Braidotti are part of this research's view of mediation, but in this chapter I also want to push further in certain directions relevant to my case study. In the following sections, I will therefore focus on four particular aspects of mediation: (1) its situatedness; (2) its processuality; (3) its relationship with the body; and (4) its manifestation through gestures and mediators.

5.2.1. Situated Mediation: Who Mediates and Why?

I am interested to put forward a notion of mediation that accounts for the *milieu* or the situation that it derives from. In this sense, mediation runs on an informal circuit, alongside hegemonic communication, as a parasite, with its nicknames, jokes, anecdotes, oral history, popular music, and many other manifestations. These means of circulating information were also employed before the revolution, despite and because of the censorship of the regime. This particular field of production is to be regarded as oppositional in the sense that it counteracts the specific organization of the sensible and of the desires operated by the hegemonic media. In this sense, it could be termed *mediation from below*, because it indicates a battle over the meaning of the revolution but also the galaxy of knowledges tactically rotating around the actions of the people who promoted the revolution in the first place.

The first issue that is often ignored in this type of approach is *which* expressions the focus is put on. Whose mediation are the studies interested in? What unfolds alongside the tweets, the blog posts, the citizens' YouTube videos relayed by *Al Jazeera*, and the Facebook profiles of the most prominent activists from Tunis? Are there any "specific communication networks that do not overlap either with national or with global television"? (Terranova, 2004: 16). Since the communities that this research is interested in are those of the revolutionaries, who have later become *harraga* or "undocumented" migrants, the latter offer an interesting example of mediation from below and of how/for what it is being used.

The following descriptions are mainly based on the experience of people asking for asylum in Europe in 2017, but I draw from them because they are highly similar to the experience of the Tunisian *harraga*.

> When refugees leave their homes, they enter an "informational no-man's-land."
> Where should they go, and whom should they trust? Phones become a lifeline. Their importance goes well beyond staying in touch with people back

home. They bring news and pictures of friends and family who have reached their destination, thereby motivating more migrants to set out. They are used for researching journeys and contacting people-smugglers. Any rumour of a new, or easier, route spreads like wildfire. "It's like the underground railroad, only that it's digital," says Maurice Stierl of Watch the Med, an NGO that tracks the deaths and hardships of migrants who cross the Mediterranean, referring to the secret routes and safe houses used to free American slaves in the 19th century. (*Economist*, 2017)

In this regard, scholars of the autonomy of migration have pointed out the importance of communication technologies for the construction of the common, precisely from within practices of unruly and dissident mobility, thanks to what they call "mobile commons" (Trimikliniotis, Parsanoglou, and Tsianos, 2014).

On the level of mobility practices, technological mediation is a constant battlefield between the agents who enact containment[16] and the mobile communities: "people in northern Iraq use Whatsapp and Viber to talk to friends who have made it to Germany; UNHCR (the UN Refugee Agency) uses iris scans for identification in camps in Jordan and Lebanon; migrants on flimsy rubber boats in the Mediterranean use satellite phones provided by people-smugglers to call the Italian coastguard" (Ibidem). Technology is omnipresent, true, but it often animates the folds of control, therefore the proliferation of connectedness is always situated and weaponized according to the distribution of power relations. Within the territory of contained mobility, technology corresponds to a deadly touch for disobedient bodies, as the research on the "Left-to-Die-Boat" shows, with its exemplary biopolitical title. In this work, the Forensic Oceanography collective reverted the use of surveillance technologies to show the unfolding of a tragedy, the death of sixty-six people on a boat in distress, left unassisted. "The Forensic Oceanography report turned the knowledge generated through surveillance means into evidence of responsibility for the crime of non-assistance," showing how the control grid that striates the Mediterranean and its crossers totally disregarded their survival (Forensic Architecture, 2012).

The second issue that is often ignored when discussing matters of technological mediation is the distribution of the access to connectivity. Some underline, for example, the leading role of social media in the Tunisian revolution, or, worse, allude that connectivity has somehow supported a process of alleged political "maturation," therefore promoting what some have called "technofetishism" or "techno-optimism" (Mejias, 2012). This framework silences precisely the uneven economic development that has led the people of the south of Tunisia to put an end to the rule of Ben Ali. In fact, even if connectivity were equal to freedom or democracy, "in many parts of the world electricity is still a rare commodity [. . .]. Connecting depends on pancapitalist enterprises—to be free you have to pay" (Fernández, 1999). This is undoubtedly the case in Tunisia, whose southern and central arid regions survive struggling against unimagined peaks of poverty and precarity. "Utopian rhetorics of electronic media occlude the practical project of creating new markets and workforces for capitalist enterprises. In electronic media, this applies to all levels of production, from writing code to the assembly line" (Idem: 60).

Moreover, this is demonstrated by the capitalization upon affects carried out by corporate social media, such as Facebook or Twitter. "One cannot dissociate the manufacture and distribution of these technologies from economic profits made in the developed world or from an ongoing process of the colonisation of knowledge that began with the book and continued with media such as film and television" (Ibidem).

It is clear that connectivity is a discontinuous resource for many of the communities that this research takes into consideration. This is why the operations of mediation—which I directly link to the aspect of circulation of ideas and bodies—also follow different lines of transmission, made of material networks, which go beyond Internet cables or satellite frequencies. Alongside the rumors, the WhatsApp groups, the solid networks of fellow travelers who became witnesses (who informed the families when they witnessed a drowning in the Mediterranean), the erratic Facebook posts of photos, the infrastructure of mediation is formed of human and non-human components: private cars, dusty routes, boats, trains, *passeurs*,[17] car trunks, and safe houses. Even the places of detention along the borders play a crucial role in the transmission of information among the mobile communities.

5.2.2. Processuality and Topologies

Another aspect that I want to keep in mind when working on this understanding of mediation is to account for the dynamic and ever-changing sets of relations that mark most of the environments that the Tunisians have crossed after the revolutionary climax. In this sense, movement—of narratives, bodies, affects, ideas, pieces of information—is key, especially as a component of mobility practices, such as marches or migration. But as Terranova points out, drawing from Bergson, "movement is not about passage, but about duration. We are therefore ignoring the virtuality of duration," in the sense of what the permanence and crossing of a certain space make possible (Terranova, 2004: 50–51). This way of understanding movement draws attention to a crucial aspect of these mobility practices; namely, to what extent they affect the environments they encounter. In other words, as was illustrated with the examples of the struggles relocated through mobility, when the Tunisian protesters crossed their country (moving from the south and west to the North), but mostly when they crossed the Mediterranean and then Italy and France, both with their bodies as well as with their practices, they determined qualitative change that has gone way beyond the mere toppling of a dictatorial government. In fact, "the qualitative change that every movement brings (is) not only that which moves but also to the space that it moves into and to the whole into which that space necessarily opens up" (Ibidem).

More importantly, from a political point of view, focusing on qualitative modifications allows one to conceive of change as possible, which is among the most important achievements of the struggle of the Tunisians, both at home and abroad. "It is at the level of the micro, however, that mutations and divergences are engendered and it is therefore in the micro that the potential for change and even radical transformation lie" (Terranova, 2004: 37).

For the sake of clarity, the potential for change of the micro, in this case, refers strictly to events such as the events of resistance that were listed in chapter 3.[18] As Deleuze points out, a "revolutionary machine" must act at different levels, both punctual and general. In this sense, the micro transformations are part of what—in absence of absorption by the power system—builds up a revolutionary movement. "It is obvious that a revolutionary machine cannot content itself with local, punctual struggles: hyper-desiring and hyper-centralized, it must be all of that at once" (Deleuze, 1977: 104–5 in Thoburn, 2002: 457).

One way to account for all these existing levels is, as Massumi suggests, that of finding "a semiotics willing to engage with continuity," able to put the emphasis "on process before signification or coding" (Massumi, 2002: 4, 7). The idea of topology is one of the conceptual frames able to account for the overlapping of dynamic relations. It is drawn from the study of non-Euclidean geometry and employed recently by critical geographers and political philosophers who want to account for the ever-changing patterns of transformation and mobility.

> In a topological society, we no longer live in or experience "movement" or transformation as the transmission of fixed forms in space and time but rather movement—as the ordering of continuity—composes the forms of social and cultural life themselves. This is not, of course, a matter of one rationality displacing the other, but of their overlapping and mutual implication such that the continuity of movement—or the continuum—becomes fundamental to contemporary culture. (Lury, Parisi, and Terranova, 2012: 6)

More importantly, the topological rationality is able to imagine levels "beyond and beneath the law-like symbolic system of signification" (Idem:

28), therefore overcoming the centrality of the structure promoted by the Structuralist approach or the linguistic semiotic model (based on the relation signified/signifier). In this sense, Massumi refers to what Guattari described as "diagrammatics," drawing from the work of Charles Sanders Peirce. Guattari's diagrammatics are "a-signifying or signal-etic semiotics that describes the processuality of signs and not their position on a structural grid" as "processes in which ideas, intensities, functions are transmitted without having to pass through a structure of (symbolic signification)" (Guattari, 1977: 281 in Massumi, 2002: 17). The reason the concept of diagrammatics is relevant for the event of this case study is that it opens up the possibility of imagining political gestures beyond the mere discursive politics model. In this sense, a gesture such as a self-immolation or the arson of a building associated with abusive forms of power holds political importance, whether or not a clearly structured discursive claim is attached to it. In the same way as, looking at it from the other side of the barricade, "affective facts"—mainly a tool of the power apparatus—hold a crucial political undertone, although they are characterized by what seems to be a total focus on affective intensities only. This brings me to the third aspect of mediation that needs further attention.

5.2.3. The Body as Mediator

The physical body is obviously omnipresent in the practices of protest and mobility that this research has considered. Important reflections have been made so far on the body of the protester, in the act of self-immolation, and the body as a terrain of necroresistance. The body also appears to be a fundamental element of the operations of mediation, as it is seen to "always already be subject to technological mediation" (Blackman, 2012: 8). Yet, when scholars focus on the electronic media, they sometimes dematerialize that same body. As María Fernández notes, "In postcolonial theory, the body is conceived as a palimpsest on which relations of power are inscribed. In electronic media, the body is irrelevant to those relations," as if suggesting that "marginality and subalternity exist only *outside* of cyberspace in the masses yet to be linked to the global network" (Fernández, 1999: 63). Along these lines of reflection on the interaction between cyberspace and the rebel bodies, when Judith Butler speaks of the 2011 series of protests, she refers to the media as the "scene" of politics, in which the "bodies carrying the camera, audio-recorder or cellphone become the frame or border between the scene and the media, included and excluded at the same time and because of this vulnerable to the violence of the state" (Butler, 2011 in Lury et al., 2012: 11).

While this description is certainly pertinent, I would instead argue that the bodies are more than a frame, they are also the *medium* itself, and as such, they can be regarded as primary mediators in many instances. In this sense, it still makes sense to distinguish the "materiality of embodiment" and the "vectors of digital information" in order to be able to reflect on how they interact, since "the materiality of embodiment has a particular way of receiving and generating meaning that gives it a vector of movement that may be parallel to or out of sync with but definitely not the same as vectors of digital information" (Hayles, 1996 in Munster, 2001).

This observation stimulates a reflection on the intra-action between the way meaning is received and generated through embodiment vis-à-vis the modalities of production and circulation of digital information. Although the body is a constant participant to and hyper-mediated by the digital flows, in the Tunisian case the materiality of the bodily gesture and the way its consequences propagate through other bodies is what ignited the revolutionary spark, especially given the poor connectivity and the censorship of the Internet that characterized the digital landscape of Sidi Bouzid in 2010.

5.2.4. Gestures and Mediators

Furthermore, in order to look at the mediation patterns keeping in mind the three aspects that have been so far discussed—(1) the situatedness of mediation; (2) the focus on processuality and topologies; and (3) the body as a mediator—two reflections have proved their utility. On the one side is the understanding of *gesture* developed by Giorgio Agamben in *Means without End* (Agamben, 2000). On the other side is Nicholas Thoburn's idea of *mediator* as an element that represents "the agency of the minority" (Thoburn, 2016). Both working concepts, the gesture and the mediator, are most relevant to the understanding of the forms of the political linked to the Tunisian protests and mobility. These concepts speak against the prescriptive political approaches, which, in order to recognize the emergence of politics, seek consolidated political bodies and discourses with continuity in space and time. By imposing these standards, often what is ignored is the fact that the practices of struggle are developed under the pressure of abusive power and marked by a constant unruly mobility.[19]

In relation to the gesture, Agamben argues that "any communication is first of all communication not of something in common but of communicability itself" (Agamben, 2000: 10). This observation is caused by his reflection on how media establishments of the "spectacular-democratic society" nurture alienation, while actively attempting to prevent revolutionary movements.

For Agamben,

> what characterizes gesture is that in it nothing is being produced or acted, but rather something is being endured and supported. [...] *The gesture is the exhibition of mediality: it is the process of making a means visible as such.* It allows for the emergence of the being-in-medium of human beings and thus it opens the ethical dimension for them. [...] Gesture is a moment of life subtracted from the context of individual biography as well as a moment of art subtracted from the neutrality of aesthetics: it is pure praxis. (Agamben, 2000: 57, 58, 80, original emphasis)

In this sense, the gesture can be understood as the distillation of certain embodied lineages or memories of affects. Once the gesture's praxis unfolds, the nature of its mediality projects a significant wave of intensities in all directions. These intensities are welcomed and retransmitted within those communities that hold the experiential background that grants them access to those gestures. In this sense, the "Game Over" banner, the attack on police headquarters, the employment of the notion of "dignity," or the anti-Western symbols plug the relative gestures to very particular and situated ecologies of meanings. It can be argued that the locations of these meanings are spread globally. In other words, different communities across the globe can resonate with the same gesture according to specific patterns of relation. Significantly, many such political gestures, linked to the event of the revolution and its aftermath, express anger, as an "outlawed emotion." "The magic of anger is a response not to injustice, but to a frustrated political impulse to speak and be heard, and the existence of anger itself is an evidence of the denial of a right to social participation" (Lyman, 1981: 71 in Lugones, 2003: 106).

An important aspect of anger in this setting is that it operates as a moral assessment. In other words, "to be angry is to make oneself a judge and to express a standard against which one assesses the person's conduct, both of which are marks of a moral agent." This anger "makes a claim on respect and signals one's own ability to make judgments about having been wronged, one's own respectability" (Spelman, 1989: 271 in Lugones, 2003: 109–10). Anger is the type of "outlawed emotion" that riots are mainly connected to. In fact, most political gestures within the setting that this research works on are somehow relatable to instances of riots. Considering the riot as an example of moral assessment, with its agents implicitly asserting their respectability, starts to reveal more of the political significance of forms of dissent often labeled as only self-destructive. Given this focus on anger, one of the most frequent critiques of instances of protest or revolutions is that they are solely relief valves for accumulated *ressentiment* and that they are lacking in terms of political construction (this is a critique broadly discussed in Caygill, 2013). Drawing from Frantz Fanon, this research argues that instances of mass action are unavoidably an example of construction, even when they are pioneered by categories of people with no ideological or organizational background. For categories of people who aren't granted the access to the tool of respectable politics, their anger and their bodies become crucial political tools. Especially since, as Maria Lugones notes, anger functions as a moral challenge to the legitimacy of those in power by bracketing the manageability of the governed (Lugones, 2003). Anger is what animates the gesture of disobedience, which opens up the possibility of negotiation between two groups involved in the conflict. Rather than an irrational self-destructive explosion, often critiqued for its lack of political vision, anger is what opens up the possibility of politics, while signaling not only the historical absence of a dialogue with the administrators of power but, most importantly, the arrival at a breaking point. In the Tunisian setting, the suburban disenfranchised population used anger to literally signal the impossibility of survival. As a consequence, the event raises the problem of survival in terms of cohabitation and exploitation between different groups. This is why I have argued that one of the revolution's main implicit demands is that of redistribution of wealth. The stakes of the negotiations are precisely the margins of survival.

Moreover, certain forms of dissent, such as the Tunisian riots, also make visible the limits of forms of politics centered on recognition,[20] intended as the "struggle to become full legal and political persons" (Bhandar, 2011: 228), which mainly informs the Western liberal understanding of politics. From an indigenous perspective, Glen Coulthard argues that "the politics of recognition in its contemporary liberal form promises to reproduce the very configurations of colonialist, racist, patriarchal state power" (Coulthard, 2014: 3). In this sense, one of the ways for the dialectics of recognition to overcome the logic of subordination is for it to acknowledge the centrality of the body. In other words, Brenna Bhandar argues, recognition politics is relevant as long as it accounts for that which exceeds it. "The body from which the demand for recognition issues makes an appearance, it is here and there, it exposes and reveals a 'breakthrough of sense' (Nancy, 2008: 24 in Bhandar, 2011: 237) that is an excess." Much like the Tunisian revolutionaries and the Kasserine 13's practice, the struggle for recognition requires a body that can fight this battle and risk death (Idem: 240). The devastated body of necro-resistance, which has devoted its organic being to making visible the deadly action of power, "presents us with a materialist theory of being, a theory that carries with it the potential for political resistance to the violence of dispossession" (Idem: 242).

Furthermore, thinking beyond the contradictions of recognition-based politics, Coulthard, for example, advocates for the alternative of the "resurgent politics of recognition" (Coulthard, 2014: 18), one that is premised on "self-actualization, direct action, and the resurgence of cultural practices that are attentive to the subjective and structural composition of settler-colonial power" (Idem: 24). Along the same line of thought of Fanon and Aimé Césaire, this form of "disalienation through affirmative reconstruction" is only seen as a means rather than an end, "as a precondition for establishing broader bonds of social solidarity and collective struggle" (Idem: 138). In the contemporary Tunisian context, the people who have been and are produced as surplus have no access to recognition-based politics. Their very existential condition is affected by the absence of recognition on behalf of their state, which devalues the lives of its poor citizens on a daily basis. This devaluation is pursued through an oscillation between state abandonment, confinement, heavy policing, and dispossession of resources, of water and land, for example, which is increasingly pushed into private hands in Tunisia. The Tunisian case indicates two ways of exiting the condition of surplus and attempting to be acknowledged by the state. On an individual level, this mission is mostly pursued through the attempted access to new resources, as in the case of migration. On a mass level, though, the only way to challenge one's own production as surplus is through persistent and collective interruptions of the existing power relations. This is the political demand of the Tunisian riots, which, once joined by the general strike, have turned into the Dignity revolution. As such, riots challenge recognition, and mostly its absence, by putting an end to the state's project of management of its peoples. In fact, "if the state's solution to the problem of crisis and surplus is prison—carceral management—the riot is a contest entered directly against this solution—*a counterproposal of unmanageability*" (Clover, 2016: 163, my emphasis).

A short-circuit brought to the continuity of manageability seems to be an accessible negotiation tool for those people for whom forms of protest such as strike are unavailable. In fact, the interruption of manageability is able to jam profit flows connected to the circulation and consumption of raw materials and commodities. Nevertheless, nowadays it can be argued that similar disruptions assist other forms of profit extraction, such as profit deriving from the increased usage of social media, for example, which is common during instances of unrest. Joshua Clover's point makes clear how a marginalized category of people—produced as underclass, "mob," surplus—employs the riot as oppositional, and how the "counterproposal of manageability" interrupts the surplus management or containment techniques operated by the state. In this sense, it is important to observe that even instances of struggles caught up in the "affirmation trap" are part of what builds up toward revolution, at least in light of the Tunisian revolution. The "affirmation trap" (Clover, 2016) indicates those cases in which laborers struggle to maintain their relationship with capital; namely, in which protests aim at keeping employment. This is mainly visible in the Tunisian example of the 2008 "Gafsa Intifada," when the unemployed started an uprising against the hiring processes, implicitly demanding to have a chance at being employed by the Tunisia Phosphate Gafsa Company. In cases of "affirmation trap," "capital and labour find themselves in collaboration to preserve capital's self-production, to preserve the labour relation along with the firm's viability. This provides near-absolute limits for bargaining. [. . .] Labour is locked into the position of affirming its own exploitation under the guise of survival" (Clover, 2016: 147).

Although Clover argues that "caught in the affirmation trap, labour ceases to be the antithesis of capital," in Tunisia, the "Gafsa Intifada" is largely recognized as the precursor of the 2010 revolution. From this perspective, the Tunisian experience shows that struggles caught up in the "affirmation trap" can also be part of a revolutionary development, especially after they are met with the state's repressive response, which increases their propagation.

In this sense, in relation to the examples so far listed, politics holds the important component of exposing mediality, the "being-into-language, the being-into-a-mean as an irreducible condition of human beings," since "politics is the sphere neither of an end in itself nor of means subordinated to an end; rather, it is the sphere of a pure mediality without end intended as the field of human action and of human thought" (Agamben, 2000: 117–18).

Agamben's focus on mediality without an end hints at the importance of political gestures—especially the ones springing out of anger—that seem to hold "no meaning." Furthermore, Thoburn expands the notion of the mediating gestures beyond human agents when he describes how mediators "have a catalytic capacity to carry, intensify, and diversify the interrogation" that is produced from within the conditions of oppression. This capacity to "carry, intensify, and diversify" is what was referred to when writing about the notion of mediation when focusing on its preservation of the dimension of the virtual of the social within the context of cultures and practices of resistance. In this context, "a mediator can be real, imaginary, animate, or inanimate—a person, an object, plants, animals, myths, a certain discourse, an image, a refrain, or a problem" (Deleuze, 1995: 125–27 in Thoburn, 2016).

So far, this section has attempted to sketch out my understanding of mediation as an agent of plurification as opposed to technologies of containment of dissent such as representation or modulation of affects. A special effort was put into imagining how these interactions unfold within the informational ecology of the Tunisian revolutionary period with regards to the ways of functioning of the contemporary informational culture. The focus of this section has been on mediation as a situated process, marked by a discontinuous and complex relationship with connectivity, whose dynamic articulation has been addressed in terms of topological rationality. Moreover, I have introduced the importance of the gesture and the notion of the body as a mediator of the political gesture, whose centrality will be further analyzed in the following section dealing with resonance.

The next section will take on the previously developed reflection around resistance as contagion and identify its limits while showing how it can be understood in a more politically sensible manner in terms of resonance.

5.3. CONTAGION VS. RESONANCE

This section addresses the question of how protests spread in the particular context of the 2010 Tunisian revolution and with regards to the struggles during its aftermath. There are two models that suggest different approaches to understanding how protests spread. On the one side, the patterns of propagation are read in terms of contagion or virality (Nunes, 2014). This approach, which I illustrated in chapter 2, has proven essential in order to open up a reflection on the aspect of circulation connected to the event. On the other side, there is the approach that considers the distribution of the protest gestures to be the result of patterns of resonance (here I will mainly draw from Clover, 2016).[21] The two approaches are not incompatible, but this section will focus on the latter because I argue that this critique of a certain paradigm of contagion can help unearth further dimensions of the way an event like the Tunisian revolution comes into being.

Naturally, in looking at the patterns of propagation of protests, one must also consider issues around phenomena such as solidarity, empathy, and the construction of alliances and coalitions.

I will discuss a form of synchronization of protests that touches upon groups of people who are subjected to a similar degree of disposability by the state or other molar power systems such as the border system. I call this type of synchronization "resonance." The term refers to the way cultures and practices of struggle reverberate within the circulation of actions of disruption.

There are two preliminary assumptions that this section is based on: one traces the limits of the impact of connectedness; the second reaffirms the centrality of the body. First of all, connectedness *does not* equal empathy. As Fernández has pointed out, commenting on technological optimism "at the opening of this decade, prominent electronic media artists contended that electronic communication would help facilitate global peace as the exchange of text, sound, and image among virtual strangers would increase human empathy and understanding" (Fernández, 1999: 60).

On the contrary, based on my definition of resonance, whether connectedness, digital or otherwise, is present or not, the relation between different resistant communities is not based on an "exchange between strangers," but on a certain degree of commonality with regards to the frames of experiencing and responding to abusive forms of power.

The second assumption posits that when engaging in forms of support and solidarity, there is a centrality of the body and of the availability to alter the distribution of risk. The Egyptian Mosireen collective has articulated this idea very poignantly in their "Revolution Triptych" (Mosireen, 2014) when speaking to the way political solidarity chains are formed around the circulation of images of abuse:

> If an image does not provoke you, is it a continuation of the system you are trying to overthrow? An extension of it? The martyr doesn't want your sympathy. The martyr wants you to overthrow the system.
>
> The image that only seeks your pity only perpetuates the industrial cycle of morbid titillation. People, in this world that has been built, in this cycle, can now suffer from "compassion fatigue."
>
> F*** awareness.
>
> We do not ask for your charity, we do not ask for your prayers, or your thoughts or your words but your bodies. We do not ask for your martyrdom, we ask for your bodies on the streets of your cities, we ask for your ideas and your energy.
>
> We ask for your resistance. (Mosireen, 2014)

In some way, what needs to be achieved is a union between the aesthetic level of coordination—intended in an etymological sense, as to perceive, to openly see, to manifest, drawing from the Greek *aisthanomai*—αἰσθάνομαι—and the level of suffering, of grief—drawing from the Greek *pathos*—πάθος. This union of publicly seeing and suffering *together* (therefore *syn-aisthesis + syn-pathos*) must take into account the patterns of mimetic communication at a distance, intended as "corporally based forms of imitation, both voluntary and involuntary" (Gibbs, 2010: 186 in Blackman, 2012: 8). By this, I mean that mimetism runs along the lines of resonance both in terms of replicating patterns of abuse, not only patterns of resistance.[22]

One of my most important references for this research has been the work of Rodrigo Nunes. Here, however, I would like to reflect further on the way he has employed the ideas of contagion and virality in terms of the spread of protests in 2011. In that context, he has tied the idea of event to the idea of contagion, arguing for the event as "a process of contagion" that "spreads and replicates at once information—words, images, narratives, actions, etc.—and the *affective charges* that travel with it" (Nunes, 2014: 21–22). Nunes has further developed this approach with the help of notions such as the "structural germ" (drawing from Gilbert Simondon, 2005: 549 in Idem: 49) and the "vanguard-function" (drawing from Gabriel Tarde in Deleuze and Guattari, 2004: 264 in Idem: 52).

While I recognize the absolute relevance of these ideas since they helped me understand the broad dimension of circulation of cultures and practices of resistance, I am concerned that a focus on contagion and virality might occlude the political motivation behind these protests. In this sense, I draw from Firoze Manji's critique of the framework of contagion, when he says that

> while the media sought to portray this as some form of contagious disease, the reality was that the dispossessed across the continent and beyond recognized in the anger and demands of the Tunisians and Egyptians their own demand to reclaim their own dignity, and the aspirations of their own desires. They *recognized immediately the common experience* of the decades of neoliberalism that had impoverished them. (Manji and Sokari, 2012: 10, my emphasis)

The limit of the contagion framework is that it suggests a mobility of practices untied from the participants' intentionality. It could be willingly employed in a manner as to obliterate any reference to specific subjectivities. But this case study is mainly concerned with showing the complex texture of interactions between different specific groups that animate the event. Also, it somehow overshadows how the base of the connection of struggles lies within forms of historical and man-made inequality, rather than within mere communication. The same information of the repression of a riot will be received in a different manner depending on whether the receivers consider themselves part of the group that has been targeted. In this sense, the circulation of a piece of information is not enough to spread a riot.[23] A certain type of intensely embodied recognition of an experience—for example, of the abuse lived by Bouazizi—and the organization of a riot in response to this experience both run along a community infrastructure built upon a shared condition of marginalization. The recomposition lies within the shared experience of everyday precariousness and also within the common, restless *course à el khobza*, the "race for bread." In other words, what I am suggesting is that the *affective charges* that Nunes refers to are not the same for all the receivers.

Moreover, this reflection is influenced by the way the geography of protests in Tunisia unfolded in December 2010 after the self-immolation of Mohamed Bouazizi in Sidi Bouzid, as opposed to January 2016, after the suicide of Ridha Yahyaoui on an electricity pillar in Kasserine. Both gestures—carried out by Mohamed and Ridha—have intensively rippled through the volatile system of the "two Tunisias." Yet twice, the riots generated by the two suicidal gestures did not *spread by contamination, but by resonance*, because, as Clover observes, "riot goes looking for surplus populations, and these are its basis for expansion" although "this is not to deny the agency of rioters" (Clover, 2016: 154). Just like information, riot "propagates by autonomously finding the lines of least resistance" (drawing from Terranova, 2004: 65), usually determined by how well people resonate with its signal. In this sense, resonance can be read in terms of interference patterns and connected to the way the echo propagates through the emptiness between surfaces. As "interference pattern arises where the sound wave intersects with itself," "resonance can be seen as converting distance, or extension, into intensity," therefore, transforming distance in common affect by means of riot and protest. In this sense, "it is a qualitative transformation of distance into an immediacy of self-relation" (Massumi, 2002: 14). Furthermore, resonance signals the switch from competition or indifference between certain groups to cooperation and coordination between those same groups. And because information has the potential to "amplify or inhibit the emergence of commonalities and antagonisms," the space of commonality is marked by the formation of a "public as counter-weapon," which makes it possible for local responses to oppression to be shared across distant spaces, creating a sort of live archive of tactics and languages. The public I am referring to is the one recomposed by the act of witnessing the event, which inhabits a virtual space that hypothetically "multiplies the chances of re-invention of possible shared worlds" (Terranova, 2004: 2; Terranova, 2007: 140–42). Maybe the public as "event of possibility" and a "starting point for an affirmative activity" (Ibidem) is one of the lines of flight that Deleuze invokes when he says: "There is no need to ask which is the toughest or most tolerable regime, for it's within each of them that liberating and enslaving forces confront each other. [. . .] There is no need to fear or hope, but only to look for *new weapons*" (Deleuze, 1990).

Resonance interrupts the pattern of competition and opposes an alliance-based politics to the hegemonic attempts linked to *divide et impera* strategies of fragmentation and isolation, promoted through the production of internal conflicts such as "ethnic" conflicts, sectarianism, or "war on the poor." In this sense, it can be argued that resonance questions the Malthusian functioning of the "selfish gene as a technique of capture of value."

> The selfish gene is the subjectifying function that turns a multitude into an assemblage of isolated individuals. [. . .] Selfishness closes the open space of a multitude down to a hole of subjectification. The selfish gene is a simple diagram of the apparatuses of subjectification that the abstract machine of soft control distributes and perpetuates not so much among molecules as among collectivities. (Terranova, 2004: 126)

In addition to interrupting the functions of soft control, resonance is powered by a certain memory or trace of an embodied experience. To give an example, the suicide of Mohamed or Ridha didn't represent "the breaking point" for *all* Tunisian citizens, but just for some particular categories of Tunisians. In this sense, the patterns of reception such as the patterns of production of political gestures come from within particular receptacles of experience. "The poetics of sense memory involves not so much speaking of but *speaking out of* a particular memory of experience—in other words, speaking from the body sustaining sensation" (Bennett, 2000 in Munster, 2001). This is why it can be argued that the features of the contemporary riot connect dots crossing the globe, from Clichy-sous-Bois to Tottenham and Baltimore (as Clover suggests) including Sidi Bouzid, Kasserine, and the suburbs of Tunis. Along these lines, "the riot is the form of collective action that features participants with no necessary kinship but their dispossession" (Clover, 2016: 16). Thus, "the global *classes dangereuses* are united not by their role as producers but by their relation to state violence. In this is to be found the basis of the surplus rebellion and of its form, which must exceed the logic of recognition and negotiation" (Idem: 157).

In this sense, from an analytical standpoint focused on the American setting, Clover makes it clear that, in his understanding, the surplus is not synonymous with race and that it includes the diaspora. On another occasion, he underlines the pioneering function of what he calls the "expanded proletariat"; namely, a category including "the women, children, peasantry, aged people and the unemployed" (Idem: 169–70, 189).

In conclusion, the patterns of resonance are based on the commonality of shared experience. Some important aspects of this common experience are (1) people sharing the same spatiality; (2) people sharing the same sense of temporality; and (3) people sharing the same unruly mobility practices. These are the terrains out of which the politics of events such as the Tunisian revolution and its aftermath are born.

First of all, in terms of commonality of spatiality, it is the urban ghetto, the "internal colony," that is the source of a shared experience since it cements the element of kinship. It can be argued that in the Tunisian case, the life in the poor suburb, the *houma* (plural *hwem*), is what rearticulates a sense of class belonging. As Griziotti points out regarding the proletarian class composition in Italy, "being forced to spend the largest part of the day together in the same physical space and the rest of the day in the typical neighbourhoods next to the factory is an important element of the origin of the sense of class belonging" (Griziotti, 2016: 161, my translation).

In the same way, the Tunisian under- and unemployed spend most of their time in the poor suburbs struggling for subsistence. This permanence in space, as Olfa Lamloum observes, ties the group cohesion (*asabiyya*) to the territory of the neighborhood, especially in absence of a professional occupation, other than the *course à el khobza*. Moreover, if the *coup d'état* can be seen as "a temporary departure from laws and legality (that) goes beyond ordinary law" or an "irruptive assertion of *raison d'état*," as the visibilization of a power structure, then the ghetto is the *spatialization* of that same structure (Foucault, 2007: 261, 264). This is a space where power is always absolute and where the conflict with the state apparatus is always open. In this sense, this form of "internal colonialism" is intended as a "geographically-based pattern of subordination of a differentiated population, located within a dominant power or country" (Pinderhughes, 2011: 236 in Cowen and Lewis, 2016), with the state's police operating "like an army of occupation" protecting the interests of outside exploiters and maintaining the domination over the ghetto by the central metropolitan power structure" (Blauner, 1969: 404–5 in Cowen and Lewis, 2016). In this setting, "urbanization has supplanted industrialization as the engine of capital accumulation on a world scale" (drawing from Lefebvre, 2003 in Cowen and Lewis, 2016).

Second, in terms of the sense of shared temporality, it has already been argued that the temporality of the *houma* oscillates between existential anxiety and panic related to the *course à el khobza* of informalized labor and the suspension of time, in an eternally depressing time of waiting: waiting for the chance to earn something, waiting for a job, waiting for an answer on one's asylum claim. This suspension is described in the hip-hop anthem of the *houma*, "Houmani": "We wake up late; we never see the time passing / I don't even have a clock / Here the atmosphere is suffocating" (Hamzaoui and Kafon, 2013). The damage inflicted by the imposition of a constantly suspended temporality, one that drastically reduces the power to act of the people—the *houmani*, the asylum seekers—shows a repeated weaponization of the waiting time employed as a strategy of management (Povinelli, 2011). In this sense, it is suggestive to see how central this form of abuse is in the work of the artists of the suburbs (such as the rappers I've quoted or street artists).

Third, and most important, resonance runs easier across lines of communalities in terms of unruly mobility practices. For the case of the Tunisian revolution, I believe that the most important mobility practice was the one from the rural toward the suburban setting, motivated by the historical and progressive dispossession and isolation of the rural environment. As I discussed in the previous chapter, this occurred during the colonial state first and the post-independence state later; increasingly so after the '80s when the neoliberal "structural adjustments" were implemented under pressure from international financial institutions such as the World Bank and the International Monetary Fund. From the initial position of the suburban,[24] the location of most of the urbanized informal labor, which pioneered the revolution, Tunisians have moved—mostly illegally—following at least three directions: (1) toward the center of the richer cities, either to work or to protest; (2) toward Europe; and (3) toward the Islamic militancy fronts in Syria and Iraq.

In this sense, an inhabitant of the poor neighborhoods, a *houmani*, would cross the border between the ghetto and the city, usually heavily policed. Sometimes the same person would cross the border between the Tunisian city and Europe, being caught in the containment technologies of the hotspot or the detention centers at the gates of Europe. If the person were able to continue their mobility plan, they could then reach the center of European cities, as in the case of the Tunisians protesting in the center of Paris. But that person would then only end up in the same ghetto-dimension, this time of European cities, unless this person got arrested, deported, or decided to go back home. As for the mobility practices that take Tunisians toward the Islamic militancy fronts in the East, the routes depend uniquely on the traveler's status and economic resources. In order to reach Syria, the "foreign fighters" might either reach Turkey by airplane, reach it by sea or air from Libya, or fly toward Turkey from a third country.

In these examples, borders assume a topological character in the sense that they become "parameters that enable the channelling of flows and provide coordinates within which flows can be joined or segmented, connected or disconnected" (Lury et al., 2012: 11). All the while, the *refugee*, as subject of mobility, becomes "the only thinkable figure of our time and the only category in which one may see today—at least until the process of dissolution of the nation state and of its sovereignty has achieved full completion—the forms and limits of a coming political community" (Agamben, 2000: 16).

CONCLUSION

This final chapter dealt with one of the most complex aspects of the Tunisian revolution, namely the aspect of communication around, about, and from within the folds of the event.

This aspect is problematic because of the thick stratum of recurrent technofetishism, mostly supported by the idea of social media "facilitating" the revolutionary transformation. I have repeatedly shown, in chapter 1 and in the present chapter, how this assumption is animated by Orientalism and how detrimental it is if one wants to flesh out the sophisticated articulation of subjects and drives at work within this event. Starting from this point of rejection of technofetishism or techno-optimism, this chapter looked deeper into the infrastructures of circulation of signs and affects that lie in between and alongside the networks of corporate and state communication. In this sense, I have drawn upon relevant reflections within media studies, yet always tried to keep the reflection grounded around the questions that my case study has raised.

Many of this chapter's proposals—namely, the reflections around mediation and resonance—derive directly from the architecture of the event but are also intended to go beyond it.

My notion of mediation emerges (1) out of a critique of technofetishism and (2) as a question of what proliferates alongside the grand narratives of social and state media, which I label as instances of representation. With this, I attempt to account for the highly productive level of communication populated by counter-knowledges able to explain the circulation and propagation of cultures of resistance during and after the revolution. In addition, mediation signals the existence of additional infrastructures operating alongside the digital ones, in those cases in which access to connectivity is poor.

Furthermore, resonance and alliance are my proposals as to that which directly propagated the revolutionary climax. Resonance, rather than contagion, I argue, is what allowed riots to spread in Tunisia, based on a process of recognition that occurs between different oppressed groups, and that is grounded upon a commonality of temporality, inhabited space, and practices of mobility. Taking the propagation a step forward, alliance enacts the synchronization between the category that ignited the protests—the suburban poor—and the more established workers: more specifically, the unionized workforce. Their alignment of the general strike with the protests is what transformed a national network of riots into a revolution.

Conclusion

> The passage from the micro to the macro, from the local to the global must not be done through abstraction, universalization or totalization, but rather through the capacity to keep together and progressively assemble networks and patchworks.
>
> —Maurizio Lazzarato, *La politica dell'evento*, 2004

> The painter does not paint on an empty canvas, and neither does the writer write on a blank page; but the page or canvas is already so covered with preexisting, pre-established clichés that it is first necessary to erase, to clean, to flatten, even to shred, so as to let in a breath of air from the chaos that brings us the vision.
>
> —Gilles Deleuze and Félix Guattari, *What Is Philosophy?*, 1991

> Whether they are candidates for illegal emigration, self-immolation, hunger strike or for being recruited by Daesh, all of them repeat united: "We are already dead." The body becomes the last battlefield of resistance to the physical and symbolical violence that they are subjected to. And to the absence of hope.
>
> —Hela Yousfi, *Tunisian activist*[1]

The Tunisian revolution has raised a question. Not answering it won't make it go away. Emigration and its capture within forms of "corporate terrorism," such as the Islamic militancy fronts in Syria and Iraq, will not manage to break the futurity of this question, as has been proven by the ongoing social unrest in Tunisia. The 2010–2011 wave of protests has successfully challenged the long-standing entanglement between state and corporate interests while confronting their most taxing manifestations: dispossession and state violence. In this confrontation, people's bodies, often far removed from the much-heralded social media infrastructure, were the crucial mediators of both despair and insurgent knowledges.

This research was born out of the need to supersede certain approaches toward what happened in Tunisia in 2011. This endeavor is rooted in frustration about the way in which the 1989 Romanian revolution was similarly first praised and later ridiculed; used as confirmation of the incontestable political superiority of the West or fetishized in the way that historical revolutions such as the French or Russian revolutions have been. This is why I argued for an interruption of the recognition-based knowledge practice (described in chapter 2) focused on identifying and applying traditional references in terms of what revolutions, in particular, and transformative politics, in general, should look like. In this sense, prescriptive politics is no longer acceptable. I, therefore, underlined this event's singularity: first, in terms of its *irreducible* specificity; second, in terms of it being a trace of a highly risky process of singularization or subjectivation that deserved to be acknowledged.

Moreover, it is not only the Orientalization of the Romanian revolution that motivated this engagement with the Tunisian event. In fact, there are three main and very entrenched clichés that this research is born against, which have been addressed in a variety of ways. These clichés worked like well-masked traps since even some of the most radical among this event's observers didn't manage to avoid them.

The first cliché is the Orientalism of the twenty-first century, enforced by post-9/11 Islamophobia and the mobilization of fear connected to the "Arab" and "Muslim" world in light of the attacks that occurred in Europe and of the media campaign run by the Islamic militancy outlets. It is not enough to simply contextualize the current geopolitical setting, as Edward Said had marvelously done in the 1970s. Beyond the interests in fossil fuels, monopolies, cheap labor, and geo-strategic alliances, the Western distrust toward the Arab and Muslim world, expressed in the paradigm of Arab exceptionalism, is grounded in the implicit sense of superiority, hence the urgency to deconstruct it.

The second cliché follows from the first; it is the way in which instances of political "progress" outside the West need to be somehow attributed to Western interventions, and this explains the fetishist focus on social media in relation to the Arab revolutions, alluded to as an agent of "democratization." In this sense, it is important to clarify, as I briefly mentioned in chapter 5, that the Tunisian case shows how technology and the techno-social assemblage work toward mediating the struggle. What I mean is that I am not dismissing the importance of this assemblage, and I am acknowledging how it has worked creatively around scarcity and containment. What I critique is rather a focus on a particular usage of technology; namely, the employment of social media by a particular category of people, the middle class, the bloggers, the artists, whose actions are used to enforce the exclusionary and flattening narrative of the Arab Spring.

Finally, at a deeper level—one that transcends the boundaries between the West and the rest, or maybe at a level that reveals how these boundaries have been internalized—the main cliché this work intends to oppose is that of prescriptive politics and of its teleology. According to this framework, various instances of collective and organized action are deemed more or less sufficient or complete depending on the presence or absence of practices, languages, and proposals in tune with certain expectations.

In this sense, this work advocates for the highly unpredictable, risky, and creative nature of politics, intended less as stepping inside the expectations of an external observer and more like "tracing paths between impossibilities" (Thoburn, 2003: 19).

Drawing from Lazzarato's warning, "Those who hold predetermined answers, miss the event," I tried to listen and develop one way to inhabit and think through this event while being aware that I am part of it (Lazzarato, 2004: 13). In fact, the Tunisian revolution represented a highly dense "exemplary terrain" of how different practices of resistance and transformative politics unfold in the contemporary (Scott, 2014).

In this sense, this research engages with the topic of the "Arab Spring," which is used as an entry point for different reflections. The term refers to the revolutions that toppled the governments in Tunisia and Egypt in 2011, but it also refers to a broad series of protests in other countries, such as Yemen, Syria, Libya, Bahrain, Morocco, and on the rest of the African continent. This massive event has been considered a significant—yet temporary— "democratic" update for the "Arab" world, especially in light of the distrust connected to post-9/11 Islamophobia. These revolutions allegedly aimed to topple their dictatorships and establish Western-like liberal democracy centered on freedom of expression and economic prosperity. Nevertheless, the first elections put Islam-oriented parties in power—Ennahda in Tunisia and the Muslim Brotherhood in Egypt—and after 2011 most of the countries touched by the Arab Spring started experiencing "terrorist" attacks, bloody internal conflicts, or full-blown civil wars. These phenomena dampened the initial Western enthusiasm for the event and reinstated the convictions and ideas promoted by the paradigm of Arab exceptionalism.

There are five main debates that this work makes a contribution to. First is the debate around the political relevance and internal organization of the "Arab Spring" in terms of which elements are noteworthy of inspiring political practices across the East-West divide, be it the use of technology or the leaderless forms of organization.

Second, there is a difference in conceiving of instances of interruption of the traditional power relations, which opposes a dialectical view—conveyed by authors such as Alain Badiou and implicit in the notion of resistance—to a view devoted to seeing the continuous and its modulations—promoted by Deleuze's understanding of the event.

Third, my case study is also a field of debate, which regards the hypotheses around the causes, aims, and actors of the revolution, with a particular focus on the protagonism of artists and bloggers, as well as on the relevance of the general trade union, the UGTT.

Fourth, there is an interrogation of the modalities of propagation of protest, which is a particularly popular question that arose from the 2011 protests around the world. Some consider contagion to be the principle of propagation, while others stress the importance of the "structural similarities" (Manji and Sokari, 2012).

Finally, this research addresses the debate around class composition and political subjectivity in the twenty-first century. Who is a significant political subject today? Is it the working class, the "Lumpenprecariat," the refugee, or the "mob"? There are several hypotheses around how the actor of the Tunisian revolution is to be classified in terms of class belonging. But it is also a challenge to reflect on how class is articulated, if ever, with the increasing disappearance of formal employment and the enforcement of border imperialism.

This work argues that the Arab Spring is a discursive configuration aimed to make an instance of dissent more familiar and less threatening to Western observers while silencing the responsibilities of the West. An in-depth analysis of the case study is necessary because one of the limits of this "domination narrative" is precisely its generalization (Rizk, 2014). Therefore, focusing on the Tunisian revolution, what emerges is that the 2011 disruptive movement is made of both moments of rupture—which I list as events of resistance—and of significant roots and ramifications in space and time, which I drew a diagram of with the help of a historical overview of struggles before and after 2011. In other words, the revolutionary assemblage mobilizes both moments of discontinuity *and* of continuity. In terms of moments of discontinuity, instances of necroresistance function as aggregating gestures, as mediators of a minor politics emerging out of the constraints of disenfranchisement, in Tunisia as well as abroad (Bargu, 2015). Starting from the Tunisian setting, I chose to bring together the lineage of resistance traced by the Imazighen and the *fellaga* to the contemporary figures of the inhabitants of the suburb, the *houmani*, while acknowledging the challenge posed by the triad figure of the revolutionary, the "undocumented" migrant, and the Islamic militant. Furthermore, I argued that gestures of resistance are echoed by resonance rather than contagion, and that this synchronization is based on the commonality of the experience of dispossession and state violence (Clover, 2016). In addition, against instances of hegemonic representation and divisive modulation of affects, I proposed mediation as a form of transmission of counter-knowledges, focused on preserving rather than containing the virtual dimension of dissent. Forms of minor composition—both minor art and minor politics—are crucial for this research because they allow one to see the inspiring examples of art and politics that unfolded beyond representation.

In chapter 1, I deconstructed the narrative of the "Arab Spring" and showed how it conveyed a series of stereotypical assumptions around the "Arab" world. Since some activists have even called it a "domination narrative," I labeled it as a "discursive configuration" and fleshed out its functioning. Beginning this work in this way was crucial because it constituted an immediate example of the performativity of ways of reading events of resistance. In this sense, I drew from the work of Michel Foucault in Iran and of Guattari in Brazil in order to receive inspiration on how revolutionary events can be approached in a way that is not based on representation but on a responsible receptivity.

In chapter 2, I addressed one of the main methodological conundrums of this work, initiating a reflection on the debate between theories of the event and theories of resistance. Drawing from the work of Badiou and Deleuze on the notion of event, I integrated the valuable work of Claudia Aradau, Lazzarato, and Rodrigo Nunes in order to build a concept of the event of resistance able to account for the importance of both continuity and discontinuity.

In chapter 3, I put to work the notion of the "event of resistance," mainly drawn from Aradau's work, and employed a diagrammatic methodology while tracing a different snapshot of the Tunisian revolution, one based on flows of struggles. I identified four crucial categories—the underclass, the migrants, the refugees, and the Islamic militants—and reflected on the intersection of their practices of mobility. The triadic figure of the revolutionary-migrant-Islamic militant also allowed me to continue working on the class composition of the revolutionary subject, this time employing Aradau and Jef Huysmans's revisited understanding of "mob."

In chapter 4, I engaged with the genealogy of the different waves of dispossession and resistance that touched upon the Tunisian territory: from the colonial French Protectorate defeated by the *fellaga*, to the modern-day violence of the neoliberalized oligarchy challenged by the *houmani*, before and after the revolutionary climax. Moreover, this chapter looked into the practice of the Ahl Al Kahf collective in more depth, showing how its commitment and remarkable methods of interaction have articulated forms of minor art within and beyond the national borders.

Finally, in chapter 5, I addressed issues around communication and propagation of protests. Against the common approach of technofetishism, I argued that the tactical information functional to resistance traveled across a diversified infrastructure, which held a discontinuous and complex relationship with technology and connectivity. I suggested mediation as a notion in order to imagine what lies alongside hegemonic representation instances and attempts to harness affects in order to extract value. Furthermore, this chapter laid out my understanding of propagation of the protests in terms of resonance.

As Lazzarato points out, the mode of the revolution is the problematic; that of raising questions rather than providing answers. The Tunisian revolution starts off as a question around colonial legacies and neoliberalized oligarchies and ends up touching the rotten heart of the European neoliberalism when the *harraga* claim in Paris, "We made the democratic revolution, we are here to help you do the same" (*Archives du Jura Libertaire*, 2011). The Tunisian revolutionaries claim freedom, justice, and democracy from within a space in which all of them are systematically denied. They also show that advancing this claim from within a liminal position can prove deadly.

Therefore, this event indicates where transformative politics begins and what its price is for the ones who enact it. These are some of the nuances that I tried to touch upon by utilizing a vast array of terms in order to engage with the subject of the Tunisian revolution. Each of the terms refers to a particular feature of this group of people. *Underclass* was first used in order to start the reflection on the category of those who find themselves outside the working class in terms of formal labor. Aradau and Huysmans's revisited *mob* accounted for the centrality of mobility practices, for the criminalization of these protesters, and, more importantly, for how they were fearlessly stretching the margins of the political. The idea of *vanguard* emerged as a direct consequence of the 2016 Kasserine paradox in the aftermath of the beginning of the Islamic militancy phenomenon. Joshua Clover's concept of *surplus* population resonated with Marx's notion of a reserve army and made visible the contemporary conflicts between capital and labor through the lens of the struggles around production vis-à-vis the struggles around circulation, such as the riot.

Ultimately, this work sets out to reflect on how contemporary examples of rupture—such as the Tunisian revolution—challenge and expand paradigms of understanding political processes. This is why I start by thinking different approaches to discontinuity together, illustrated by the theories around event and resistance that I engage with in chapter 2. Nunes's work (Nunes,

2013) is a crucial contribution that helps me think of the event of resistance in terms of contagion, as a "glitch," and as a "germ of action" (or an instance of "proto-subjectivation," as Lazzarato would call it [Lazzarato, 2014: 219]). This approach accounts for the modalities of transformative politics within the global unevenly hyper-mediated semiosphere, but it also stimulated me to look deeper into how cultures and practices of resistance propagated across big distance, which was the focus of the first two sections of chapter 5. Eventually, though, I went beyond the concept of resistance as contagion in order to underline the importance of the embodied commonality of marginalization as a pre-condition for the propagation of dissent, referred to as resonance. Both mediation and resonance are notions that I developed thinking *through* the Tunisian revolution and the questions it raised. In a certain sense, these two notions overlap. In fact, they relate to the same event from two different angles, as do different terms, like underclass, "mob," and vanguard. Mediation is supposed to underline the existence of an anti-hegemonic mode of organization of meaning and affects, which is a situated declination of the techno-social assemblage and which is significantly animated by gestures of necroresistance (as the Tunisian case shows). Resonance, instead, speaks to the ground behind the aspect of propagation; it draws attention to the fact that gestures of necroresistance, for example, are met with further mobilization by *those* people who perceive a commonality with the subject of necroresistance. This commonality is based on a shared embodied experience of dispossession, containment, and social marginalization.

In terms of future developments, this work aims in three directions. First of all, it only marginally touched upon the question of value, in terms of the revolutionary "transvaluation" and of how new values can be perpetuated. Moreover, the Tunisian revolutionaries, the *harraga*, and the refugees struggling at Choucha actively challenged the way their lives were valued to the point of weaponizing their vulnerability and of presenting us with a "materialist theory of being [. . .] that carries with it the potential for political resistance to the violence of dispossession" (Bhandar, 2011: 242).

Along these lines, more work is needed around examples of collective action and organization from within police state–type articulations, whether located in the "internal colony" of the metropolitan ghetto or, more broadly, in the increasingly militarized societies. In addition, this reflection must account for the different ways of weaving together discipline and control in the contemporary setting marked by the informational culture.

Finally, more needs to be said about strategizing new modalities of recomposition—whether around Tiziana Terranova's "formation of publics as counter-weapons" or around cross-class alliances. Beyond molar models of identity formation and beyond a politics based on equivalence, the future, as the Tunisian revolution teaches, challenges us to build relations—in other words, to "keep together and progressively assemble networks and patchworks" (Lazzarato, 2004: 137).

> What? If.
> Trust was built
> Trust was earned
> New ways and worlds assembled (?)
> Because there is nowhere else to go
> We need fugitives of the spirit
> And the heart and the mind.
>
> —Deborah Cowen, "What? If." *[Infrastructures for the Future]*[2]

Notes

INTRODUCTION

1. This term should always be intended as contested in this thesis, yet on some occasions, I will not use scare quotes in order to render the reading more fluid.

2. Some selected references include Achcar, 2013; Al-Zubaidi & Cassel, 2013; Amin, 2012; Beinin & Vairel, 2013; Castells, 2012; Dabashi, 2008; Garelli et al., 2013; Gerbaudo, 2012; Gerges, 2014; Ghonim, 2012; Haddad et al., 2012; Hanieh, 2013; Kilani, 2014; Lynch, 2012; Macchi, 2012; Mason, 2012; Massarelli, 2012; Noueihed & Warren, 2012; Ramadan, 2012; Žižek, 2012.

3. Deleuze draws the concept of virtual from Henri Bergson's understanding of duration. The "virtual" is not opposed to the "real," but to the "actual," whereas the real is opposed to the "possible" (Deleuze, 1966: 96–98). The virtual is constituted by a multiplicity of potentials, and it is "inseparable from the movement of its actualization" (Deleuze, 1966: 42–43, 81; Deleuze, 2002: 44).

4. My initial discussion of contagion will mainly draw from Nunes's work on the 2011 protests, *Organisation of the Organisationless* (Nunes, 2014), in which he reflects on how "affective charges" become contagious in the context of political mobilization, leading to mass movements in the absence of mass organization.

5. I am here specifically referring to the episode that occurred on November 16, 2015, when the sixteen-year-old shepherd Mabrouk Soltani was beheaded by Islamic militants who were training close to his village, allegedly because he refused to hand his sheep to them (Marzouk, 2015). Two years later, his brother, who had returned to his village leaving his job on a construction site in Sfax to support his mother, was also kidnapped and beheaded by the militants of the Islamic State as a punishment for his lack of allegiance toward the organization (AFP, 2017).

6. Before the start of its Arabization in the seventh century AD, Tunisia—as much of North Africa—was inhabited by indigenous nomadic peoples that called themselves Amazigh (Tamazigh for the women, and Imazighen for the plural). They

speak the Amazigh language and worship the cult of the sun and moon. Non-Amazigh people call them Berbers.

7. Ahl Al Kahf, literally "the people underground," is a prolific collective of artists who have operated from Tunis between 2011 and 2013, producing street art that would promote the messages of the revolution and who have engaged in a tireless social critique in the post-revolution period. Their work has been of crucial inspiration for this research, and I will discuss their practice in chapter 4.

8. On January 16, 2016, twenty-eight-year-old Ridha Yahyaoui committed suicide on a light pillar protesting in front of the Kasserine governorate against the practice of blacklisting former activists from the public employment lists. His gesture originated extensive protests all over Tunisia (Alba Rico, 2016b; Sana, 2016).

CHAPTER 1

1. Ahl Al Kahf, literally "the people underground," is an art collective born in 2011 in Tunis, engaged in street art practices until 2013, and whose works I will be drawing from throughout this research. I will specifically focus on their practice in section 4.2. *The Ahl Al Kahf Collective: The Exiled Believers and the Seeds of Revolution*.

2. I am here using parentheses for two main reasons. First, there are colonial reasons behind the delimitation of the "Arab" space from the African continent. Therefore, choosing to call the 2011 wave of unrest "Arab" carries certain implications, while erasing the propagation of protests beyond the Suez Canal or the Sahara desert. Second, a focus on the "Arab" identity levels out the diversity of peoples that inhabit countries such as Tunisia. Most significantly, a focus on the "Arab" specificity does not account for the historically determinant discrimination and Arabization of the Amazigh peoples (also known as Berbers).

3. This aspect of temporality and of the processual nature of political transformation will also be addressed in the following section, in which I will discuss the stereotypical features of the "Arab Spring." Furthermore, I will attempt to engage with the processual character of the events through a diagrammatic practice in chapter 3.

4. In the contemporary Egyptian context that Giordani is looking at in her work, *inquilab* has developed its original meaning and is used now to refer to instances of "coup d'état" (Giordani, 2013).

5. Before the revolution, Tunisia was regarded as one of the "good examples" of the "Arab world," and gender discrimination was hardly debated in the Western public space. During the revolution, the mobilization of Tunisian women and girls didn't receive enough media attention, or was, on the contrary, thematized as exceptional. After the revolution and the electoral victory of the Islamists, increasing concerns about gender discrimination have become common in the Western discourse around gender in Tunisia. In this sense, there is an extensive literature, which explores the way gender has been strategic for the post-9/11 Orientalist paradigm (Delphy, 2015; Ghani & Fiske, 2017; Hasso & Salime, 2016; Hunt, 2006; Zayzafoon, 2005).

6. J. Cole and S. Cole have written, "That the female element in the Arab Spring has drawn so little comment in the West suggests that our narratives of, and preoccupations with, the Arab world—religion, fundamentalism, oil and Israel—have blinded us to the big social forces that are altering the lives of 300 million people" ("An Arab Spring for Women," *The Nation*, April 26, 2011).

7. I am here referring mainly to the importance of groups such as that of the Eleven Widows, active during the 2008 Gafsa Intifada, and to the enduring activism of the mothers of the Tunisian *desaparecidos* in the Mediterranean in 2011–2012, to name just two significant examples.

8. This "fear of Islamists," intended as a fertile soil for anti-Western terrorism, is particularly strong when it regards countries that, unlike Turkey or Saudi Arabia, are not declaredly aligned to the American foreign policies or commercial interests (Haddad et al., 2012: 44).

9. These brief historical observations are meant to only hint at the complexity of the history of Tunisian secularism to suggest why the 2011 protests can't simply be read in terms of secularism vs. Islam unless one is willing to engage with the past manifestations of secularism.

10. This stereotypical assumption sounds relevantly similar to other tropes of otherization, which have contributed to naturalize the production of conflict in non-Western spaces. I am here referring to the assumptions of conflictuality linked to the so-called Balkans or the African "tribal society," for example.

11. The literature taken into consideration in this section can only be a partial selection, as the work around the 2010–2011 events is constantly being updated and integrated by new inspiring lines of research.

12. El Mahdi, 2011, but also Hosni, 2014, and Rizk, 2014.

13. Mainly discussed in Gobe, 2010, but also in Achcar, 2013; Amin, 2012; Ayeb, 2011; Beinin & Vairel, 2013; Hanieh, 2013; Kilani, 2014; Missaoui & Khalfaoui, 2011.

14. In chapter 3, I will be discussing the relevance of the mobility of tens of thousands of Tunisians in the immediate aftermath of the revolutionary climax of January 14, starting with the same night after Ben Ali's flight to Saudi Arabia.

15. In chapter 5, I will be reflecting on how a notion of singularity can be thought beyond the representation that the event has received in mainstream global corporate and local state media. By singularity, I seek to allow the space of reflection on the specificity of the Tunisian event, free from categories and expectations emitted by the West.

16. A similar previous example of this type of approach was the European Leftist *intelligentsia*'s dismissal of the 1979 Iranian revolution. On that occasion, Michel Foucault engaged courageously with the events in his 1979 *Le Monde* article "Useless to Revolt?" fundamentally raising a crucial issue for this research; namely, how does one relate to practices of politics that are not one's own? (also discussed in Tazzioli, 2013a, and more recently in Ghamari-Tabrizi, 2016).

17. This line of research will be further developed in chapter 2, "The Event of Resistance and Its Capture," in which I reflect on different philosophical conceptions around the notion of rupture, discontinuity, and interruption symbolized by the con-

cept of the event. While doing this, I will keep in mind the Tunisian revolution as a starting point of a series of research questions around temporalities of transformation.

18. This line of research will be further developed in chapter 2, "The Event of Resistance and Its Capture," in which I reflect on different philosophical conceptions around the notion of rupture, discontinuity, and interruption symbolized by the concept of the event. While doing this, I will keep in mind the Tunisian revolution as a starting point of a series of research questions around temporalities of transformation.

19. This is not at all unproblematic in the Western world either.

20. Although I am aware how important this aspect of the mobilization is, this research won't specifically focus on the molecular transformations brought into being by the revolutionary process, except for the description of the importance of the Kasbah occupations, addressed in chapter 3.

21. I am arguing that the Tunisian revolution cannot be limited to being recognized by its Western observers. Instead, space must be made for its unfamiliarity to exist and be embraced. Throughout this research, recognition will be addressed in different capacities: (1) in terms of processes of recognition imposed upon potentially unfamiliar events as a mechanism of containment (as in the "Facebook revolution" narrative); (2) in political terms, along the lines of the Hegelian theorization; and (3) as stemming out of the critique of recognition politics, focusing on processes of recognition between different equally oppressed categories. This capacity is something like an inter-subaltern recognition (for lack of a better term), which I will refer to in terms of resonance in chapter 5.

CHAPTER 2

1. As I state in the introduction, my understanding of singularity uses Guattari's work as a starting point (Guattari, 1986) in order to develop it as a concept that acknowledges (1) an event's irreducible originality and (2) its relevance as a trace of singularization or subjectivation as an example of transformative politics.

2. I choose to use the term "immunitary" uniquely because of the centrality of the idea of "germ" in Nunes (2013) and that of microbe in the work of Parisi and Goodman (2005).

3. While in this chapter I will develop the reflection around the notion of contagion, in connection to the event, later on, in chapter 5, I will suggest how this frame can go beyond a mere focus on contagion, introducing the notion of resonance as an explanation for the way forms of protest spread across different communities.

4. The concept of hegemony theorized by the Italian political theorist Antonio Gramsci generally refers to "the ways in which a governing power wins consent to its rule from those it subjugates" (Eagleton, 1991).

5. Despite problematizing the term "revolution," I will still refer to the events as the "Tunisian revolution." As I have mentioned in the first chapter, I critique the state use of the term, but respect its use when it comes from the participants to the events. With this term, I refer not only to the more violent weeks of protests (between December 2010 and January 2011) but also to the significant events before and after

that period, which have involved relevant moments of mobilization, as I illustrate in the following chapters.

6. In this sense, I use the term "event" as an indication of the general situation that I am engaging with—as another way of referring to the Tunisian revolution—as opposed to the expression "network of events of resistance," which I develop in order to account for a more complex level of the same phenomenon, as if it were a more detailed snapshot of the Tunisian revolution.

7. Caygill also underlines the necessary connection between the experience and the reflection around resistance, pointing out that "while resistance has continuously to be reinvented, its history of inventions demands philosophical reflection" (Caygill, 2013: 6).

8. I will be referring to this political subjectivity as "underclass" or "mob" in the following chapter and carry on the reflection on the appropriate terminology until chapter 5.

9. In the next chapters, I will reflect further on these practices of communication. In chapter 4, I will bring to attention the work of the Ahl Al Kahf street art collective and show how it has facilitated the propagation of political messages in Tunisia and beyond its borders. In chapter 5, I will focus on the counter-hegemonic organization of meaning but also affects to make sense of the circulation of cultures and practices of resistance across the Mediterranean after the revolution.

10. To give an example of how contagion and transversal alliances can differ in terms of intentionality, one can consider the relationship between the American Black Lives Matter (whose activity intensified in 2013) and the Palestinian resistance movements. The American movement can feel inspired and circulate or reinterpret images and symbols of the Palestinian resistance (which they easily relate to), but transversality is built when the movements intentionally meet (as has happened) and publicly declare their convergence. Precisely this aspect will be further discussed in chapter 5.

11. The anti-globalization movement, also known as the No Global movement, refers to a series of protests starting in the late '80s and continued until the '00s, aimed at exposing the economic, environmental, and social inequality produced by processes of globalization increasing the wealth gap between the global north and the global south. The movement is often associated with Seattle because it reached one of its peaks of participation and repression in the protests organized against the World Trade Organization meeting in Seattle in November of 1999.

12. I am aware and very inspired by the debate initiated by Deleuze on the comparison between his and Foucault's view over resistance, illustrated in the seminal article *Désir et plaisir* (Deleuze, 1994), in which he draws a parallel between his primacy of lines of flight and Foucault's primacy of resistance as the only thing that goes against the *dispositifs* (systems of power) (as discussed in Thoburn, 2003: 41). Yet this section will engage with a different set of debates around the notion of resistance.

13. Although, as many critiques to Deleuze have pointed out, desire doesn't necessarily involve the development of a politics of resistance, as such.

14. Especially in his last book, *Signs and Machines* (2014), Lazzarato is very careful in distinguishing between the plane of signification and cognition and the asignifying one, which informs, in his vision, instances of proto-subjectivation on a

political level, framed as an existential non-discursive affirmation. He explains that the moments of the interruption of dominant signification dynamics (such as strikes, riots, revolts) allow the articulation of political innovation. It can be argued that Lazzarato holds a significant suspicion toward the domain of the discursive, privileging the non-discursive one as the fertile ground for emancipation. I argue that both planes play a crucial role, starting with the moment defiance spreads like a virus, which I see in non-discursive terms, and ending up with the construction of narratives able to account for the development and outcomes of revolutionary ruptures, which is all about the way power relations interact with and produce discourses.

15. I am aware that the notion of resistance (inherently positing a dialectic articulation) doesn't fit with Deleuze's understanding of the event (in non-dialectical terms), yet this inquiry is intended to expand both the definition of "event" (as has been done in the previous section) and "resistance," drawing from the theorists who help build a more sensitive approach toward the singularity of the event under scrutiny.

16. In chapter 5, these same reflections will be developed more in-depth through the concept of resonance.

17. The concept of resistance as glitch, bug, or germ will be further discussed since it offers the possibility of addressing the modalities of capture of resistance. I have privileged this interpretation in biological terms because later on I will be looking at the strategies of capture of resistance in terms of immunitary response of the dominant regime.

18. In the case of the Tunisian revolution, this was visible when the dominant discourse went from ignoring the unrests to glorifying them once it became clear that no intervention could stop the process of transformation. What happened when the "Arab" revolutions exploded was an extremely visible reconfiguration of the signification regime. Mainstream Western media operated a shift in their discourse, suspending two crucial assumptions: that the Middle Eastern countries in general bred anti-Western "terrorists" and that Ben Ali's Tunisia, in particular, was a Western-like modern economy (the World Bank being the leading promoter of the "Tunisian miracle" narrative).

19. Modulation of affects has played a crucial role in the capture of the resistances unchained in the "Arab" world in 2011. Here are some examples of how I understand this strategy of capture to be working (I realize some of them can be quite controversial). In terms of modulation of affects, Western corporate media has largely fostered collective media panic around the electoral victory of Islam-inspired parties in both Egypt and Tunisia. In Egypt, for example, this previous campaign helped to "normalize" the military coup in the summer of 2013 and the bloody repression connected to it. In terms of what I will later define as preemption, one can look at the case of the Libyan civil war and the way Western countries have legitimized their military intervention. Finally, at the end of this section, I argue (drawing from Luciana Parisi and Steve Goodman's analysis of nanotechnologies) that contagious affect that can foster emancipatory resistance can also be hijacked by power in its interests. In my view, this is the case of highly organized and financed forms of global armed struggle, such as the Islamic State, which partially functions as an accumulation dispositive

of the dissent and frustration of the underclass of both the "Arab" and the Western world. I claim that corporate terrorism captures and exploits dissent, thus canceling its radically emancipatory potential by reproducing it under the form of a "deadly, self-poisoning line of flight." I will further discuss this phenomenon in chapter 4.

CHAPTER 3

1. I still employ the term "revolution" because this is the translation of what Tunisians have called the transformative event that happened in 2011, the English translation of *al-thawra*. I don't share the Western gaze based on the essentialization of the idea of "revolution," but I respect the will to employ the Arabic term coming from the participants to the Tunisian revolution.
2. In fact, in the first two sections of chapter 5, I will be discussing how the resistance connected to the Tunisian revolution and to the struggles that followed was propagated not only by technological communication but mainly by the mediation of a sociopolitical assemblage, for which the practices of the "mob" were crucial.
3. The term shares the etymologic origin of the English "barbarous," a term that ancient Greeks employed to refer to all those peoples who didn't use their language, Greek. Bar-bar is, in fact, the onomatopoeic restitution of an incomprehensible language.
4. I traveled to Tunis in March 2013, when I took part in the World Social Forum, and in July 2014. On these occasions, I had the chance to meet and discuss with many participants in the revolution about their experience and expectations. I met men and women of different ages, some of whom were longtime Leftist activists, journalists, or contemporary artists. I was also able to meet some of the refugees coming from Libya, who decided to protest and remain in Tunisia. Moreover, throughout my research period, I also had the chance to meet some of the young and politicized participants to the revolution during their stay or travel in Europe.
5. This entire work has been inspired by the artists' claims. For example, they have informed my critique of the narrative of the Arab Spring (chapter 1) as well as my focus on the protagonism of the "mob" (which I discuss and develop in chapters 3, 4, and 5).
6. This aspect of that day has been heavily debated, with agent Hamdi even being temporarily imprisoned as the authorities identified her as responsible for having triggered the protests. Yet regardless of the slap—and of the highly significant debates that one might develop around it—I think the attention should remain on the way the Tunisian state suffocated the "bread race" of the disenfranchised, therefore driving large segments of the population to the desperation that the revolution was born from.
7. This remarkable form of protest—by which groups from the periphery would march toward the central power's headquarters in Tunis—has a historical lineage in the ancient marches that the people from the south pursued in the nineteenth century—when the Tunisian territory was under Ottoman rule—to take their demands to the Bey, the prefect of the Ottomans (Massarelli, 2012: 59).

8. In North African cities, the *Kasbah* represents the administrative center, which hosts the government, and is opposed to the *medina*, which hosts the central mosque and the market (*suq*).

9. It is very important to understand that the repressive regime of Ben Ali had suffocated any attempt of politicization of its citizens. As a consequence, the revolution was initiated by an apolitical category, later joined by traditionally politicized categories such as the wider unionized workforce, but, most importantly, by the previously persecuted Leftist and Islamist activists.

10. As explained previously, "literally *harga* means 'to burn' and *harraga* in the Maghreb indicated 'those who burn,' meaning both young people who 'burn' frontiers as they migrate across the Mediterranean Sea and those who are ready to burn their documents (but also their past and eventually their lives) in order to reach Europe" (Garelli et al., 2013: 14).

11. I refer here to the fact that many rejected refugees chose to remain on the location of the refugee camp that the UNHCR "closed down," even after access to water and electricity was cut. Since Choucha is placed in a desert area, the choice of remaining in the camp was possibly a suicidal choice, which the refugees were consciously taking on in order to enforce their demand to be relocated.

12. Grégoire Chamayou summarizes the American *Department of Defense Dictionary of Military and Associated Terms'* definition of "terrorism" as "all illegal and calculated use or threat of violence aimed at producing a feeling of terror for political ends" and critiques this vague conception as being "not defined by certain operational modes, but by an intention whose objective is to produce a subjective effect, an emotion—fear" (Chamayou, 2015). As revealed by the diagram in Figure 3.5, this flow is made of different events involving Muslim activists, both in terms of charity, protests, as well as armed struggle. My claim, drawing from Fabio Merone's reflection (Merone, 2015a), is that the "Islamic bloc" has undergone a significant radicalization due to its progressive political exclusion and massive state-repression after 2013.

13. It is important to specify that the Islam-inspired participation was largely influenced by the financial aid and impulse coming from the Gulf monarchies, especially Saudi Arabia, pushing for a Wahhabist hegemonization, based on a radical interpretation of Islam (Haddad et al., 2012).

14. Mosireen, literally "we are determined," is an Egyptian media-activism collective that has recorded, archived, and shared videos and works around the Egyptian revolution. They are very relevant for this research, both for their practice and for their theorizations. Their work is available at http://mosireen.org/?page_id=6.

15. At this point, it might be worth restating my relation to the Tunisian (and Egyptian) artists and intellectuals I have quoted so far. I don't intend to speak on their behalf, just like they clearly reject the role of representatives of their revolutions. Rather, the thinkers I worked with have allowed me to elaborate and ground my critique and understanding of the construction of narratives around contemporary resistance. From a privileged position—of knowledge and empathy—they have shown me the way out of the totalizing narratives.

16. Karl Marx, with his theorization of the *Lumpenproletariat*, had already proposed a conception of the categories below the working class. "Underclass" instead emerges

in the sociological field in the second half of the twentieth century in the United States. In 1963, Gunnar Myrdal defined it as the "class of unemployed, unemployable and underemployed who are more and more set apart from the nation at large" (Myrdal, 1963: 10). The American genealogy of the "underclass" contains some assumptions that must be problematized. In fact, the underclass doesn't only imply a structural position (below the working class), but also the lack of skills (due to low education) and will to be employed, the dependency on welfare, and the employment of deviant behavior, habitually set in an urban environment. The term has been critiqued as being derogatory synonymous with the impoverished Afro-Americans, whose behaviors are routinely criminalized and disproportionately policed (Gans, 1996).

17. I am not mentioning, yet not excluding, the potentially reactionary nature of the politics of the mob. Wilhelm Reich has, after all, documented the genuine popular desire for fascism in the twentieth century. I am here specifically referring to the struggles carried on by the unemployed, migrants, and refugees who advanced claims such as regional equality and end of state violence, alongside freedom of movement and stay in Europe.

CHAPTER 4

1. This phenomenon almost seems to bear similarities with what in other territories (such as the US, South Africa, India, Israel, etc.) has been deemed as internal colonialism, as

> a *geographically-based* pattern of subordination of a differentiated population, located within the dominant power or country. This subordination by a dominant power has the outcome of *systematic* group inequality expressed in the policies and practices of a variety of societal institutions, including systems of education, public safety (police, courts, and prisons), health, employment, cultural production, and finance. This definition includes the subordinated population—the colonized—and the land on which they reside within a former settler colony or settler colony system. (Pinderhughes, 2012)

2. The foreword *baldi-* indicates an urban *Tunsiois* family, as opposed to *afaqi-*, rural outsider, *al-mackzan-*, state, or *ulema-*, learned scholar of Islam (Zoubir and Amirah-Fernández, 2008: 115).

3. A structure of local administration inherited from the time the territory was under Ottoman domination.

4. As a further detail about this project, Lacquaniti explains how the project wasn't completed since the initial idea was that of drawing the Palestinian flag in the background. Only the green and black sections had been completed because the project was blocked by the intervention of a local Salafist group who threatened the artists and tried to cancel the poet's face. By the time the photo was taken, the portrait's right eye was smeared with red paint (Lacquaniti, 2015).

5. Amel's reflection applied the Marxist thinking to the West-Asian context, considering the existing conditions on the ground and integrating the colonial past

and the imperial present. He fought alongside the tobacco peasants in Lebanon and inaugurated a new way of conceiving the type of pressure labor *could* put on capital, therefore liberating the horizon of the Arab resistance (*Jadaliyya*, 2012; al-Saadi, 2014; Prashad, 2014).

6. As Deleuze points out:

> The difference between minorities and majorities isn't their size. A minority may be bigger than a majority. What defines a majority is a model you have to conform to. A minority, on the other hand, has no model, it's a becoming, a process. (Deleuze, 1990: 173)

7. I employ the term "corporate" mainly in order to draw attention to the impressive economic articulation of the organization.

8. This is the suggestive definition of "sectarianism" provided by the Marxist scholar and activist Mahdi Amel, reworked by Hanieh:

> Sectarianism is a modern technique of political power, a means through which ruling classes attempt to establish their legitimacy and social base while fragmenting the potential for any kind of popular opposition. Post-invasion Iraq and the subsequent rise of ISIS provide a tragic confirmation of this thesis. (Hanieh, 2015)

9. Sidi Bouzid and Kasserine, the most rebel cities where the revolutionary protests were most active, are also the cities where most of the foreign fighters come from.

10. I should make it clear that my assumptions are somewhat approximated in the sense that Europe and the Eastern fronts are privileged destinations for the poorer Tunisians, but this trend doesn't exclude also a broad participation of middle-class Tunisians to the Islamic militancy project, for example. Other more qualified Tunisians also chose to emigrate toward Gulf countries.

11. On November 16, 2015, Mabrouk Soltani, the only supporter of a family of seven, a sixteen-year-old shepherd from Daouar Slatniya, in the governorate of Sidi Bouzid, was beheaded in front of his fourteen-year-old cousin by Islamic militants who had set their training camp in the Mghila mountains where Mabrouk brought his sheep. He was killed because he refused to hand over his sheep to them (Marzouk, 2015). Two years later, his brother, who had come back home leaving his job on a construction site in Sfax, was also kidnapped and beheaded by the militants of the Islamic State as a punishment for his non-allegiance toward the organization. This time, the organization also made public a video of the execution (AFP, 2017). These two tragic episodes show the dimension of civil war between the poorest categories of the Tunisian society, but they also reveal the absence of the state in supporting the most vulnerable.

12. For the sake of clarity, it might be worth mentioning again that in my understanding the term "vanguard" is uniquely derived from the Tunisia setting and is not intended to draw from previous philosophical traditions. By vanguard, I refer to the under- and unemployed Tunisians who have *initiated* the revolutionary process in extremely risky situations and who continue to struggle in Tunisia and Europe for their lives to be respected, often using their bodies as a political tool. In this sense, while I am aware of Deleuze and Guattari's anti-populist position, I don't intend to oppose "mob" and vanguard. The latter is my response to the Kasserine paradox; it's

my attempt to seek a more affirmative term able to account for the determination of the protagonists of the revolution.

CHAPTER 5

1. Written by Franco Berardi "Bifo" and Massimiliano Guareschi (Guattari, 2007: 15).

2. My stay and activism in Italy in the post-2011 period gave me the opportunity to informally come into contact with many Tunisian migrants, some of whom were involved in housing rights struggles in the Italian capital, as I will further discuss in this section.

3. I borrow this term from Terranova's reflection on the Negrian Hyper-network Empire, and I find it relevant because it stresses the level of development of global networks and the way networks animate cultural articulations, both in terms of control and in terms of forms of resistance. To put it simply, the Tunisian revolution occurs in a historical setting significantly marked by some people's access to wide-range networks bearing a further complexity in comparison to the cybernetic ones. The way these networks have the potential to work directly forge the unfolding of events (Terranova, 2004).

4. With regards to my case study, it was particularly the work of collectives such as Ahl Al Kahf and Mosireen that made it possible to imagine what an antihegemonic circulation of meaning could look like.

5. When I speak of populations produced as surplus, I mainly draw on Clover's work, who defines this group as expelled from formal labor and destined to "informal economies, often semi- or extralegal," a "portion of humanity that earns less than subsistence amounts" often at great risks (Clover, 2016: 156). For a more detailed discussion, see Pârvan, 2017.

6. Although it could also be argued that many of these instances are what transformed a series of gestures into the event of the revolution in the first place. In this sense, there would be no preeminence of the event over the mediation; rather, the mediators would have determined the eventfulness of the revolution as such.

7. The Italian capital carries a long tradition of housing rights activism promoted through occupations of empty public and private facilities. One of the most notable examples is the occupation by 150 families of the empty social houses in the suburban neighborhood of San Basilio (in 1974), followed by the violent eviction, known as the "battle of San Basilio," during which Fabrizio Ceruso, a nineteen-year-old activist of *Autonomia Operaia*, was shot to death by the police (Progetto San Basilio, 2014).

8. https://www.facebook.com/Blocchi-Precari-Metropolitani-675076152611908/.

9. When demanding 100 million Euros from the EU so Italy could face the migration "emergency," Maroni declared in February 2011: "We are witnessing the fall of the Berlin Wall of Maghreb. It's the new '89" (*Il Sole 24 ORE*, 2011).

10. From a personal conversation with A., a member of the Metropolitan Precarious Blocs in Rome, on March 21, 2012.

11. In this case, by "affective intensities" I mainly refer to the anger, the frustration. Different modalities of extraction based on affects are possible in this case. The most common one that I haven't referred to yet is the one that involves the profit of netarchical corporations (such as Facebook, Twitter, etc.) whose flows increment the more dissent is stimulated by a certain event.

Furthermore, in terms of modulation of affect, the Tunisian state media outlets, for example, tend to either neutralize it with celebrations of the "achieved" revolution or to criminalize it. Finally, as I have argued in the previous chapter, organizations of Islamic militancy are heavily stimulating and extracting value out of these affective formations by capitalizing on the cheap military labor they make possible.

12. I have placed the artistic gestures within the field of mediation too, especially bearing in mind instances of organic or minor art.

13. As Said had already alluded to in the '70s with the term neo-Orientalism.

14. Although it should be noted that in 2017 in the central Western countries, threat has been largely normalized, alongside the state of exception it legitimizes.

15. Although on that occasion he wasn't necessarily reflecting on the interaction between media establishments and disruptive events.

16. When I refer to "containment" in relation to practices of mobility, I mainly draw upon the work of Tazzioli and Garelli, who have widely studied the European border regime and have looked into strategies of immobilization that go beyond detention as a management tool against migration. In this sense, they refer to *containment* as "mechanisms for *channelling and capturing mobility* deployed by state and non-state actors" (Tazzioli & Garelli, 2017, my emphasis).

17. Literally "the ones who help you pass" in French. This is what Tunisian citizens call those informal workers called "people-smugglers" in Europe.

18. In other words, I am here, by no means, encouraging a comforting view of change mediated by social media gestures, for example, or the so-called clicktivism.

19. This is an aspect I will be developing in the following sections in which I will discuss the notion of politics within a police state setting.

20. When discussing paradigms of recognition, I refer to the originally Hegelian dialectical view of the slave-master relationality, which authors such as Glen Coulthard critique (Coulthard, 2014).

21. Though other authors such as Mezzadra and Neilson have also addressed the issue of resonance in political terms (Mezzadra & Neilson, 2013).

22. I have first reflected on this aspect when I noticed the police in my home country, Romania, perform the same choreographic moves of American police during arrests. These moves have become viral thanks to cultural industry products and videos of police brutality. But the imitation of these moves—mainly focused on brandishing weapons and brutalizing the arrestee with specific gestures, which are both highly uncommon for the Romanian police—add a further layer of aggressiveness.

23. I am here strictly referring to the Tunisian case. I am aware that riots can be both weaponized by the state and enact heavily reactionary practices. Such was the case in the Tunisian context when informal militias—the *baltaghias*—attempted to destabilize the rebel neighborhoods with the intention of legitimizing the forceful interventions of the state after Ben Ali's escape from Tunis, or when locals from Ben

Guerdane launched a racist arson attack on the refugee camp of Choucha. I am listing these two examples since they could be easily associated with forms of rioting.

24. By "suburban," I refer to the impoverished peripheries of the Tunisian capital.

CONCLUSION

1. *Osservatorio Iraq*, 2016: 25, my translation.

2. This is a poem that Deborah Cowen published on her social media profile on November 16, 2016. Dr. Cowen is a philosopher and an urban geographer whose writing on the politics of infrastructure (Cowen, 2014) and suburbanization of poverty (Cowen & Lewis, 2016) has been inspirational for this research.

Bibliography

Achcar, G. (2013) *The People Want: A Radical Exploration of the Arab Uprising.* Berkeley: University of California Press.
Achcar, G. (2015) "What Happened to the Arab Spring?" *Jacobin.* December 17, 2015.
Ackerman, B. (1992) *The Future of Liberal Revolution.* New Haven, CT: Yale University Press.
Agamben, G. (1998) *Homo Sacer: Sovereign Power and Bare Life.* Stanford, CA: Stanford University Press.
Agamben, G. (2000) *Means without End: Notes on Politics.* Minneapolis: University of Minnesota Press.
Ahl Al Kahf. (2012a) *"Ahl Al Kahf": Founder Manifesto.* https://www.facebook.com/notes/أهل-الكهف-ahl-alkahf/ahl-al-kahf-founder-manifesto-transition-eng/387527047994290 (accessed May 13, 2015).
Ahl Al Kahf. (2012b) "Performative Intervention at the Academy of Fine Arts, Vienna (text)." https://www.facebook.com/notes/ف-هكل-ا-ل-اه/-ahl-alkahf/ahl-al-kahf-performative-intervention-jan-2012/593074547439538 (accessed May 15, 2016).
Ahl Al Kahf. (2013) *Interview with Ahl Al Kahf.* http://www.workandwords.net/uploads/files/Ahl_Al-Khaf_interview_FRANCAIS.pdf (accessed October 1, 2014).
Al-Ali, N. (2012) "Gendering the Arab Spring." *Middle East Journal of Culture and Communication* 5, no. 1: 26–31.
Alba Rico, S. (2012) "Siliana: Dernier épisode en date de la révolte permanente en Tunisie." *Avanti4.* December 2, 2012. http://www.avanti4.be/analyses/article/siliana-dernier (accessed May 15, 2015).
Alba Rico, S. (2015) "Perché il terrore sulle spiagge della Tunisia." *Comune Info.* June 29, 2015.
Alba Rico, S. (2016a) "Tunisia, normalità ed eccezione." *Tunisia in Red.* January 20, 2016.
Alba Rico, S. (2016b) "Tunisia: Torna la rivoluzione?" *Tunisia in Red.* January 24, 2016.

Alcoff, L. (1991) "The Problem of Speaking for Others." *Cultural Critique* 20: 5–32.
Alessandrini, A. (2014) "Foucault, Fanon, Intellectuals, Revolutions." *Jadaliyya*. April 1, 2014.
al-Saadi, Y. (2014) "Mahdi Amel's Revival Manifests Ache for Local Revolutionaries." *Al-Akhbar*. April 9, 2014.
Al-Zubaidi, L., and Cassel, M. (Eds.) (2013) *Writing the Revolution*. London: I. B. Tauris.
Amin, S. (2012) *The People's Spring: The Future of the Arab Revolutions*. Oxford: Fahamu Press.
Aradau, C. (2004) "(In)Different Politics: Resistance as Event and Trafficking in Women." Paper presented at the annual meeting of the International Studies Association, Le Centre Sheraton Hotel, Montreal, Quebec, Canada. March 17, 2004.
Aradau, C., and Huysmans, J. (2009) "Mobilising (Global) Democracy: A Political Reading of Mobility between Universal Rights and the Mob." *Millennium: Journal of International Studies* 37, no. 3: 583–604.
Archives du Jura Libertaire. (2011) "Occupation du 51 avenue Bolivar—3eme Kasbah à Paris." May 4, 2011. http://juralibertaire.over-blog.com/article-occupation-du-51-avenue-bolivar-3e-kasbah-a-paris-73136659.html (accessed May 15, 2015).
Ayad, C. (2011) "La revolution de la gifle." *Libération*. June 11, 2011.
Ayeb, H. (2011) "Social and Political Geography of the Tunisian Revolution: The Alfa Grass Revolution." *Review of African Political Economy* 38, no. 129: 467–79.
Ayeb, H. (2013) "Le rural dans la révolution en Tunisie: Les voix inaudibles." *Demmer*. https://habibayeb.wordpress.com/2013/09/28/le-rural-dans-la-revolution-en-tunisie-les-voix-inaudibles/ (accessed May 15, 2016).
Ayeb, H. (2016a) "La frontiera cancella il territorio." *Comune Info*. http://comune-info.net/2016/04/la-frontiera-cancella-territorio/ (accessed May 15, 2016).
Ayeb, H. (2016b) "Tunisie: Jemna, ou la résistance d'une communauté dépossédée de ses terres agricoles." *Associations Autogestion*. http://www.autogestion.asso.fr/?p=6428 (accessed August 10, 2017).
Badiou, A. (1985) *Peut-on penser la politique?* Paris: Seuil.
Badiou, A. (1988) *L'Etre et l'événement*. Paris: Seuil.
Badiou, A. (1992) *Manifesto for Philosophy*. Translated by N. Madarasz. New York: State University of New York.
Badiou, A. (1998a) *Abrégé de métapolitique*. Paris: Seuil.
Badiou, A. (1998b) *Court traite d'ontologie transitoire*. Paris: Seuil.
Badiou, A. (2000) *Deleuze: The Clamour of Being*. Minneapolis; London: University of Minnesota Press.
Badiou, A. (2001) "Politics and Philosophy: An Interview with Alain Badiou." In *Ethics: An Essay on the Understanding of Evil*, 95–144. London: Verso.
Badiou, A. (2002) *Ethics: An Essay on the Understanding of Evil*. London: Verso.
Badiou, A. (2003) "Beyond Formalisation: An Interview," interview with Peter Hallward. *Angelaki: Journal of the Theoretical Humanities*. Special Issue: The One and the Other: *French Philosophy Today*, vol. 8, no. 2: 111–36.
Badiou, A. [2006] (2009) *Logics of Worlds*. Translated by A. Toscano. London: Continuum.

Badiou, A. (2012) *The Rebirth of History? Times of Riots and Uprisings.* London: Verso.
Bargu, B. (2014) *Starve and Immolate: The Politics of Human Weapons.* New York: Columbia University Press.
Bargu, B. (2015) *Why Did Bouazizi Kill Himself? Fatal Politics and the Politics of Fate.* Conference at SOAS (School of Oriental and African Studies). September 21, 2015.
Bateson, G. (1969) "Conscious Purpose versus Nature." In *The Dialectics of Liberation*, edited by D. Cooper. London: Penguin.
Bayle, T. (2015) "Sidi Bouzid, le berceau de la revolution infiltré par le djihadisme." *Mondafrique.* June 15, 2015.
Beinin, J., and Vairel, F. (2013) *Social Movements, Mobilization, and Contestation in the Middle East and North Africa.* Stanford, CA: Stanford University Press.
Ben Hamdi, M., and Khadraoui, M. (2016) "Siliana: La vie dans le foret, entre misère et terreur." *Inkifada.* January 28, 2013.
Ben Mhenni, L. (2011) *Tunisian Girl: Bloguese pour un printemps arabe.* Barcelona: Indigène Editions.
Bennett, J. (2000). "The Aesthetics of Sense-Memory: Theorising Trauma through the Visual Arts." In *Trauma and Memory: Cross-Cultural Perspectives*, edited by F. Kaltenbeck and P. Weibel. Graz, Austria: Passagen Verlag.
Bensédrine, S. (2011) "La transition tunisienne va peut-être durer des années." *Jeune Afrique.* March 30, 2011. http://www.jeuneafrique.com/Article/ART JAWEB20110329184420/corruption-islamistes-droits-de-l-homme-rcd-tunisie-sihem-bens-drine-la-transition-tunisienne-va-peut-tre-durer-des-ann-es.html (accessed May 15, 2015).
Berger-Levrault. (1896) *La Tunisie: Histoire et description, Tome I.* http://www.e-corpus.org/notices/104460/gallery/876977/fulltext (accessed May 15, 2016).
Berry, D. M., and Galloway, A. (2015) "A Network Is a Network Is a Network: Reflections on the Computational and the Societies of Control." *Theory, Culture & Society*, 1–22.
Bhandar, B. (2011) "Plasticity and Post-Colonial Recognition: 'Owning, Knowing and Being.'" *Law Critique* 22(3): 227–49.
Bignall, S. (2010) *Postcolonial Agency: Critique and Constructivism.* Edinburgh: Edinburgh University Press.
Blackman, L. (2012) *Immaterial Bodies: Affect, Embodiment, Mediation.* Sage Publications.
Blauner, R. (1969) "Internal Colonialism and Ghetto Revolt." *Social Problems* 16, no. 4: 393–408.
Bogues, A. (Ed.) (2006) *After Man, towards the Human: Critical Essays on Sylvia Wynter.* Ian Randle Publishers.
Bogues, A. (2010) "Sylvia Wynter and the Black Radical Anti-Colonial Intellectual Tradition: Towards a New Mode of Existence" (introduction). In *The Hills of Hebron*, by S. Wynter. Kingston, Jamaca: Ian Randle Publishers.
Bojadzijev, M., and Mezzadra, S. (2016) *Logistics and Migration: New Challenges for Migration Studies.* Colloquium in Berlin.

Boltanksi, L. (1999) *Distant Suffering: Morality, Media and Politics*. Cambridge: University Press.
Braidotti, R. (2014) *Il postumano: La vita oltre l'individuo, oltre la specie, oltre la morte*. Rome: DeriveApprodi.
Burke, J. (2016) "The New Threat from Islamic Militancy: Q&A with Jason Burke." *Five Dials*. http://fivedials.com/portfolio/the-new-threat-from-islamic-militancy-a-qa-with-jason-burke/ (accessed May 15, 2016).
Business News. (2013) "Tunisie: Les victimes des événements du bassin minier de Gafsa seront indemnisées, Selon Dilou." January 13, 2013.
Butler, J. (1993) *Bodies That Matter: On the Discursive Limits of "Sex."* New York: Routledge.
Butler, J. (2011) "Bodies in Alliance and the Politics of the Street." European Institute for Progressive Cultural Policies. September 2011. http://eipcp.net/transversal/1011/butler/en (accessed May 15, 2015).
Cantaloube, T. (2011) "A Kasserine, là où naquit la revolution tunisienne." *Mediapart*. https://www.mediapart.fr/journal/international/200111/kasserine-la-ou-naquit-la-revolution-tunisienne?onglet=full (accessed August 10, 2017).
Castells, M. (2012) *Networks of Outrage and Hope: Social Movements in the Internet Age*. Cambridge: Polity Press.
Caygill, H. (2013) *On Resistance. A Philosophy of Defiance*. London: Bloomsbury.
Césaire, A. (1996) "Poetry and Knowledge." In *Aimé Césaire: The Collected Poetry*, translated by C. Eshleman and A. Smith. Berkeley: University of California Press.
Chamayou, G. (2015) "Oceanic Enemy: A Brief Philosophical History of the NSA." *Radical Philosophy*, 191 (May/June). https://www.radicalphilosophy.com/commentary/oceanic-enemy (accessed June 15, 2015).
Chennaoui, H. (2016) "La criminalization des mouvements sociaux de retour." *Nawaat*. January 30, 2016.
Chennaoui, H. (2017) "Blessés et martyrs de la revolution: Un combat contre l'oubli," *Nawaat*. https://nawaat.org/portail/2017/01/17/blesses-et-martyrs-de-la-revolution-un-combat-contre-loubli/ (accessed July 3, 2017).
Chouti, L. (2011) "Popular Protests in Burkina Faso." *Pambazuka News*, https://www.pambazuka.org/governance/popular-protests-burkina-faso (accessed August 17, 2020).
Clover, J. (2016) *Riot. Strike. Riot: The New Era of Uprisings*. London: Verso.
Cole, J., and Cole, S. (2011) "An Arab Spring for Women." *The Nation*. April 26, 2011.
Coulthard, G. (2014) *Red Skin, White Masks: Rejecting the Colonial Politics of Recognition*. Minneapolis: University of Minnesota Press.
Cowen, D. (2014) *The deadly life of logistics: Mapping violence in global trade*. Minneapolis: U of Minnesota Press.
Cowen, D., and Lewis, N. (2016) "Anti-Blackness and Urban Geopolitical Economy: Reflections on Ferguson and the Suburbanization of the 'Internal Colony.'" *Society and Space*. August 2, 2016. https://societyandspace.com/2016/08/02/deborah-cowen-and-nemoy-lewis-anti-blackness-and-urban-geopolitical-economy-reflections-on-ferguson-and-the-suburbanization-of-the-internal-colony.

Cowen, D., Garelli, G., and Tazzioli, M. (2018) "Editors' Interview with Deborah Cowen." *South Atlantic Quarterly*, 117(2): 397–403.
Crisis Group. (2014) *L'exception tunisienne: Succès et limites du consensus.* Briefing Moyen Orient et Afrique du Nord Nr. 37. Tunis/Bruxelles. June 5, 2014.
Cubitt, S. (1999) "Orbis Tertius." *Third Text* 13, no. 47: 3–10.
Dabashi, H. (2008) *Post-Orientalism: Knowledge and Power in Time of Terror.* Piscataway, NJ: Transaction Publishers.
Dabashi, H. (2012a) *The Arab Spring: The End of Postcolonialism.* London: Zed Books.
Dabashi, H. (2012b) *Corpus Anarchicum: Political Protest, Suicidal Violence and the Making of the Posthuman Body.* New York: Palgrave Macmillan.
Dakhli, L. (2013) "A Betrayed Revolution? On the Tunisian Uprising and the Democratic Transition." *Jadaliyya*. March 5, 2013.
Danielli, J. F. (1980) "Altruism and the Internal Reward System or the Opium of the People." *Journal of Social and Biological Structures* 3, no. 2: 87–94.
Dardot, P., and Laval, C. (2014) *The New Way of the World: On Neoliberal Society.* London: Verso.
Darwish, M. (2007) *The Butterfly's Burden.* Newcastle, UK: Bloodaxe.
Darwish, M. (2015) *State of Siege.* Syracuse, UK: Syracuse University Press.
Da Silva, D. F. (2017) "Reading the Dead: Denise Ferreira da Silva in Conversations with Shela Sheikh." Conference at The Showroom, London, Arts Council England. May 25, 2017.
De Genova, N. P. (2002) "Migrant 'Illegality' and Deportability in Everyday Life." *Annual Review of Anthropology* 31, no. 1: 419–47.
Deleuze, G. [1964] (1973) *Proust and Signs.* Minneapolis: University of Minnesota Press.
Deleuze, G. [1966] (1991) *Bergsonism.* Translated by H. Tomlinson and B. Habberjam. New York: Zone Books.
Deleuze, G. [1968] (2003) *Différence et Répétition.* Paris: Presses Universitaires de France.
Deleuze, G. [1969] (2002) *Logique du sens.* Paris: Minuit.
Deleuze, G. (1977) "Three Group Problems." Translated by M. Seem. *Semiotext(e): Anti-Oedipus* 2, no. 3: 99–109.
Deleuze, G. [1986] (2006) *Foucault.* London: Bloomsbury.
Deleuze, G. (1987) *Qu'est-ce que l'acte de création?* Conference during the Tuesdays of the Femis Foundation. May 17, 1987. http://www.lepeuplequimanque.org/en/acte-de-creation-gilles-deleuze.html (accessed May 15, 2015).
Deleuze, G. (1989) *Cinema 2: The Time-Image.* Translated by H. Tomlinson and R. Galeta. London: Athlone Press.
Deleuze, G. (1992a) "What Is an Event?" In *The Fold: Leibniz and the Baroque.* Minneapolis: Minnesota University Press.
Deleuze, G. (1992b) "Postscript on the Societies of Control." *October* 59: 3–7.
Deleuze, G. (1994) "Désir et plaisir." *Magazine littéraire* 325: 59–65.
Deleuze, G. (1995) *Negotiations, 1972–1990.* Translated by M. Joughin. New York: Columbia University Press.

Deleuze, G. (1998) "On the New Philosophers and a More General Problem: An Interview with Deleuze." *Discourse* 20, no. 3: 37–43.
Deleuze, G. (2001) *Pure Immanence: Essays on a Life*. Translated by A. Boyman. New York: Zone Books.
Deleuze, G. [2002] (2004) *Desert Islands and Other Texts, 1953–1974*. Translated by D. Lapoujade, edited by M. Taormina. Los Angeles: Semiotext(e).
Deleuze, G., and Guattari, F. [1972] (2008) *The Anti-Oedipus*. London: Bloomsbury.
Deleuze, G., and Guattari, F. [1973] (2002) "Sur le capitalisme et le désir." In *L'Ile déserte*, 365–80. Paris: Minuit.
Deleuze, G., and Guattari, F. [1980] (2004) *A Thousand Plateaus: Capitalism and Schizophrenia*. London: Bloomsbury.
Deleuze, G., and Guattari, F. [1984] (2003) "Mai 68 n'a pas eu lieu." *Deux régimes de fous*. Paris: Minuit.
Deleuze, G., and Guattari, F. (1986) *Kafka: Toward a Minor Literature*. Minneapolis: University of Minnesota Press.
Deleuze, G., and Guattari, F. (1987) *A Thousand Plateaus: Capitalism and Schizophrenia*. Minneapolis: University of Minnesota Press.
Deleuze, G., and Guattari, F. [1991] (1994) *What Is Philosophy?* Translated by H. Tomlinson and G. Burchell. New York: Columbia University Press.
Delphy, C. (2015) *Separate and Dominate: Feminism and Racism after the War on Terror*. London: Verso Books.
Di Lampedusa, G. T. [1958] (2002) *Il gattopardo* (Vol. 4). Milan: Feltrinelli Editore.
Dosse, F. (2011) *Gilles Deleuze and Félix Guattari: Intersecting Lives*. New York: Columbia University Press.
Downey, A. (Ed.) (2014) *Uncommon Grounds: New Media and Critical Practice in the Middle East and North Africa*. London: I. B. Tauris.
Eagleton, T. (1991) *Ideology: An Introduction*. London: Verso.
The Economist. (2013) "The Arab Spring: Has It Failed?" July 13, 2013.
The Economist. (2017) "Migrants with Mobiles: Phones Are Now Indispensable for Refugees." February 11, 2019. https://www.economist.com/news/international/21716637-technology-has-made-migrating-europe-easier-over-time-it-will-also-make-migration (accessed August 10, 2018).
Eickelman, D. F. (2012) "The Arab Spring and Social Anthropology." Lecture available at http://www.youtube.com/watch?v=3rjtXLlvg4I (accessed January 11, 2014).
El Hammi, E. (2011) "Liberté d'expression en Tunisie: La justice, nouveau fer de lance de la censure?" *Nawaat*. December 30, 2011. http://nawaat.org/portail/2011/12/30/liberte-dexpression-en-tunisie-la-justice-nouveau-fer-de-lance-de-la-censure/ (accessed May 15, 2015).
El-Houri, W. (2016) "Revolutions beyond Failure and Success." *TRAFO: Blog for Transregional Research*. http://trafo.hypotheses.org/796 (accessed July 3, 2017).
Ellison, R. [1952] (2010). *Invisible Man*. New York: Vintage Books.
Elloumi, M. (2015) "Capacité de resilience de l'agriculture familiale tunisienne et politique agricole post revolution." In *Accaparement, action publique, stratégies individuelles et ressources naturelles: Regards croisés sur la course aux terres et*

à l'eau en contextes méditerranéens, edited by G. Vianey, M. Requier-Desjardins, J.-C. Paoli. Montpellier, France: CIHEAM (Centre International de Hautes Études Agronomiques Méditerranéennes).

El Mahdi, R. (2011) "Orientalising the Egyptian Uprising." *Jadaliyya*. April 11, 2011.

Esposito, R. (2013) *Terms of the Political: Community, Immunity, Biopolitics*. New York: Fordham University Press.

Esposito, R. (2015) *Biological Life, Political Life*. Lecture at Goldsmiths, University of London. October 1, 2015.

Étudiant Tunisien. (2012) A post on the meaning of *jabri*. https://www.facebook.com/Tun.Meme/posts/387265954676278 (accessed August 10, 2017).

Eudell, D. L. (2010) "Toward Aimé Césaire's 'Humanism Made to the Measure of the World': Reading *The Hills of Hebron* in the Context of Sylvia Wynter's Later Work." In *The Hills of Hebron*, by S. Wynter. Kingston, Jamaica: Ian Randler Publishers.

Fanon, F. [1961] (2004) *The Wretched of the Earth*. Translated by R. Philcox. New York: Grove Press.

Fanon, F. [1952] (2008) *Black Skin, White Masks*. Translated by R. Philcox. New York: Grove Press.

Fanon, F. (1967) "This Africa to Come." In *Toward the African Revolution*. New York: Grove Press.

Fernández, M. (1999) "Postcolonial Media Theory." *Art Journal* 58, no. 3: 58–73.

Firth, C. (2014) "'On Resistance: A Philosophy of Defiance' by Howard Caygill." *Dandelion* 5.1 (Summer).

Forensic Architecture. (2012) "The Left-to-Die Boat: The Deadly Drift of a Migrants' Boat in the Central Mediterranean." https://www.forensic-architecture.org/case/left-die-boat/#toggle-id-2 (accessed August 10, 2017).

Foucault, M. (1979) "Inutile de se soulever?" *Le Monde*. May 11–12, 1979.

Foucault, M. (1980) "Entretien avec Michel Foucault." (Interview with D. Trombadori taken in 1978.) *Il Contributo*, Salerne, 4e année, janvier-mars, 23–84. In Foucault, M. (1994) *Dits et ecrits* 4, no. 281. Paris: Gallimard.

Foucault, M. (2001) *Dits et ecrits* 3. Paris: Gallimard.

Foucault, M. (2007) *Security, Territory, Population: Lectures at the Collège de France, 1977–1978*, edited by M. Senellart and translated by G. Burchell. New York: Palgrave Macmillan.

Foucault, M., and Deleuze, G. (2001) "Les intellectuels et le pouvoir." In *Dits et écrits* 1, 1174–83. Paris: Gallimard.

Foucault, M., and Sassine, F. (2014) *Entretien inedit avec Michel Foucault 1979*, August 22, 2014. http://fares-sassine.blogspot.de/2014/08/entretien-inedit-avec-michel-foucault.html (accessed May 15, 2016).

Francois, M., and Sadik, N. (2013) "Argument: Has the Arab Spring Failed?" *New Internationalist*. October 2013.

Frangeul, F. (2011) "D'où vient 'la revolution du jasmin'?" *Europe 1*. January 17, 2011. http://www.europe1.fr/international/d-ou-vient-la-revolution-du-jasmin-375743 (accessed May 15, 2015).

Fuller, M. (2005) *Media Ecologies: Materialist Energies in Art and Technoculture*. Cambridge, MA: MIT Press.

Fuller, M., and Goffey, A. (2012) "Digital Infrastructures and the Machinery of Topological Abstraction." *Theory, Culture & Society* 29, nos. 4–5: 311–33.

Gans, H. (1996) "From 'Underclass' to 'Undercaste': Some Observations about the Future of the Post-Industrial Economy and Its Major Victims." In *Urban Poverty and the Underclass*, edited by E. Mingione, 141–52. Cambridge, MA: Blackwell Publishers.

Garelli, G., Sossi, F., and Tazzioli, M. (Eds.) (2013) *Spaces in Migration: Postcards of a Revolution*. London: Pavement Books.

Garelli, G., and Tazzioli, M. (2013) "Arab Springs Making Space: Territoriality and Moral Geographies for Asylum Seekers in Italy." *Environment and Planning D: Society and Space* 31, no. 6: 1004–21.

Gerbaudo, P. (2012) *Tweets and the Streets: Social Media and Contemporary Activism*. London: Pluto Press.

Gerges, F. (Ed.) (2014) *The New Middle East: Protest and Revolution in the Arab World*. New York: Cambridge University Press.

Ghamari-Tabrizi, B. (2016) *Foucault in Iran: Islamic Revolution after the Enlightenment*. Minneapolis: University of Minnesota Press.

Ghani, B., and Fiske, L. (2017) Book review of *At the Limits of Justice: Women of Colour on Terror*, edited by S. Perera and S. H. Razack. *Continuum: Journal of Media & Cultural Studies* 31, no. 5: 731–33.

Ghonim, W. (2012) *Revolution 2.0: The Power of the People Is Greater Than the People in Power—A Memoir*. Boston: Houghton Mifflin Harcourt.

Gibbs, A. (2010) "After Affect: Sympathy, Synchrony, and Mimetic Communication." In *The Affect Theory Reader*, Seigworth, 186–205. Durham, NC: Duke University Press.

Gilmore, R. W. (2007) *Golden Gulag: Prisons, Surplus, Crisis, and Opposition in Globalizing California* (Vol. 21). Berkeley: University of California Press.

Giordani, A. (2013) "Keywords: Revolution/Coup d'état." *Jadaliyya*. August 3, 2013. http://www.jadaliyya.com/pages/index/13309/keywords_revolution-coup-d'état (accessed April 1, 2014).

Glissant, É. (1997) *Poetics of Relation*. Translated by B. Wing. Ann Arbor: University of Michigan Press.

Gobe, E. (2010) "The Gafsa Mining Basin between Riots and a Social Movement: Meaning and Significance of a Protest Movement in Ben Ali's Tunisia." https://halshs.archives-ouvertes.fr/halshs-00557826 (accessed May 13, 2015).

Griziotti, P. (2016) *Neurocapitalismo: Mediazioni, tecnologiche e linee di fuga*. Rome: DeriveApprodi.

Guattari, F. (1977) *La révolution moléculaire*. Collection 10/18. Paris: Editions Recherches.

Guattari, F. (1985) "Machine abstraite et champ non-discursif." Seminar of March 12, 1985.

Guattari, F. (1996) "Subjectivities for Better and for Worse." In *The Guattari Reader*, edited by G. Genosko, 198–99. Oxford: Basil Blackwell.

Guattari, F. (2007) *Caosmosi*. Milan: Costa & Nolan.

Guattari, F., and Rolnik, S. [1986] (2008) *Molecular Revolution in Brazil.* Translated by K. Clapshow, B. Holmes, and R. Nunes. Cambridge, MA: Semiotext(e)/MIT Press.

GVC (Groupe de Volontariat Civil). (2013) *Recherche-Action: La société civile et la diffusion des TIC au sein du Gouvernorat de Sidi Bouzid.* The project is cofinanced by the European Union.

Haddad, B., Bsheer, R., and Abu-Rish, Z. (Eds.) (2012) *The Dawn of the Arab Uprisings: End of an Old Order?* London: Pluto Press.

Haleh Davis, M. (2014) "Justification of Power: Neoliberalism and the Role of Empire." *Jadaliyya.* March 25, 2014.

Hall, S. (2001) "Encoding/Decoding." In *Media and Cultural Studies: KeyWorks*, edited by M. G. Durham and D. M. Keller. Oxford: Blackwell Publishing.

Hall, S. (2006) "Old and New Identities." In *Beyond Borders: Thinking Critically about Global Issues*, edited by P. S. Rothenberg. New York: Worth Publishers.

Hamzaoui, M. A., and Kafon. (2013) "Houmani." https://www.youtube.com/watch?v=jlYZPm9TOEo (accessed July 2020).

Hanieh, A. (2013) *Lineages of Revolt: Issues of Contemporary Capitalism in the Middle East.* Chicago: Haymarket Books.

Hanieh, A. (2015) "A Brief History of ISIS." *Jacobin.* December 3, 2015.

Harb, S. (2013) "Interview with Philip Rizk." June 18, 2013. www.tabulagaza.blogspot.co.uk (accessed May 15, 2015).

Hardt, M., and Negri, A. (2009) *Commonwealth.* Cambridge, MA: Harvard University Press.

Hardt, M., and Negri, A. (2011) "Arabs Are Democracy's New Pioneers." *The Guardian.* February 24, 2011.

Hardt, M., and Negri, A. (2012) *Declaration.* http://antonionegriinenglish.files.wordpress.com/2012/05/93152857-hardt-negri-declaration-2012.pdf (accessed May 15, 2015).

Harendt, A. (1963) *On Revolution.* London: Pelican Books.

Harvey, D. (2006) "The Political Economy of Public Space." In *The Politics of Public Space*, edited by N. Smith and S. Low, 17–34. New York: Routledge.

Harvey, D. (2007) *A Brief History of Neoliberalism.* Oxford: Oxford University Press.

Hasso, F. (2013) "Alternative Worlds at the 2013 World Social Forum in Tunis." *Jadaliyya.* May 1, 2013. http://www.jadaliyya.com/pages/index/11396/alternative-worlds-at-the-2013-world-social-forum (accessed August 10, 2017).

Hasso, F. S., and Salime, Z. (Eds.) (2016) *Freedom without Permission: Bodies and Space in the Arab Revolutions.* Durham, NC: Duke University Press.

Hayles, N. K. (1996) "Virtual Bodies and Flickering Signifiers." In *Electronic Culture: Technology and Visual Representation*, edited by T. Druckrey, 262–63. New York: Aperture Foundation.

Hibou, B. (2011) *The Force of Obedience: The Political Economy of Repression in Tunisia.* Cambridge: Polity Press.

Hosni, A. (2014) "Revolution as Aesthetics (Part I)." Interactive: A Platform for Contemporary Art and Thought. https://interartive.org/2014/01/revolution-as-aesthetics-part-i/ (accessed May 15, 2015).

Hudis, P. (2015) *Frantz Fanon: Philosopher of the Barricades*. London: Pluto Press.
Human Rights Watch. (2016) *Submission to the United Nations Committee against Torture on Tunisia*. April 4, 2016. https://www.hrw.org/news/2016/04/04/submission-united-nations-committee-against-torture-tunisia (accessed August 10, 2017).
Hunt, K. (2006) "'Embedded Feminism' and the War on Terror." In *(En)Gendering the War on Terror: War Stories and Camouflaged Politics*, edited by K. Hunt and K. Rygiel, 51–71. Aldershot, UK: Ashgate.
Huntington, S. (1996) *The Clash of Civilizations and the Remaking of the World Order*. New York: Simon & Schuster.
Il Sole 24 ORE. (2011) "'Servono 100 milioni di euro': Maroni chiede aiuto alla UE per far fronte all'emergenza immigrazione." February 14, 2011. http://www.ilsole24ore.com/art/notizie/2011-02-14/polemica-maroni-commissaria-immigrati-140124.shtml?refresh_ce=1#continue (accessed August 10, 2017).
Infoaut. (2013) "Sciopero della logistica del 15 Maggio (Diretta minuto per minuto)." May 15, 2013. http://www.infoaut.org/precariato-sociale/sciopero-della-logistica-del-15-maggio-diretta-minuto-per-minuto (accessed August 10, 2017).
Jadaliyya. (2012) "Hassan Hamdan 'Mahdi Amel': A Profile from the Archives." October 3, 2012.
Jünemann, R. (1989) *Materialfluß und Logistik: Systemtechnische Grundlagen mit Praxisbeispielen*. Berlin: Springer.
Kaldor, M. (1999) *New and Old Wars: Organized Violence in a Global Era*. London: Polity Press.
Kaldor, M. (2003) *Global Civil Society: An Answer to War*. Cambridge: Polity Press.
Kapoor, I. (2004) "Hyper-Self-Reflexive Development? Spivak on Representing the Third World 'Other.'" *Third World Quarterly* 25, no. 4: 627–47.
Kassir, S. (2013) *Being Arab*. London: Verso Books.
Katsiaficas, G. (1999) "Ibn Khaldun: A Dialectical Philosopher for the 21st Century." *New Political Science* 21, no. 1: 45–57.
Kember, S., and Zylinska, J. (2012) *Life after New Media: Mediation as a Vital Process*. Cambridge, MA: MIT Press.
Khaldun, I. (1969) *The Muqaddimah: An Introduction to History; In Three Volumes*, vol. 1, no. 43. Edited by F. Rosenthal and N. J. Dawood. Princeton, NJ: Princeton University Press.
Kilani, M. (2014) *Quaderni di una rivoluzione: Il caso tunisino e l'emancipazione del mondo contemporaneo*. Milan: Eleuthera.
Lacquaniti, L. (2014) "La vera resistenza viaggia sui muri." *Il Manifesto*. April 3, 2014.
Lacquaniti, L. (2015) *I muri di Tunisi: Segni di rivolta*. Rome: Exorma Edizioni.
Lamloum, O. (2016) *Politics on the Margins in Tunisia: Vulnerable Young People in Douar Hicher and Ettadhamen*. International Alert, www.international-alert.org.
Landler, M. (2011) "Obama Cites Poland as Model for Arab Shift." *The New York Times*. May 28, 2011.
Landzelius, K. M. (1999) "Hunger Strikes: The Dramaturgy of Starvation Politics." In *Einstein Meets Magritte: An Interdisciplinary Reflection on Science, Nature, Art, Human Action and Society*, vol. 5, edited by D. Aerts, J. Broekaert, and W. Weyns, 83–90. Dordecht: Kluwer Academic.

Lazzarato, M. (2003) "Struggle, Event, Media." *Republicart*, no. 13: Culture and Protest http://www.republicart.net/disc/representations/lazzarato01_en.htm (accessed April 1, 2015).

Lazzarato, M. (2004) *La politica dell'evento*. Soveria Mannell, Italy: Rubbettino Editore.

Lazzarato, M. (2014) *Signs and Machines: Capitalism and the Production of Subjectivity*. Los Angeles: Semiotext(e).

Lefebvre, H. (2003) *The Urban Revolution*. Minneapolis: University of Minnesota Press.

Léger, T. A. (2014) "Tunisie: Menzel Bouzaiane la rebelle." *Jeune Afrique*. October 3, 2014. http://www.metamute.org/editorial/articles/lessons-2011-three-theses-organisation (accessed May 15, 2015).

Liauzu, C. (1976) "Un Aspect de la crise en Tunisie: La naissance des bidonvilles." *Revue française d'histoire d'outre-mer*, 63, no. 232–33: 607–21.

Lugones, M. (2003) *Pilgrimages/Peregrinajes: Theorizing Coalition against Multiple Oppressions*. Lanham, MD: Rowman & Littlefield Publishers.

Lury, C., Parisi, L., and Terranova, T. (2012) "Introduction: The Becoming Topological of Culture." *Theory, Culture & Society* 29, nos. 4–5: 3–35.

Lyman, P. (1981) "On Politics of Anger: On Silence, Resentment, and Political Speech." *Socialist Review* 11, no. 3: 55–74.

Lynch, M. (2011) "Obama's 'Arab Spring'?" *Foreign Policy*. January 6, 2011.

Lynch, M. (2012) *The Arab Uprisings: The Unfinished Revolutions of the New Middle East*. New York: Public Affairs.

Lyotard, J.-F. (1989) *The Differend: Phrases in Dispute*. Translated by G. Van Den Abbeele. Minneapolis: University of Minnesota Press.

Macchi, A. (2012) *Rivoluzioni S.p.A.: c'è dietro Chi la Primavera Araba*. Lecco, Italy: Alpine Studio.

Mandraud, I. (2011) "A Tunis, une commission enquete sur les victims de la revolution." *Le Monde*. February 5, 2011, p. 7.

Manji, F., and Ekine, S. (Eds.) (2012) *African Awakening: The Emerging Revolutions*. Oxford: Pambazuka Press.

Marx, K. [1867] (2015) *Capital: A Critique of Political Economy. Book One: The Process of Production of Capital*. Moscow: Progress Publishers.

Marzouk, Z. (2015) "Obituary: Mabrouk Soltani, Shepherd." *TunisiaLive*. http://www.tunisia-live.net/2015/11/19/obituary-mabrouk-soltani-shepherd/ (accessed September 26, 2017).

Marzouki, N., and Aliriza, F. (2015) "In Defense of Tunisia's Democratic Sovereignty." *Opendemocracy*. September 23, 2015.

Mason, P. (2012) *Why It's Kicking Off Everywhere: The New Global Revolutions*. London: Verso.

Massad, J. (2012) "The 'Arab Spring' and Other American Seasons." *Al Jazeera*. August 29, 2012.

Massarelli, F. (2012) *La collera della casbah: Voci di rivoluzione da Tunisi*. Milan: Agenzia X.

Massumi, B. (1987) "Translator's Foreword: Pleasures of Philosophy." In *A Thousand Plateaus*, G. Deleuze and F. Guattari [1980] (2004). London: Bloomsbury.

Massumi, B. (1993) "Everywhere You Want to Be: Introduction to Fear." In *The Politics of Everyday Fear*, edited by B. Massumi, 3–38. Minneapolis: University of Minnesota Press.

Massumi, B. (2002) *Parables for the Virtual: Movement, Affect, Sensation*. Durham, NC: Duke University Press.

Massumi, B. (2007) "Potential Politics and the Primacy of Preemption." *Theory and Event* 10, no. 2. http://muse.jhu.edu/journals/theory_and_event/v010/10.2massumi.html (accessed April 1, 2015).

Massumi, B. (2010) "The Future Birth of the Affective Fact: The Political Ontology of Threat." In Gregg, M., and Seigworth, J. G. The Affect Theory Reader (pp. 52–70). Durham, NC: Duke University Press.

Massumi, B. (2015) *Ontopower: War, Powers, and the State of Perception*. Durham, NC: Durham University Press.

Massumi, B., and Zournazi, M. (2009) *An Interview with Brian Massumi*. https://archive.org/stream/InterviewWithBrianMassumi/intMassumi_djvu.txt (accessed July 2020).

Mbembe, A. (2003) "Necropolitics." *Public Culture* 15, no. 1 (Winter): 11–40.

Mbembe, A. (2016) "The Society of Enmity." *Radical Philosophy* 200: 23–35.

McKittrick, K. (Ed.) (2015) *Sylvia Wynter: On Being Human as Praxis*. Durham, NC: Duke University Press.

Meddeb, H. (2011) "L'ambivalence de la course à 'el khobza': Obéir et se révolter en Tunisie." *Politique Africaine* 121: 35–51.

Mejias, U. A. (2012) "Liberation Technology and the Arab Spring: From Utopia to Atopia and Beyond." *The Fibreculture Journal*. http://twenty.fibreculturejournal.org/2012/06/20/fcj-147-liberation-technology-and-the-arab-spring-from-utopia-to-atopia-and-beyond (accessed August 10, 2017).

Mengue, P. (1994) *Gilles Deleuze ou le système du multiple*. Paris: Kimé, p. 227.

Merone, F. (2013a) "Tunisia and the Divided Arab Spring." *OpenDemocracy*. August 9, 2013. https://www.opendemocracy.net/fabio-merone/tunisia-and-divided-arab-spring (accessed May 14, 2015).

Merone, F. (2013b) "Salafism in Tunisia: An Interview with a Member of Ansar al-Sharia." *Jadaliyya*. April 11, 2013. http://www.jadaliyya.com/pages/index/11166/salafism-in-tunisia_an-interview-with-a-member-of- (accessed May 15, 2015).

Merone, F. (2015a) "Explaining the Jihadi Threat in Tunisia." *OpenDemocracy*. March 21, 2015. https://www.opendemocracy.net/arab-awakening/fabio-merone/explaining-jihadi-threat-in-tunisia (accessed May 14, 2015).

Merone, F. (2015b) "Ibn Khaldun." YouTube lecture. August 26, 2015. https://www.youtube.com/watch?v=nz1avfT7Bfo&index=2&list=PLcNNw9rf9dNZaJWBTCyXU6kOvylmipMO4.

Mezzadra, S. (2006) *Diritto di fuga: Migrazioni, cittadinanza, globalizzazione*. Verona, Italy: Ombre Corte.

Mezzadra, S., & Neilson, B. (2013) *Border as Method, or, the Multiplication of Labor*. Durham: Duke University Press.

Mignolo, D. W. (2009) "Epistemic Disobedience, Independent Thought and Decolonial Freedom." *Theory, Culture & Society*, 26, nos. 7–8: 159–81.

Migration Policy Centre. (2013) *Migration Facts Tunisia*. April 2013. http://www.migrationpolicycentre.eu/docs/fact_sheets/Factsheet%20Tunisia.pdf (accessed May 13, 2015).

Mioc, M. (2009) "Programul TVR in zilele de 21 si 22 decembrie 1989." http://altmarius.ning.com/profiles/blogs/programul-tvr-in-zilele-de-21 (accessed August 10, 2017).

Missaoui, N., and Khalfaoui, O. (2011) *Dégage, dégage, dégage: Ils ont dit dégage!* Tunis: Éditions Franco-Berbères.

Mosireen. (2014) "Revolution Triptych." In *Uncommon Grounds: New Media and Critical Practices in North Africa and the Middle East*, edited by A. Downey, 47–52. London: I. B. Tauris.

Moussaoui, R. (2016) "Les vies brulées des jounes chomeures de Kaserine." *L'Humanité*. February 10, 2016.

Munster, A. (2001) "Digitality: Approximate Aesthetics." ctheory.net. February 14, 2001. In *Life in the Wires: The CTheory Reader*, 407–21.

Murray, C. (1999) *The Underclass Revisited*. Washington, DC: American Enterprise Institute.

Myrdal, G. (1963) *Challenge to Affluence*. New York: Random House.

Nail, T. (2013) "Deleuze, Occupy, and the Actuality of Revolution." *Theory and Event* 16, no. 1.

Nancy, J. L. (2008) *Corpus*. New York: Fordham University Press.

Nawaat. (2014) "Films 'Jiha' et 'Thawra ghir draj' de Ridha Tlili: Deux ondes autour d'une revolution." February 1, 2012. http://nawaat.org/portail/2012/02/01 (accessed October 10, 2014).

Noueihed, L., and Warren, A. (2012) *The Battle for the Arab Spring: Revolution, Counter-Revolution and the Making of a New Era*. New Haven, CT: Yale University Press.

Nunes, R. (2010) "Subject, Event, Separation: On the Politics of Badiou and Deleuze and Guattari." In *Treue zur Wahrheit: Die Begründung der Philosophie Alain Badious*, edited by J. Knipp and F. Meier. Munich: Unrast.

Nunes, R. (2012) "The Lessons of 2011: Three Theses on Organisation." *Metamute*. June 7, 2012. http://www.metamute.org/editorial/articles/lessons-2011-three-theses-organisation (accessed May 15, 2015).

Nunes, R. (2013) "Rethinking the Militant." In *Volume III: The Future of Communism*, third volume of *Communism in the 21st Century*, edited by S. Brincat. Santa Barbara, CA: Praeger.

Nunes, R. (2014) *Organisation of the Organisationless: Collective Action after Networks*. London: Mute.

Organisation Non Gouvernamentale de défense des droits des Imazighen (2008) *Les Berbères en Tunisie. Rapport de Tamazgha. Présenté au Groupe de travail sur l'examen périodique universel*. Genève: United Nations. https://lib.ohchr.org/HRBodies/UPR/Documents/Session1/TN/TAMAZAGHA_TUN_UPR_S1_2008_Tamazgha_uprsubmission_F.pdf (accessed August 15, 2018).

Osman, T. (2013) *Egypt on the Brink: From Nasser to the Muslim Brotherhood*. New Haven, CT: Yale University Press.

Osservatorio Iraq and Un ponte per... (2016) *Rivoluzioni violate. Cinque anni dopo: attivismo e diritti umani in Medio Oriente e Nord Africa*. Rome: Edizioni dell'asino.

O'Sullivan, S. (2005) "Notes Towards a Minor Art Practice." *Drain* 2, no. 2.

O'Sullivan, S. (2008) "The Production of the New and the Care of the Self." In *Deleuze, Guattari and the Production of the New*, edited by S. O'Sullivan and S. Zepke, 91–103. London: Continuum.

O'Sullivan, S. (2014) *On the Production of Subjectivity: Five Diagrams of the Finite-Infinite Relation*. London: Palgrave Macmillan.

Papadopoulos, D., and Tsianos, V. (2007) "The Autonomy of Migration: The Animals of Undocumented Mobility." In *Deleuzian Encounters: Studies in Contemporary Social Issues*, edited by A. Hickey Moody and P. Malins, 223–35. New York: Palgrave Macmillan.

Parisi, L., and Goodman, S. (2005) "The Affect of Nanoterror." *Culture Machine* 7.

Pârvan, O. (2010) *La rivoluzione rumena in diretta: Analisi dei discorsi televisivi del 22 dicembre 1989*. MA Thesis for the University of Bologna, Italy.

Pârvan, O. (2017) "Unruly Life: Subverting 'Surplus' Existence in Tunisia." *Metamute*. February 2, 2017.

Pinderhughes, C. (2011) "Toward a New Theory of Internal Colonialism." *Socialism and Democracy* 25, no. 1: 235–56.

Popovici, V. (2014) *(Collective) Dignity and (the Rhetorics of) Belonging: A Fragmented History of the Production of National Identity in Arts and the Cultural Realm in Romania from the 70s up to Now*. Course at the National University of Arts, Bucharest. http://veda-popovici.blogspot.ro/2015/02/collective-dignity-and-rhetorics-of.html (accessed August 10, 2017).

Povinelli, E. A. (2011) *Economies of Abandonment: Social Belonging and Endurance in Late Liberalism*. Durham, NC: Duke University Press.

Prashad, V. (2014) "The Arab Gramsci." *Frontline* (India's National Magazine). March 21, 2014.

Progetto San Basilio. (2014) "Chi Siamo." *San Basilio: Storie de Roma*. http://www.progettosanbasilio.org/?page_id=213 (accessed August 10, 2017).

Ramadan, T. (2012) *Islam and the Arab Aawakening*. New York: Oxford University Press.

Rancière, J. (1999) *Disagreement: Politics and Philosophy*. Minneapolis: University of Minnesota Press.

Rancière, J. (2004a) *The Politics of Aesthetics*. London: Continuum.

Rancière, J. (2004b) "The Politics of Literature." *SubStance* 33, no. 1: 10–24.

Rancière, J. (2009) *The Emancipated Spectator*. London: Verso.

Read, J. (2003) "A Universal History of Contingency: Deleuze and Guattari on the History of Capitalism." *Borderlands* (e-journal) 2, no. 3.

Revel, J. (2013) "The Event and the Epiphany." Paper presented at Colloque Ulm, *L'évenement dans la philosophie francaise*. December 6, 2013.

Rizk, P. (2014) "2011 Is Not 1968: An Open Letter from Egypt." *Roar Magazine*. January 25, 2014. http://roarmag.org/2014/01/egyptian-revolution-working-class/ (accessed January 13, 2015).

Rua Wall, I. (2016) "This Agitated Veil: A Spatial Justice of the Crowd?" In *Spaces of Justice: Peripheries, Passages, Appropriations*, edited by C. Butler and E. Mussawir, 150–65. London: Routledge.

Said, E. [1978] (2003) *Orientalism*. London: Penguin Books.

Said, E. (1997) *Covering Islam: How the Media and the Experts Determine How We See the Rest of the World*. New York: Random House.

Saliba and Fils. (1911) *L'Agriculture indigene en Tunisie: Rapport general de la commission d'amélioration de l'agriculture indigene constituée par le décret du 13 mai 1911*. http://www.e-corpus.org/notices/104481/gallery/883214/fulltext (accessed May 15, 2016).

Salwen, M. (1991) "Cultural Imperialism: A Media Effects Approach." *Critical Studies in Media Communications* 8, no. 1: 29–38.

Sana, E. (2016) "En Tunisie, 'du travail ou la mort'." *Mediapart*, https://www.mediapart.fr/studio/portfolios/en-tunisie-du-travail-ou-la-mort (accessed August 18, 2020).

Sassen, S. (1991) *The Global City: New York, London, Tokyo*. Princeton, NJ: Princeton University Press, p. 41.

Scott, D. (2000) "The Re-enchantment of Humanism: An Interview with Sylvia Wynter." *Small Axe* 8, no. 120: 173–211.

Scott, D. (2014) *Omens of Adversity: Tragedy, Time, Memory, Justice*. Durham, NC: Duke University Press.

Scott-Heron, G. (1971) "The Revolution Will Not Be Televised." https://www.youtube.com/watch?v=QnJFhuOWgXg (accessed July 15, 2020).

Shihade, M., and Shihade, M. (2012) "On the Difficulty in Predicting and Understanding the Arab Spring: Orientalism, Euro-Centrism and Modernity." *International Journal of Peace Studies* 17, no 2 (Winter 2012): 57–70.

Silverman, K. (1996) *The Threshold of the Visible World*. London: Routledge.

Simondon, G. (1992) "The Genesis of the Individual." In *Incorporations* (Zone 6), edited by J. Crary and S. Kwinter, 297–319. Zone Books.

Simondon, G. (2005) *L'individuation à la lumière des notions de forme et information*. Grenoble: Jerôme Millon.

Soli, E., and Merone, F. (2013) "Tunisia: The Islamic Associative System as a Social Counter-Power." *OpenDemocracy*. October 22, 2013. https://www.opendemocracy.net/arab-awakening/evie-soli-fabio-merone/tunisia-islamic-associative-system-as-social-counter-power (accessed May 13, 2015).

Soltani, N. (2015) *Testimony of Mr. Nassim Mabrouk, Cousin of the Martyr Mabrouk Soltani*. https://www.facebook.com/notes/ommi-sissi/testimony-of-mr-nassim-soltani-cousin-of-the-martyr-mabrouk-soltani-translation/10153821998597074/ (accessed May 15, 2016).

Spelman, E. (1989) "Anger and Insubordination." In *Women, Knowledge, and Reality*, edited by A. Garry and M. Pearsall, 263–73. Boston: Unwin Hyman.

Spivak, G. (1988) "Can the Subaltern Speak?" In *Marxism and Interpretation of Culture*, edited by C. Nelson and L. Grossberg, 271–313. Chicago: University of Illinois Press.

Spivak, G. (1996) *The Spivak Reader*. Edited by D. Landry and G. MacLean. New York: Routledge.

Spivak, G. (1999) *A Critique of Postcolonial Reason: Toward a Critique of the Vanishing Present*. Cambridge, MA: Harvard University Press.

Spivak, G. (2003) "A Conversation with Gayatri Chakravorty Spivak: Politics and the Imagination." Interview by Jenny Sharpe. *Signs: Journal of Women in Culture and Society*, 28, no. 2: 609–24.

Stark, A. (2011) "Arab Exceptionalism? Tunisia's Islamist Movement." *E-International Relations (Students)*. January 31, 2011.

Steyerl, H. (2013) *The Wretched of the Screen*. Berlin: Sternberg Press.

Stinco, G. (2013) "Sciopero facchini Granarolo: '40 sospesi per aver parlato in un video su YouTube.'" *Il Fatto Quotidiano*. May 7, 2013. http://www.ilfatto quotidiano.it/2013/05/07/sciopero-facchini-granarolo-40-sospesi-per-aver-parlato-in-video-su-youtube/586075/ (accessed August 10, 2017).

Tazzioli, M. (2013a) "Une revolution n'est pas seulement une revolution: Non-exemplarité et arrachement du fil de l'histoire à la lumière des soulèvement iraniens." Paper presented at *Foucault insurrectionnel*, Séminaire intensif du Collège international de philosophie, Paris. January 21, 2013.

Tazzioli, M. (2013b) *Countermapping Migration Governmentality: Arab Uprisings and Practices of Migration across the Mediterranean*. PhD Thesis submitted at Goldsmiths College, University of London. August 2013.

Tazzioli, M. (2014) "People Not of Our Concern." *Radical Philosophy* 184. March/April 2014.

Tazzioli, M. (2015) "Troubling mobilities: Foucault and the hold over 'unruly' movements and life-time." In *Foucault and the History of Our Present* (pp. 159–75). London: Palgrave Macmillan.

Tazzioli, M. (2016) "Revisiting the omnes et singulatim bond: The production of irregular conducts and the biopolitics of the governed." *Foucault studies*, June 28, 2016: 98–116.

Tazzioli, M., and Garelli, G. (2018) "Containment beyond Detention: The Hotspot System and Disrupted Migration Movements across Europe." *Environment and Planning D: Society and Space*. https://journals.sagepub.com/doi/abs/10.1177/0263775818759335 (accessed July 15, 2020).

Terranova, T. (2004) *Network Culture: Politics for the Information Age*. London: Pluto Press.

Terranova, T. (2007) "Futurepublic: On Information Warfare, Bio-racism and Hegemony as Noopolitics." *Theory, Culture & Society* 24, no. 3: 125–45. http://tcs.sagepub.com/content/24/3/125.abstrac (accessed February 18, 2015).

Terranova, T. (2016) "A Neomonadology of Social (Memory) Production." In *Memory in Motion: Archives, Technology, and the Social*, edited by I. Blom, T. Lundemo, and E. Røssaak, 287–306. Amsterdam: University of Amsterdam Press.

The New Arab (2017) "Brother of IS beheaded Tunisian shepherd killed," https://english.alaraby.co.uk/english/news/2017/6/4/brother-of-is-beheaded-tunisian-shepherd-killed (accessed August 17, 2020).

Thoburn, N. (2002) "Difference in Marx: The Lumpenproletariat and the Proletarian Unnamable." *Economy and Society* 31, no. 3: 434–60.

Thoburn, N. (2003) *Deleuze, Marx and Politics*. London: Routledge.
Thoburn, N. (2016) "The People Are Missing: Cramped Space, Social Relations, and the Mediators of Politics." *International Journal of Politics, Culture, and Society* 29, no. 4: 367–81.
Tichindeleanu, O. (2010) Paper presented at the conference Art Always Has Its Consequences in Zagreb, WHW. https://www.academia.edu/38096081/Where_Are_We_When_We_Think_in_Eastern_Europe_2010_ (accessed July 15, 2020).
Tlostanova, M. (2017) *Postcolonialism and Postsocialism in Fiction and Art: Resistance and Re-existence*. New York: Springer.
Totten, J. M. (2012) "Arab Spring or Islamist Winter?" *World Affairs*. January/February 2012. http://www.worldaffairsjournal.org/article/arab-spring-or-islamist-winter (accessed May 13, 2015).
Trimikliniotis, N., Parsanoglou, D., and Tsianos, V. (2014) *Mobile Commons, Migrant Digitalities and the Right to the City*. New York: Springer.
Trimikliniotis, N., Parsanoglou, D., and Tsianos, V. S. (2016) "Mobile Commons and/in Precarious Spaces: Mapping Migrant Struggles and Social Resistance." *Critical Sociology* 42, nos. 7–8: 1035–49.
Turner, G. (1996) *British Cultural Studies: An Introduction*. New York: Routledge.
Valayden, D. (2014) "The Dangers of Liberalism: Foucault and Postcoloniality in France." *Jadaliyya*. March 17, 2014.
Valeriani, A. (2012) "La Primavera Araba e il web come forma culturale." http://barbapreta.wordpress.com (accessed May 15, 2015).
Walia, H. (2012) *Undoing Border Imperialism*. Chico, CA: AK Press/Institute for Anarchist Studies.
Weibel, P. (1990) "Medien als Masken: Videocratie. Das Erhebene Object ded revolutionaeren Blicks." In *Von der Buerokratie zur Telekratie: Rumaenien in Fernsehen*, edited by P. Weibel. Berlin: Merve.
Weibel, P. (2005) "Mediile ca masca: Videocratia. Obiectul sublim al privirii revolutionare." *IDEA arta + societate*, online magazine, no. 22, 2005.
Weizman, E. (2014) "Roundabout Revolution." Lecture available at http://vimeo.com/83507978 (accessed May 15, 2015).
Wittes, T. C. (2012) "Learning to Live with the Islamist Winter." *Brookings*. July 19, 2012.
Wynter, S. ([1962] 2010) *The Hills of Hebron*. Kingston: Ian Randle Publishers.
Zarocostas, J. (2015) "More Than 7,000 Tunisians Said to Have Joined Islamic State." *McClatchyDC*. March 17, 2015. http://www.mcclatchydc.com/2015/03/17/260058/more-than-7000-tunisians-said.html (accessed May 15, 2015).
Zayzafoon, L. B. Y. (2005) *The Production of the Muslim Woman: Negotiating Text, History, and Ideology*. Lanham, MD: Lexington Books.
Ziarek, E. P. (2012) "Bare Life." In *Impasses of the Post-Global: Theory in the Era of Climate Change*, vol. 2, edited by H. Sussman, 194–211. London: Open Humanities Press.
Žižek, S. (2012) *The Year of Dreaming Dangerously*. London: Verso.
Zoubir, Y. H., and Amirah-Fernández, H. (Eds.) (2008) *North Africa: Politics, Region, and the Limits of Transformation*. London: Routledge.

Zubaida, S. (1993) *Islam, the People and the State: Political Ideas and Movements in the Middle East*. London: I. B. Tauris.

FILMOGRAPHY

Alberti, L., Clementi, A., and Magoni, E. (2013) *TRAsGUARDI IN RIVOLUZIONE. Le voci delle donne tunisine a due anni dalla primavera araba*. Tunisia.
Ayeb, H. (2014) *Ghabès Labass*. Tunis.
Bayoudh, S. (2014) *Legge 52: Proibizionismo e repression in Tunisia*.
Ben Cheikh, M. (2011) *Plus jamais peur*. Tunis.
Ben Slama, M. (2011) *14 janvier (Chronique d'une vérité)*. Tunis.
Fellah, W. (2014) *Boza*. Tunis.
Levin, B. (2014) *Regarding the Revolution of Others*.
Marker, C. (1977) *Le fond de l'air est rouge*.
Mejri, K., and Peterson, M. (2014) *Scenes from a Revolt Sustained*. US.
Minissale, M. (2013) *Printemps en Exil*, http://leprintempsenexil.webdocs.mediapart.fr/fr/credits/.
Piccinnini, C. (2014) *Eco de femmes*. Italy.
Tlili, R. (2010) *Jiha*. Sidi Bouzid: Ayen Ken.
Tlili, R. (2011) *Revolution under 5 Minutes*. Sidi Bouzid: Ayen Ken.
Tlili, R. (2013) *Controlling and Punishment*.
Tlili, S. (2012) *Maudit soit le phosphate*. Tunis.

SITES

http://biosmove.com/
https://www.facebook.com/أهل-الكهف-ahl-alkahf-115175015229496/
http://fortresseurope.blogspot.it
https://habibayeb.wordpress.com/
http://www.iom.int
http://jadaliyya.com/
https://krieger.jhu.edu/arrighi/research/socialprotest/
http://nawaat.org/portail/
http://www.tunisiainred.org/
https://vimeo.com/biosmove
https://vimeo.com/user10725480
https://voiceofchoucha.wordpress.com
http://watchthemed.net
http://www.zoo-project.com

Index

Page references for figures are italicized.

Agamben, Giorgio, 164–65, 168, 175
Ahl Al Kahf, 95, 111–31, *114*, *116–17*,
   120, *121*, *122*, *125*, *126*, *127*, *129*,
   150, 186n1
Amazigh (pl. *Imazighen*) 72, 109–10,
   128, 142, 186n2
Arab Spring, 13–34, 61, 65, 158

Bargu, Banu, 140–42
Berber. *See Amazigh*
Bouazizi, Mohamed, 1, 79–80, 118,
   122, 141, 149, 171, 191n6

capture, 34, 45, 60–66, 137, 190n16
Caygill, Howard, 44–46, 55–56, 189n7
Choucha, refugee camp of, 87–90, *91*,
   183, 191n11, 196n23
contagion, 44–45, 53–54, 59, 62–63, 65,
   138, 169–71, 185a4, 189n10

Deleuze, Gilles, 34, 44, 47–53, 59–60,
   66, 111, 118, *122*, 126, *127*, 130,
   158, 162, 168, 172, 185n3, 189n11,
   189n14, 193n6, 194n12
dispossession, 33, 101–11, 150, 166,
   173

event, theories of, 43–55

Facebook revolution, 20, 22–23, 27, 77,
   147, 154, 188n21
flows of struggle, 69–71, 75–99, *85*, *88*,
   91, *93*
Foucault, Michel, 35–37, 53, 118–19,
   174, 187n16, 189n11

Guattari, Félix, 34, 36–37, 47–50, 53,
   56–57, 59–60, 112, 126, 130, 163,
   188n1, 194n12

Hanieh, Adam, 18, 27, 33, 135–37,
   193n8
Harraga, 70, 74–75, 84–87, *88*, 146,
   159, 182, 191n10
Houma (pl. *hwem*), 134–35, 139, 146,
   150, 173–75
Houmani, 95, 135, 146, 150, 174–75,
   180

Kasbah, occupation of, 29, 59, 72,
   81–84, *85*, 114, 191n8

Lazzarato, Maurizio, 48, 55–64, 189n13

media, social, 20, 23–24, 33, 54, 147–48, 160–61, 167
mediation, 145–61
mediator: body as, 163–64; gesture as, 164–69
migration. *See Harraga*
militancy, Islamic, 75, 90–94, *93*, 138, 175, 185n5, 194n11, 195n11
minor art, 130–31, 150, 195n12
mob, 70–71, 78, 94–98, 101–2, 132, 139, 142, 150, 167, 190n2, 192n17
modulation: of affects, 60–67, 146, 150, 155–58, 190n18, 195n11
Mosireen, art collective, 22, 94, 112, 170, 192n14, 195n4

necroresistance, 140–43, 148, 163, 166, 180, 183
Nunes, Rodrigo, 44, 47, 49–54, 56, 59, 61, 63, 139, 169–70, 185n4, 188n2

Orientalism, 17–18, 20, 64, 111, 178

peasant struggles, 102–10, 142, 173, 193n5

recognition, 47, 54, 150, 166–67, 178, 188n21, 196n20
refugee, 87–90, *91*, 159–60, 175, 191n11
representation, 13–15, 26, 34, 37, 47, 56–58, 60–64, 131, 149, 153–59
resistance, network of events of, 45–55, 64, 66, 98, 99, 188n6

resonance, 147, 150–51, 155, 157, 169–76
riot, 30–32, 50–51, 57, 59, 72, 79–80, 82–84, 86–87, 102, 109, 134, 140, 149, 150, 165–67, 171–73, 196n23
Rizk, Philip, 16, 20, 22–23, 25, 32, 77–78, 94, 132

singularity, 36, 43, 47–50, 150, 188n1
surplus population, 78, 132–34, 150, 195n5

technofetishism, 146, 147–48, 160–61, 167, 172–73
Terranova, Tiziana, 64, 147, 149, 152, 154, 158, 159, 161–62, 172, 194n3
terrorism, 65–66, 90, 92, 127, 187n8, 192n12; corporate, 135, 137, 190n18
Thorburn, Nicholas, 49, 162, 164, 168, 179, 189n11
Tlili, Ridha, 19, 69, 72, 79, 95, 110, 113

underclass, 23, 51, 74, 77–84, *85*, 94–97, 132, 167, 192n16
United Nations High Commissioner for Refugees (UNHCR). *See* Choucha, refugee camp of

vanguard, 101–2, 131–41, 146, 194n12

Yahyaoui, Ridha, 137–38, 141, 146, 171, 173, 186n7

Lightning Source UK Ltd.
Milton Keynes UK
UKHW011836061220
374652UK00001B/28